ARTIFICIAL INTELLIGENCE

CHAPMAN AND HALL COMPUTING SERIES

ARTIFICIAL INTELLIGENCE

Concepts and applications in engineering

Edited by

A.R. Mirzai

Research Fellow
School of Mechanical Engineering and
Computer Aided Design
Polytechnic of Central London

CHAPMAN AND HALL
LONDON • NEW YORK • TOKYO • MELBOURNE • MADRAS

UK   Chapman and Hall, 11 New Fetter Lane, London EC4P 4EE

JAPAN   Chapman and Hall Japan, Thomson Publishing Japan,
                Hirakawacho Nemoto Building, 7F, 1-7-11 Hirakawa-cho,
                Chiyoda-ku, Tokyo 102

AUSTRALIA   Chapman and Hall Australia, Thomas Nelson Australia,
                480 La Trobe Street, PO Box 4725, Melbourne 3000

INDIA   Chapman and Hall India, R. Sheshadri, 32 Second Main Road,
                CIT East, Madras 600 035

First edition 1990

© 1990   A.R. Mirzai and contributors

Printed in Great Britain by
T.J. Press (Padstow) Ltd, Padstow, Cornwall

ISBN 0 412 37900 7

British Library Cataloguing in Publication Data
Artificial intelligence: concepts and applications in
engineering.
    1. Artificial intelligence
    I. Mirzai, A.R.
    006.3

ISBN 0 412 37900 7

To my parents

Contents

Preface

In recent years, artificial intelligence (AI) has become a vibrant topic in the field of science. There have been many attempts to define AI but still no single definition has been given which adequately encompasses every aspect of the subject. Minsky defines AI as the task of making machines perform functions which, if done by human beings, would require intelligence. This then begs the question of defining intelligence. In general, intelligence is the ability to make primitive judgements by logical arguments. In nature, man is consider to be an intelligent organism because when faced with some information from his senses about the current environment he is capable of understanding the situation and selecting an appropriate course of action. Of course, in some cases this action may not be correct, but an intelligent human being would learn from his mistakes. With this in mind, we define AI to be the development of techniques which can be used to reproduce this ability in computers and other machines.

One product of AI is the development of expert systems and during the last 30 years many researchers have been working on the application of these systems to specific problems. In general, an expert system is a highly sophisticated computer program capable of making human-like decisions by representing the human expertise in the form of explicit rules. In traditional expert systems knowledge is represented in the form of fixed IF...THEN... rules, but researchers are now realizing that the human experts do not always make decisions in such rigid fashion. They also learn from experience by way of analyzing the consequences of previous decisions. Their responses may also be based on what is often described as "intuitive understanding" of the situation with no obvious analytical component. Therefore, recent years have seen a growing interest in development of computer programs that are capable of learning and synthesizing their own knowledge from previous experience.

With AI advancing so rapidly, it is necessary to keep up with the new developments in this field in both theoretical and practical issues. The main objective of this book is to present the concepts and the principles of AI in a language understandable to engineers. It also gives representative examples of the way in which AI techniques are being applied in different fields of engineering.

The book is divided into two main parts. The first five chapters are devoted to the concepts and the principles of artificial intelligence and expert systems. The chapters also illustrate how the field of artificial intelligence has evolved over the last 30 years. The first chapter looks at expert systems from a historical point of view. The second and the third chapters cover some aspects in classical expert systems, ranging from architectures for expert systems to learning strategies. The subsequent chapters in the first part of the book present a number of techniques for the design of intelligent systems which implement the expert systems philosophy in different ways. These techniques include neural networks, pattern recognition and adaptive signal processing.

Part two of the book is entirely devoted to the applications of artificial intelligence. Here, intelligent and expert systems are described which have been applied to a number of problems in the field of communication, instrumentation, medical and sonar signal processing and speech recognitions. In each case it is shown how the concepts presented in the first part have been adapted for these specific problem areas. Although there is a electrical engineering bias in the selection of the applications, the chapters highlight many problems encountered when adapting AI techniques to a wide variaty of practical problems.

*****

Chapter 1 looks at artificial intelligence as a scientific discipline from the invention of the digital computer to the late 1980's. It illustrates the progress of the field as a whole by looking at some typical systems such as the Pandemonium, the Perceptron, WISARD, NETtalk, GPS, SHRDLU, MYCIN and EURISKO, each of which marked a change in the prevailing ethos of AI research. A number of selected commercial systems are used to illustrate the kind of work that is being done in this field. The chapter concludes with a look towards the 21st century and 6th generation computers.

Chapter 2 provides an introduction to the blackboard architecture and discusses issues that arise when designing or using systems with that architecture. In particular, issues of blackboard consistency, control strategy and system efficiency are considered. As an example of a blackboard architecture, the HASP system is described in detail. Some related technologies, such as chart parsing, assumption-based truth maintenance and dynamic databases, are also discussed. Finally, the strengths and the weaknesses of blackboard architecture are evaluated and some open research issues in this field presented.

As already mentioned, recent years have seen a growing interest in systems which are capable of synthesizing the knowledge of an expert. One way of achieving this is through the use of machine learning systems (MLS) and the rest of the chapters in this part of the book look at the theoretical developments in this field. The concept of machine learning, as a general area of research in the field of AI, is the subject of chapter 3. Here learning is formulated as a problem of heuristic search and the relationship between expert system methodology and inductive rule-learning is discussed. Two inductive systems, ID3 and AQ, are discussed in detail and the main limitations of these systems are highlighted. The extensions for including probabilistic classifications and fuzzy matching with rules are also mentioned. The chapter also describes some other learning techniques which are more suitable to noisy data. The chapter concludes by outlining some current research and developments in the field of machine learning.

Another form of learning involves the use of neural or connectionist systems. Neural networks offer an alternative approach to building intelligent systems and chapter 4 studies multi-layer perceptrons (MLP) which are one of the most widely used neural network architectures. The chapter describes the back-propagation algorithm used to train MLP. The performance of this algorithm depends on a number of parameters such as the network complexity (i.e. number of nodes), the adaptation rate, momentum and also the presentation of the training examples. The effects of these parameters on the performance of the network are investigated by looking at an artificial problem: the learning of the concept of a "right-angle triangle" by looking at the sides of a valid triangle. The chapter also reports on the performance of a MLP used for the classification of different types of back pain.

The last chapter in this part of the book reports on the development of a MLS which employs techniques from the field of pattern recognition and adaptive signal processing. Pattern recognition has been used for many years in different areas such as weather forecasting, hand-print character classification, speech recognition, medical signal and image processing, remote sensing and satellite image interpretation. Similarly, adaptive signal processing has been used in different areas of communications such as channel equalization and modelling, echo cancellation and voice coding. This chapter illustrates how these two techniques are combined for the design of intelligent systems. The chapter gives an introduction to pattern recognition and classification using multi-dimensional discriminant analysis methods. It also reviews and compares a number of adaptive algorithms which can be used as a learning strategy for a class of adaptive architectures, namely the linear combiners. Finally, the chapter describes a data analysis program developed to improve the performance of the linear combiners by providing information on the relationships between the inputs and the outputs of the system under observation.

The first chapter in the second part of the book illustrates the application of AI techniques to improve spectral estimation of signals in the restricted domain of biomedical signal analysis. Spectral estimation is one of the fundamental problems in signal processing and here a Prolog blackboard shell is used to estimate the correct autoregressive model order for the best performance. This estimation technique is then used to track the fundamental frequency of real foetal heart signals.

Chapter 7 is devoted to the application of expert systems for the estimation of systolic time intervals of foetal heart sounds. The systolic time intervals are often used by doctors and obstetricians to decide on the well-being of the foetus before birth. In this approach a combination of conventional signal processing and rule-based reasoning is adopted to form "solution islands" in areas of good signals and these islands are joined making maximum use of a *priori* knowledge of foetal heart rate behaviour. A proposal is outlined for intelligently combining the information from three different types of tranducer in order to automate the process of measuring these intervals.

Sonar interpretation is the subject of chapter 8. For many practical applications, sonar interpretation involves detecting and describing objects such as pipelines, divers and underwater vehicles. It may also involve analyzing image textures to describe different geological strata such as sand, rocks, shingle and oil. A human expert working with sonar data seems to use two levels of processing. First, he subconsciously performs image segmentation to identify the characteristic features and he then uses rule-based reasoning based on his a *priori* knowledge of the environment. To automate this task a blackboard system, BOFFIN, has been developed. This is described in detail and the chapter illustrates how different stages of the interpretation process can be carried out using this system. Finally, the system is evaluated by looking at the performance of BOFFIN on real sonar images.

Automatic speech recognition (ASR) is one of the most challenging problems in the field of AI. Chapter 9 looks at some of the important aspects of ASR problem and briefly reviews two of the established approaches to ASR, which are called the strong knowledge (conventional symbolic AI) approach and the strong algorithms (stochastic models) approach. The connectionist (or neural network) approach to ASR is considered in more detail. The chapter summarizes the strengths and weaknesses of variations on the error back-propagation technique for multi-layer perceptrons (MLP). It also compares the performance of the MLP with that of a hidden Markov model (HMM). The performance of the MLP is not as good as the HMM, but in the author's view a successful marriage of different approaches will be part of the developments in ASR in the future.

At production level in industry there is a general need for built-in monitoring systems which can automate the process of fault diagnosis and calibration for final quality testing. Traditionally, the fault diagnosis and calibration have been carried out manually by skilled operators. This approach is very time-consuming and expensive and in recent years intelligent systems have been employed to carry out these tests. Fault diagnosis and calibration are the subjects of the last two chapters in this book. First, in chapter 10, the fault diagnosis of 16-QAM (quadrature-amplitude-modulated) digital radios is considered. Two approaches are investigated, these includes a rule-based expert system and the machine learning system described in chapter 5. The performance merits of both systems are highlighted and the drawbacks are also detailed. This comparison leads to the proposal for a hybrid system, using a combination of both approaches.

Finally, chapter 11 details the problems in applying a machine learning system to the alignment of waveguide filters. The MLS, described in chapter 5, is adapted in such a way that it can assist an unskilled operator to perform accurate and fast tuning of these filters. Issues such as feature extraction and methods of training the system are discussed. The chapter also highlights many practical problems encountered due to the physical structure of the filters and suggests a number of methods for improving the performance of the intelligent tuning system.

This book cannot offer answers to all the problems faced by engineers in designing intelligent systems nor can it provide examples of applications of AI in all the engineering disciplines, but the contributors, who are drawn from industry and leading AI research centres in UK, have identified some of the main difficulties that have arisen in the design of expert and intelligent systems and illustrated how these problems may be overcome. It is therefore hoped that others will profit from our experience. The book can be used as a reference or a text book for those already engaged in AI and, in particular, those practising engineers who, while not specialists in AI, are interested in learning and applying AI techniques to their practical problems.

I am first grateful to all the authors for their invaluable time and the energy they have devoted to preparing their chapters. I am also grateful to Prof. Tom Crawford, Prof. Peter Grant and Dr. Colin Cowan for their support and encouragement. Thanks are also due to many colleagues in the signal processing group in the Department of Electrical Engineering at the University of Edinburgh, in particular, Dr. Mulgrew and Dr. Gibson.

A.R. Mirzai

Edinburgh, July 1989

List of Contributors

Mr. J.S. Bridle,
Speech Processing Research Unit,
RSRE,
St. Andrews Road,
Great Malvern,
Worcestershire WR14 3PS.

Dr. K.E. Brown,
Dept. of Electrical and
Electronic Eng.,
Heriot-Watt University,
31-35 Grassmarket,
Edinburgh EH1 2HT.

Mr. P. Clark,
The Turing Institute,
George House,
36 North Hanover Street,
Glasgow G1 2AD.

Dr. C.F.N. Cowan,
Dept. of Electrical Eng.,
University of Edinburgh,
The King's Buildings,
Edinburgh EH9 3JL.

Prof. T.M. Crawford,
Queensferry Telecom Division,
Hewlett Packard,
South Queensferry,
West Lothian EH30 9TG.

Mr. B.L.F Daku,
Dept. of Electrical Eng.,
University of Saskatchewn,
Saskatoon,
Canada.

Mr. R. Forsyth,
Warm Boot Ltd.,
8 Grosvenor Ave,
Mapperley Park,
Nottingham NG3 5DX.

Prof. P.M. Grant,
Dept. of Electrical Eng.,
University of Edinburgh,
The King's Buildings,
Edinburgh EH9 3JL.

Dr. J. Hallam,
Dept. of Artificial Intelligence,
University of Edinburgh,
Forrest Hill,
Edinburgh EH1 2QL.

Dr. A. Hart,
School of Mathematics
and Statistics,
Lancashire Polytechnic,
Preston PR1 2TQ.

Dr. D.M. Lane,
Dept. of Electrical and
Electronic Eng.,
Heriot-Watt University,
31-35 Grassmarket,
Edinburgh EH1 2HT.

Mr. E. McDonnell,
Dept. of Electrical Eng.,
University of Edinburgh,
The King's Buildings,
Edinburgh EH9 3JL.

Dr. A.R. Mirzai,
Dept. of Electrical Eng.,
University of Edinburgh,
The King's Buildings,
Edinburgh EH9 3JL.

Acknowledgements

The authors wish to acknowledge the following individuals and institutions;

Dr. Jeremy Wyatt, Sye Law and Prof. Rayharris (*AH*)

British Council (*BLFD*)

Department of Education for Northern Ireland (EM)

Science and Engineering Council (Marine Technology Directorate), G.T. Russell, M.J. Chantler, D.T. Berry, E.W. Robertson, A.G. McFadzean, J.P. Stoner and H.M. Conner (*DML*)

R.K. Moore, S.M. Peeling and M.R. Russell (*JSB*)

Science and Engineering Research Council (*KEB*)

Mr Virgil Marton (*CFNC and TMC*)

Sceience and Engineering Research Council and Ferranti Industrial Electronics (Dundee) (*ARM*)

Part One: Concepts

Chapter 1

Developments in Artificial Intelligence

R. Forsyth

1 Historical Review

Mary Shelley's deranged doctor, Victor Frankenstein, is taken by many to be the fictional archetype of the AI scientist [29]. Psychiatrically speaking, his character was the portrayal of a manic depressive: he laboured long and feverishly to create his monster; but when he saw the results of his work, fell into despondency and torpor.

Thus it is highly appropriate that, since the invention of the digital computer in the mid-1940s, the discipline of AI has been characterized by a similar cycle of mania followed by depression. There have been several bouts of excessive enthusiasm (as one generation of workers overturned the ideas of their predecessors) followed by disillusionment (as the limitations of the new approach became clear).

In fact it is possible to identify five boom-then-bust episodes in the history of AI which, for the sake of simplicity, I have divided into five decade-long chunks in Table 1.

This summarizes the "mainstream" of AI development, though, of course, it should be remembered that AI researchers do not change the whole thrust of their work on 31 December in every tenth year. It should also be remembered that there are in every phase a handful of mavericks working outside the main conceptual framework — either using a previously discarded approach or one whose time has yet to come (which, as we shall see, sometimes amounts to the same thing).

Decade	Label	Main Concern
1950s	The Dark Ages	Neural Networks
1960s	The Age of Reason	Automated Logic
1970s	The Romantic Movement	Knowledge Engineering
1980s	The Enlightenment	Machine Learning
1990s	The Gothic Revival	Neural Nets Revisited

Table 1.1- Short history of AI.

1.1 The Dark Ages: Black Boxes and Grey Matter

Almost as soon as it was devised, the digital computer was seen as a natural vehicle for the exploration of intelligence. In the 1950s computers were routinely referred to as "electronic brains"; and two of the visionaries most responsible for the design of the digital computer, John von Neumann and Alan Turing, speculated on the possibility of simulating, and indeed surpassing, human intelligence with machines [31,32].

The phrase "artificial intelligence" was not coined till the Dartmouth Summer School of 1956, so the field was initially part of cybernetics. During this period the central idea was that the way to make machines intelligent was to mimic the brain. Workers took a bottom-up approach, assuming that putting together a large network of artificial neurons and subjecting it to an appropriate training schedule was the best way to build intelligent systems. In other words they thought that if they could model the brain, a mind would emerge as an inevitable consequence.

This approach freed researchers from having to analyze high-level mental processes (like thinking, remembering, understanding speech and so on). But it had two serious disadvantages: (1) the hardware of the time simply was not capable of supporting sufficiently large networks of artificial neurons to give rise to anything resembling human intelligence; and (2) the physiology of the brain was, and still is, very imperfectly understood.

Thus by the early 1960s the neural-simulation approach had fallen into disrepute — but not before some interesting systems had been built. We briefly consider just two of them: Pandemonium and the Perceptron.

Pandemonium [27,28] was a pattern-recognition system based on a four-level computational architecture. At the bottom level were *data demons* which sampled basic attributes of the input pattern, such as whether a patch in an image was light or dark. Each data demon was linked to one or more *computing demons* at the next level up. These computed simple functions (such as product, difference, maximum) of their inputs and then passed their output up to the next level, the *cognitive demons*. There was one cognitive demon for every different type of pattern that the system could be taught to recognize. Thus if the task was to discriminate between written digits (0 to 9) there would be ten cognitive demons (See Figure 1.1).

Each cognitive demon calculated the weighted sum of the inputs it received from all the computing demons and "shrieked" with an intensity proportional to this sum at the top-level demon, the *decision demon* — of which there was only one. The decision demon simply picked the cognitive demon with the "loudest shriek" as identifying the class of the input pattern.

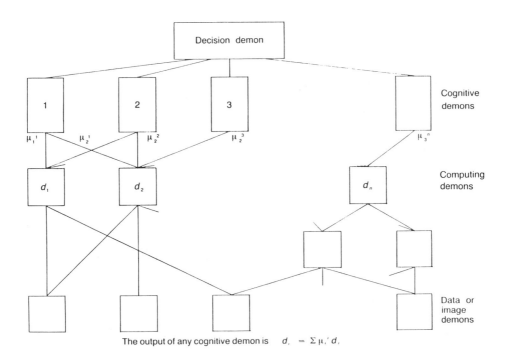

Figure 1.1- Pandemonium.

Pandemonium could learn in two ways: (1) by adjusting the weights attached to the connections between computing and cognitive demons; (2) by replacing, every so often, a few computing demons having very small weights with new ones obtained by "mutated fission" and "conjugation".

Although now of purely historical interest, Pandemonium incorporated some very important ideas. Firstly, it was explicitly, though loosely, based on theories about the nervous system, and thus represents one of the earliest connectionist models. Secondly, it employed what would now be termed a genetic algorithm [13] in its method of replacing ineffective computing subdemons by mutation and recombination of more useful ones. Thirdly, it introduced a precursor of fuzzy logic [35], in that the logical and relational operations performed by computing demons gave smoothly varying outputs. For instance, a subdemon that computed the truth value $D1 > D2$ had a logistic curve as its output rather than a step function; that is, it was scaled according to the size of the difference $D1 - D2$. Fourthly, and most importantly, Pandemonium was a learning machine. Its designer, Selfridge, like most of his contemporaries, assumed that intelligence could not be pre-programmed but would have to be taught. This is an insight which has recently been rediscovered.

Despite incorporating so many modern ideas, and despite Selfridge's picturesque language, Pandemonium had less effect on the course of AI than a slightly later and slightly simpler neural-net model, the Perceptron invented by Frank Rosenblatt [22,23]. (See Figure 1.2)

The original Perceptron was an optical pattern classification device. Its input layer was a grid of 400 photocells which corresponded (very roughly) to the retina of the vertebrate eye. The photocells responded with 1 for light and 0 for dark. They were randomly connected to the next layer, the associator units, which computed a threshold function: if an associator unit's total input exceeded its threshold its output was 1, otherwise 0. Thus the associators were simple feature detectors or pattern primitives rather like Pandemonium's computing demons.

All the associators were linked to the final layer, containing one processing element for each type of pattern. (In the simple case of only two patterns, a single processing element, with a Yes/No output, was sufficient.)

The final processing element took a weighted sum of the values on its input lines and compared it to a threshold: if the sum exceeded the threshold it signalled that its specific pattern was present, otherwise that it was absent. The way the system learned was by alteration of the weights.

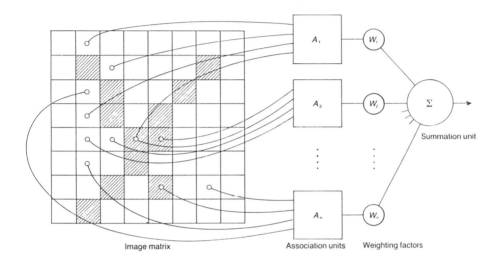

Figure 1.2- A Perceptron.

Association units combine single-pixel responses into group features. Each feature is weighted and the sum is compared to a threshold to make the final class decision.

Rosenblatt's main achievement was to devise a training strategy for Perceptrons and to prove that it would converge on an optimal set of weights provided that the input patterns were "linearly separable", which means that they could be partitioned into hypercube-shaped regions in feature space. The following error-correction algorithm was applied after every training presentation.

1. If the output is correct, leave the weights unaltered.
2. If the output should have been 1 but was 0, increment the weights on the active input lines (i.e. those with values above 0).
3. If the output should have been 0 but was 1, decrement the weights on the active input lines.

The increment could be fixed, but it was more usual for it to be proportional to the difference between the weighted sum and the desired output.

Perceptrons were trained to perform useful pattern-recognition tasks, and variants of the Perceptron learning system [33] have been built into most telecommunication lines for adaptive noise reduction over the last twenty years; but in the end the AI community grew dissatisfied with this approach. Learning the difference between linearly separable classes of patterns ceased to seem very exciting. Most AI workers drew the conclusion (somewhat prematurely) that neural models would always be limited to emulating very low levels of intelligence.

1.2 The Age of Reason: Logic and Language

In the 1960s, as it became apparent that building brains was not a viable AI strategy, a new fashion took over. This was a top-down approach, according to which computers, humans and other creatures were treated as species of information processor. The mechanisms of the nervous system were no longer a concern, since a program can be executed on many different physical systems without reference to their underlying hardware.

The chief proponents of this view were Allen Newell and Herbert Simon of Carnegie-Mellon University [20]. They argued that the correct level of description for human problem solving was in terms of comparing, storing and manipulating symbols. They were interested in the kind of rational behaviour in which a problem solver takes a symbolic description of a problem situation and systematically transforms the elements of that description by applying formal rules in a sequence of steps to achieve a new state — namely, the solution. They hoped to find broad general principles of intelligence which would be common to all forms of rational problem solving, from business decision-making to playing games, and which could equally well be carried out by humans or by computers.

This approach succeeded with formal puzzles and games, but tended to break down when applied to the kind of open-ended, ill-structured problems which people deal with in everyday life. Two systems that exemplify both its strengths and weaknesses were GPS (the General Problem Solver) and SHRDLU.

GPS [5] was given a task environment for a particular problem in terms of routines for matching pairs of objects, routines for applying operators to objects and routines to determine whether an operator could be applied to an object. These objects were symbol structures, which could also be considered as states or situations.

GPS went to work by setting goals, detecting differences between the current state and its goal, and then finding operators that would reduce those differences — a technique known as means-end analysis. Each problem generated subproblems till a subproblem was reached that could be solved in one step. The system proceeded by successive solution of its subproblems till it achieved its goal or gave up.

GPS had three main methods: (1) transforming one state into another; (2) reducing the difference between two states; and (3) applying an operator to an object or state. Methods could call each other — including themselves — as subprocesses. Endless repetition was avoided by maintaining a list of states already encountered. GPS also used a technique, called "planning", which abstracted from two objects A and B new objects A' and B' by eliminating most of the details. It then attempted to turn A' into B' (typically an easier task than turning A into B) and — if successful — used the simplified solution to guide work on the full problem.

The idea of means-end analysis was taken further in STRIPS, the Stanford Research Institute Planning System [6], where it was used for robotic planning. Here the objective was for a robot to find its way around in a household environment.

Operators in STRIPS were defined in terms of preconditions and effects. The preconditions were those facts which had to be true to apply the operator. The effects were facts that would become false (the Delete-list) or become true (the Add-list) when the action was carried out. For example the operator GO-INTO-ROOM might be defined as follows.

GO-INTO-ROOM (self, Room) :

Preconditions : at(self,P); outside(P,Room);
            near(P, D); door(D);
            connects(D,Room,P); not shut(D).

Add-List : in(self,Room).

Delete-List : at(self,P).

If the robot had a goal of entering a particular room (which might itself be a subgoal in a higher level plan) it would look for an operator which had being in a room in its Add-list, such as GO-INTO-ROOM. It would then try to satisfy the preconditions of that operator. With the above example, it might well find that all preconditions were true except that the door was not open. This would cause it to seek operators that had opening the door on their Add-lists. In the end this kind of reasoning could lead to quite long sequences of purposeful behaviour, involving, for instance, finding a key, bringing it to the door, turning it in the lock, twisting the door handle, pushing the door, and so on.

STRIPS was further developed into ABSTRIPS [25] but by that time this line of research was running out of steam. Planning based on search through a propositionally encoded state space seemed incredibly pedantic when compared to what people do. It was logical and it worked (within limits), but it failed to capture the essence of human problem-solving.

SHRDLU [34] was a rather different kind of system which could take part in a conversation, via keyboard and screen, about a simple world containing children's building blocks. This blocks-world was also represented on the screen and contained a simulated robot arm, to which the user could give orders in natural English, producing dialogues like the following (where machine replies are in capitals).

Pick up a big red block.
OK.
Grasp the pyramid.
I DON'T UNDERSTAND WHICH PYRAMID YOU MEAN.
Find a block which is taller than the one you are holding
and put it into the box.
BY 'IT' I ASSUME YOU MEAN THE BLOCK WHICH IS
TALLER THAN THE ONE I AM HOLDING. OK.
What does the box contain?
THE BLUE PYRAMID AND THE BLUE BLOCK.

Winograd's work introduced a number of new ideas about the relationship between syntax and semantics and about representing linguistic information in a computer, but — though it made a great impact at the time — it did not lead to a breakthrough in machine understanding of unrestricted natural language.

By the early 1970s, the GPS approach, based on heuristic search of a state space, was seen to have run into a dead end. Though GPS could solve cryptarithmetic and other puzzles, there was no known way of extending it to deal with the kind of fuzzy, ill-defined problems which regularly crop up in economics, medicine, meteorology and a wide range of other domains. Likewise, it was realized, when the initial euphoria had worn off, that Winograd's SHRDLU could not easily be "scaled up" from its micro-world of children's blocks to cope with the full diversity of natural language.

1.3 The Romantic Movement: Knowledge as Power

The key to the next phase of AI was the abandonment of the goal of general intelligence. Observing that human experts are competent in their field by virtue of a large body of specialist knowledge, a team led by Edward Feigenbaum at Stanford University began developing the first expert systems. This coincided with a move of the global centre of gravity in AI from the east to the west coast of the USA — roughly speaking, from MIT to Stanford.

The expert or knowledge-based system is a caricature of the human expert, in the sense that it knows almost everything about almost nothing. For example, an expert system for blood infections may not even have any knowledge about lung diseases, let alone about another area like currency trading. None the less, this narrowing of focus enabled expert-system designers to achieve impressive practical results. Among the most noteworthy systems developed during this period were DENDRAL, MYCIN and Prospector.

DENDRAL [2] was concerned with the interpretation of data obtained from a mass spectrometer. This instrument bombards a chemical sample with a beam of electrons, causing its molecules to break up. The fragments are passed through a magnetic field which deflects those with a high charge and low mass more than those with a low charge and large mass. As a result, a plot showing the relative abundance of fragments with different mass-to-charge ratios is produced.

Such plots give the trained analytical chemist an insight into the structure of the compound under test. The trouble is that a complex molecule can fragment in many ways, i.e. that different chemical bonds can be broken inside the mass spectrometer. Whereas it is relatively easy to predict that the cleavage of a specific chemical bond will give rise to a peak in the plot at a particular point, it is much harder, working in reverse, to take the plot — with many different peaks — and work out what chemical decomposition produced it. In other words, there is a problem of inverse mapping.

DENDRAL helped to solve this problem by using a constrained generator which, given a molecular formula, proposed a number of ways it could be structured. With a complex compound there might be literally millions of potential structures. DENDRAL used fragmentation rules, rules of chemistry and the data from the mass spectrometer to eliminate the vast majority of these, leaving a small candidate set for the human chemist to consider.

A further development, Meta-DENDRAL, employed a learning algorithm to refine and extend DENDRAL's rule-set. It has been reported [18] that Meta-DENDRAL made genuinely novel contributions to the science of organic chemistry.

DENDRAL was the first knowledge-based system but two other pioneering expert systems, MYCIN and Prospector, have been even more influential in the development of the field. MYCIN [30] was a system for diagnosing bacterial blood infections and prescribing appropriate drug therapy. Prospector [9] was a system for interpreting the results of geological investigations, which became famous after assisting in the discovery of large molybdenum deposits in the USA and Canada.

All three systems, though very different in application, shared some important common features which have become hallmarks of the expert system. Above all, they imposed a division between knowledge and reasoning, so that an expert system today is seen to be composed of two core parts: the knowledge base and the inference engine.

The knowledge base contains symbolic representations of experts' rules of judgement in a format that permits the inference engine to perform deductions on it. The inference engine consists of whatever search and reasoning procedures are necessary to deploy that knowledge — in other words to draw conclusions from it.

Expert systems like MYCIN brought many new ideas into AI, and into mainstream computing, but perhaps the most significant was this notion of explicit representation of knowledge and its separation from the inference process.

1.4 The Enlightenment: Learning how to Learn

AI is still living, to a large extent, off the intellectual capital accumulated in the expert-system boom of the 1970s. But during the 1980s expert systems as such have ceased to be the focal point of AI research. At the cutting edge of AI research in the 1980s has been the issue of machine learning, which is a major theme of the present book.

This is not so much because expert systems have failed as because they have succeeded. The idea of representing knowledge explicitly — as rules, frames or in other forms — has stimulated many new developments that would not otherwise have taken place. But it has also become widely recognized that knowledge elicitation and codification is a difficult and labour-intensive task [12,15]. It is therefore quite natural to think in terms of automating this knowledge acquisition process, or at least assisting it by machine. This brings us back to the problem of machine learning (see also [8]).

Successful learning programs have been developed by Michalski [17] and by Ross Quinlan [21], but these will be covered in chapter 3 of the present volume; so here we consider two other, contrasting, learning systems: EURISKO and WISARD.

EURISKO [16] was a development of an earlier system called AM [4] which explored the domain of elementary number theory. EURISKO was intended to extend AM's applicability to other domains than mathematics and to remedy some of the weaknesses which prevented AM going further than it did. It was tested in several domains: elementary mathematics (where it reproduced the discoveries of AM), designing VLSI components (where it invented a three-dimensional logic gate), and the design of battle fleets in a naval wargame called the Trillion Credit Squadron competition. In this last context, EURISKO twice won the US national championship with bizarre fleets which, essentially, exploited previously unnoticed loopholes in the rules.

EURISKO worked according to an agenda, which it could manipulate itself. Tasks on the agenda were given numeric worths, from 0 to 999, which determined how much processing time could be devoted to them. When it finished one task, EURISKO would pick the next task to work on by selecting the one with the highest worth rating. While working on a task, other tasks could be added to the agenda, or could have their worths increased or decreased. One of the interesting things about EURISKO was that it never really needed to stop: it could go on introspecting for ever — creating new tasks and revising its conceptual vocabulary until someone halted it. (What generally happened, however, was that a point of diminishing returns was reached where even the highest-scoring tasks on the agenda had low values.)

Not only could EURISKO create new concepts, by applying heuristic rules to existing concepts, it could also devise new heuristics. This was possible since rules, concepts and practically everything else in the system were represented in a uniform language known as RLL-1 (Representation Language Language 1). RLL-1 is a sophisticated object-oriented language.

Thus EURISKO could start out with a rule such as,

> **IF** a rule has fired only once
> **THEN** try to generalize it.

Treating this rule as data rather than program, it might find that the rule itself had fired only once. Then it could be applied to itself, to generate

> **IF** a rule has fired less than 4 times
> **THEN** try to generalize it.

Possibly this rule would turn out to be more useful than its parent.

Despite EURISKO's self-reflexive capacity, it did not go further in elementary mathematics than AM; and for the time being its inventor, Lenat, has turned aside from discovery programs altogether. He is currently working on a different project called CYC which aims to computerize a very large knowledge base by encoding a household encyclopaedia and adding all the unstated, 'common sense' knowledge needed to interpret it. This is a long-term project, but when it is completed Lenat believes there will at last be sufficient background knowledge for computerized discovery systems — perhaps quite similar to EURISKO in overall plan — to go beyond the barriers that held up AM and EURISKO just when they were getting really interesting. Till this 'world lexicon' is ready we will not know for sure whether EURISKO got stuck through lack of background knowledge or because of intrinsic defects in its mode of operation (See also [11]).

Another innovative learning system, of a completely different type, was the WISARD visual pattern recognizer [1]. The interesting point about WISARD is that it was a parallel computer with no processors, only memory. (See Figure 1.3)

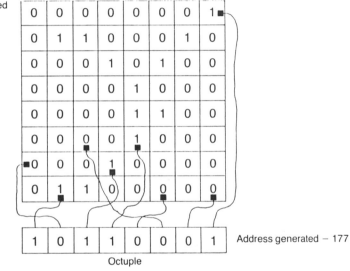

Image data digitalised as ones and zeros

Address generated – 177

Octuple

Figure 1.3- WISARD schematic.

Groups of eight pixels are arbitrarily connected to eight-bit registers to form the basis of WISARD's pattern recognition system. Each octuple corresponds to a bank of 256 memory locations. During the training phase the value in the octuple forms an address within its RAM bank dependent on the pixel pattern and a 1 is written to this address. If the same pattern is present during the recognition phase then the same RAM bank address will be generated and the 1 present will signify recognition.

It worked by inspecting a TV image digitized as 512 x 512 pixels, which were sampled in groups (normally groups of 8). Each 8-bit grouping was a random sample of 8 pixels in the image, which could be in one of 256 states, since pixels have only two values, 0 or 1. In effect these 8-bit groupings were feature detectors, and the current state of each one said something about the picture currently on view.

Each feature detector was connected to its own private bank of 256 RAM locations, using a content-addressing scheme. The state of the detector (an 8-bit value) pointed to one of its 256 RAM locations. Prior to training, all the bits were set to zero. During the training phase, the bit addressed by every detector would be set to 1 if the image being presented was a positive example of the concept to be learned, or left alone if not. There were actually 32768 detectors, requiring a total of one megabyte of RAM (not a huge memory these days).

After training, when a new image was shown to the system, each detector addressed a location within its RAM bank (as in the training phase) and retrieved the bit stored there — 0 or 1. These were just added up: a high total indicated that many detectors were in the same state as when a positive training instance had been displayed; hence that the present image was also likely to be a positive case. A low total suggested the opposite. (Extension to deal with more than two classes merely required more memory.)

WISARD, in effect, computed a 'fingerprint' of what it saw and compared this with past experience. In practice it proved highly resistant to distortions in the image. For example, it was taught to discriminate between smiling and frowning faces. This is just the sort of thing that computers, programmed in the traditional manner, have hitherto been strikingly poor at doing.

EURISKO and WISARD between them exemplify two divergent approaches to the problem of machine learning — a problem that will have to be addressed if artificial intelligence is ever to become a reality (since intelligence without learning is scarcely conceivable). At present the AI community seems to favour the route pioneered by WISARD rather than that followed by EURISKO.

1.5 The Gothic Revival

As we enter the 1990s a counter-reformation is underway within AI. Research students and research grants are being diverted away from the symbolic knowledge-based paradigm which held sway in the 1970s and 1980s towards neuro-computing or "connectionism". I call this AI's "Gothic revival" because we have now come full circle. The irony is that neural-net computing was the guiding theme of the 1950s.

Once more, extravagant claims are being made about the potential of the new (or newly rediscovered) technology, and the race is on, especially in the US and Japan, to become world leader in neuro-computing.

Why should the neural-net approach succeed now when its limitations were exposed more than 25 years ago? After all, though there has been progress in neurophysiology, there has been no tremendous breakthrough in our understanding of the brain during the intervening years.

The answer is twofold. In the first place, modern computing machinery is many orders of magnitude more powerful than anything available to the cyberneticians of the 1950s, and computer power is still increasing relentlessly. It is possible to construct neural nets with hundreds of thousands of processing elements which, while not rivalling the capabilities of higher mammals, do approach or even exceed the complexity of the nervous systems of insects, molluscs and other 'simple' creatures.

Secondly, and perhaps more importantly, learning rules for multi-layered neural networks have been discovered. A particular weakness of the Perceptron — identified by Minsky and Papert [19] when they delivered the *coup de grace* to earlier work on neural networks — was the fact that it had only one layer of internal processing elements. This was not because multi-layer systems have no advantages over single-layer systems (they have) but because Rosenblatt's error-correcting rule could not be guaranteed to converge on a solution when used with multi-layered systems.

In the 1980s a number of workers independently discovered what has become known as the back-propagation rule, which overcomes this difficulty. Perhaps the most notable success of back propagation is Sejnowksi's NETtalk [26], a text-reading system. (See Figure 1.4)

NETtalk scans seven characters at a time, and attempts to pronounce the middle item of the seven. When it has done so, the text is moved along and it does the same for the next character — again in the context of three other characters on either side. With 309 processing units and about 18000 weights, NETtalk was trained using a back-propagation algorithm on several thousand words of text. It progressed from meaningless babble to 98% correct pronunciation in 16 hours. This contrasts dramatically with the performance of DECtalk, a rule-based system built by Digital Equipment Corporation which initially inspired NETtalk: DECtalk is said to have required well over 20 man-years to encapsulate the knowledge of phonetics and English spelling needed for correct pronunciation.

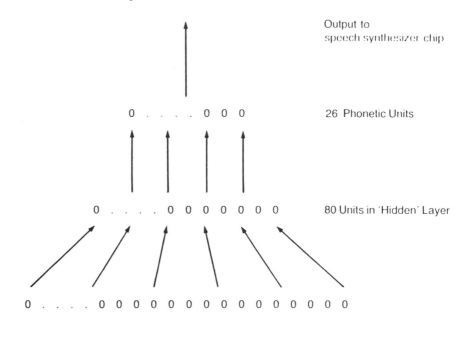

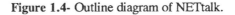

Figure 1.4- Outline diagram of NETtalk.

Back propagation computes an error term at the output layer (typically half the sum of the squared differences between the actual output values and the desired target values) and feeds this back through the network [24]. Provided that the transfer function of the processing units in the internal layers can be differentiated, the error signal can be fed back all the way to the input units, adjusting connection weights as it goes. This is a simple method of credit apportionment which does for multi-stage neural networks (which are not limited to linearly separable pattern classes) what Rosenblatt's error-correction procedure did for the Perceptron.

With a sigmoid transfer function (quite commonly used in practice), the error term (*de*) for each internal or 'hidden' processing cell (*j*) at a given level (*s*) is computed as

$$de(j,s) = o(j,s) \times (1 - o(j,s)) \times wsum(j,s+1)$$

where $o(j,s)$ is the output from unit *j* at level *s* and $wsum(j,n)$ is the product of weight times error-term summed for all units at level *n* that receive output from unit *j* on level $n-1$ ($n = s+1$). Then the weight change (*dw*) to be added to all weights at a given level (*s*) is

$$dw(j,s) = lc \times de(j,s) \times o(i,s-1)$$

where *lc* is an (adjustable) learning coefficient. Although back propagation is easy to grasp, intuitively satisfying and has become almost an "industry standard", it is not a very efficient training rule. More sophisticated weight-adjustment algorithms do exist. (See chapter 4 of this volume.)

2 Expert Systems in Practice

However, we have been anticipating events somewhat. Although the leading edge of AI has moved on to machine learning, and more recently to neural-net models of learning, the state of the art in applied AI is still the expert system. Knowledge engineering is flourishing, and the immediate future will involve progress in the techniques used in knowledge engineering.

In the early 1980s, commercial expert-system vendors tended to re-create a classic expert system like MYCIN or Prospector, remove the domain-specific knowledge, and release the resulting inference engine, together with some kind of rule editor, as an *expert-system shell*. Today that is no longer sufficient: users realize that for large-scale applications additional facilities are required, such as screen-handling, access to existing databases, procedural code and so on. Over the last four or five years, expert-system shells have evolved by acquiring extra facilities so that the more modern products are, in fact, complete software development environments. Thus the distinction between expert-system shells and AI programming environments is becoming increasingly blurred. Two commercial products that illustrate this trend are Leonardo [3] and Egeria [14]. They are used below to illustrate, with small-scale examples, the kind of work that is being done in this field.

2.1 Grand National Betting Advisor

The first example was put together with the aid of some old horse-racing yearbooks.

The Grand National — the most popular single betting event in Britain — is widely regarded as a lottery. But in fact there is enough regularity in the results over the years to make it an interesting (if sometimes frustrating) exercise in prediction.

For example, although the race is known as a 'graveyard for favourites' it is still usually won by a well-backed horse. To be quantitative, just under 40% of the winners from 1946 to 1988 were returned at odds of 10/1 or less, while 65% have been returned at odds of 20/1 or less. Yet in a typical field fewer than 10% of the horses will have odds of 10/1 or less, while only 25% will have odds at or below 20/1. Thus 65% of the winners come from 25% of the runners, indicating that the betting is a reasonable guide to a horse's prospects.

Another reliable indicator is the weight carried. An obvious thought is that the lighter the load which a horse is required to carry round 4.5 miles and over 30 fences the better. But historically horses carrying heavier weights have done well. To be specific, of the last 29 races 24 have been won by a horse carrying more than ten stone; yet in an average race only just over a third of the runners carry more than ten stone. Thus 83% of the winners come from 35% of the horses. The explanation for this seemingly puzzling fact is that the race is a handicap, so the better horses are given heavier loads. As there is a minimum weight, many of the animals carrying ten stone (the minimum weight) are carrying a greater burden than their form would warrant: they are actually overloaded.

It is also a good sign when the horse has won at least one of its last four outings. If so, as you would expect, it has a better chance of being placed than otherwise.

In addition, there has been a tendency, over the last 12 races, for 9, 10 and 11 year-olds to do better in terms of proportion finishing in the first four than other age groups. Presumably around ten years there is some kind of equine athletic peak (though this effect is weaker than those already mentioned).

Such, then, is the reasoning behind the rule-base expressed below in the Leonardo rule language.

```
grandnat                              9-Mar-89
-------------------------------------------------------------------

1 : /* Rule-base for the Grand National (Bayesian) :
2 : /* by R.S. Forsyth, April 1988
3 :
4 : control bayes
5 :
6 : control 'threshold 0.02'
7 :
8 : seek backability
9 :
10 : if start is yes then use introscreen; intro is done
11 :
12 : if intro is done
13 : and horsename is not '????'
14 : and won_in_last_4 > 0 { Ls 1.88 Ln 0.6 }
15 : then backability is ok { Prior 0.1 }
16 :
17 : if age_of_horse > 8
18 : and age_of_horse < 12 { Ls 1.2 Ln 0.7 }
19 : then backability is ok { Prior 0.1 }
20 :
21 : if forecast_odds <= 20 { Ls 2.5 Ln 0.48 }
22 : then backability is ok
23 :
24 : if weight_carried is 'more than 10 stone' { Ls 2.36 Ln 0.44 }
25 : then backability is ok
26 :
27 : if going is not heavy { Ls 1.25 Ln 0.8 }
28 : then backability is ok
29 :
30 : /* heavy going tends to produce funny results.
31 :
32 : /* Preamble is in IntroScreen
33 : /* Postscript is in Conclusion slot of Backability
```

There is not space here to explain the system in depth, but it should be noted that this example uses Leonardo's Bayesian inference method, which requires values for LS (Logical Sufficiency) and LN (Logical Necessity) to be specified.

The goal of the system is to establish a value for the variable BACKABILITY — which can be interpreted as the probability of the horse under consideration finishing in the first four (thus gaining at least place-money). The prior probability of this happening is 0.1, since the race limit is 40 entrants and it is hardly ever under-subscribed.

Leonardo, like similar systems, prompts for values of variables having a bearing on the goal to be sought (such as AGE_OF_HORSE) from the user; and then uses Bayes's rule to update the probability of BACKABILITY. The apparent simplicity of the rule-base is slightly deceptive, as there are other elements that do not appear in these rules (e.g. an introductory message). Of these background elements the most important is a little procedure that decides on acceptable odds once BACKABILITY is known, listed below.

```
Name: Vfmodds
Longname:
Type: Procedure
AcceptsText: back
LocalReal: cf, vfm
Body:

screen(63)
global
cf = certainty(back) / 400
vfm = ((1-cf)/cf)
vfm = int(vfm+0.5)
box (5,10,10,70,31,1)
at(7,15, horsename,' should be worth an each-way bet if')
at(8,15, 'you can get odds of ',vfm as 'xxx',' to 1')
```

This is Leonardo's rather roundabout way of defining a procedure called VFMODDS, which is used at the end of the consultation to tell the user what odds would represent value for money. The details are not very important here, but to understand what is going on you need to know that Leonardo is an object-oriented system. Rules implicitly declare objects, such as GOING and BACKABILITY. Each object is described by a frame that consists of a number of slots (or attributes), such as

```
Name: age_of_horse
Value: 8
Certainty: {1.0}
```

and many more besides. Some slots are filled by Leonardo with default values; others are optional. It so happens that an object of type

Procedure must have a slot called

Body:

which contains statements in Leonardo's procedural programming language. This allows a knowledge base to contain a mixture of declarative and procedural code.

VFMODDS is actually called by putting the line

Conclusion: {run vfmodds(backability)}

as a slot in BACKABILITY's frame. This is an optional slot that says what should happen when the system gets to a conclusion about an object's value.

2.2 Derby Day

Our second example concentrates on another major sporting occasion, also the medium of heavy betting, the Epsom Derby. Here we illustrate a different software package, Egeria. In Egeria there is no division, as there is in Leonardo, between the procedural programming language and the rule language.

The system listed below is the result of an afternoon spent poring over some racing annuals for the years 1983 to 1989. It is a simple betting advisor for the Epsom Derby. It won't make your fortune, but it will almost certainly save you from backing some real no-hopers, especially if you use it over a number of years.

It rates any horse according to three attributes which are fairly easy to find out about. (Some other possible attributes were considered, but they had little effect.) These are:

Odds: Forecast betting odds
Lastrace: Finishing position in horse's last race
WonTrial: Whether horse has won a recognized trial:
- Guardian Trial
- 2000 Guineas
- Lingfield Trial
- Dante Stakes.

The program applies the rule

If odds >= 20 or lastrace > 3 then 'Hopeless'
else if odds < 10 and lastrace = 1 then 'Probable'
else if WonTrial then 'Probable'
else 'Possible'

to split the runners into three categories. As a matter of interest, the results for each of those categories over the last 7 runnings of the race (1983-89) are tabulated below.

	Winners/Runners	Placed (1,2,3)
Probable	6/27	13/27
Possible	1/23	5/23
Hopeless	0/64	3/64

Table 1.2- Derby results, 1983-89.

Essentially this is a way of eliminating over half the contestants, which have very little chance of winning. A few refinements to the bare rule have been added in the Egeria program.

(Readers may find it amusing to try out either or both of these knowledge bases in practice. N.B. Please don't expect miracles!)

```
BREAK '£3£'
HALT
END BREAK /* Traps CTRL+C */

/* Betting Advisor for Epsom Derby, RS Forsyth, Feb-89 */

condition hopeless is
 odds >= 20 or lastrace > 3

condition probable is
 not hopeless and
 (odds < 10 and lastrace = 1) or WonTrial

condition question WonTrial
 'Has it won any of: Guardian Trial, 2000 Gns,
    Lingfield Trial, Dante? '

integer question odd1
 'What is the first number (before /) in the forecast odds? '
```

is 1 to 2000

integer question odd2
'What is the second number (after /) in the forecast odds? '
is 1 to 100

real odds is
odd1 / odd2 /* just simple arithmetic */

integer question lastrace
'Please enter position in last race (1 to 9) or 10
for 10th or worse ' IS 1 TO 10

string question name
'Please give the name of the horse you are interested in : '

window Welcome /* Opening screen is saved on file as a
                message window */
end window

procedure advisor (string outcome)
  /* this procedural code is called once the category is known */
  use syswindow
  if outcome = 'Hopeless' then
    writeline Name, ' has virtually no chance.'
  else
    if outcome = 'Possible' then
      if odds > 4 then
        writeline Name, ' might just be worth an each-way bet.'
      else writeline Name, ' is unlikely to be worth backing.'
      end if
    else
      if outcome = 'Probable' then
        writeline Name, ' has a reasonable chance.'
        write 'I suggest '
        writeline if odds > 4 then
                    'an each-way bet.'
                  else 'a win bet.'
      else writeline 'I cannot decide about ', Name
      end if
    end if
  end if
end procedure

```
Task Main when created
 /* Main is triggered when the program starts */
 put Welcome /* gives instructions to user */
 writeline ' ---- DERBY DAY Betting Advisor ---- '
 ask [Name, odd1, odd2, lastrace]
 if hopeless then
  do advisor ('Hopeless')
 else
  investigate [probable]
  until probable then
    do advisor ('Probable')
    finish
  otherwise
    do advisor ('Possible')
    finish
 end if
end task
```

Once again the details are not so important as the general principles, though it is worth noting the difference between *tasks* and *procedures*. This example program contains one of each, a task (Main) and a procedure (Advisor). The task calls the procedure.

Procedures are called at specific points in the program — just as in conventional programming languages like C or Pascal. Tasks, on the other hand, are executed when their triggering condition becomes true. This provides a kind of event-driven programming. In the present case, however, this flexibility is not utilized: Main is simply triggered off when the program begins.

Like Leonardo, Egeria offers:

- object-oriented structures (with class inheritance)
- uncertainty management, in various forms
- procedural code
- multiple alternative representation methods

Between them, Egeria and Leonardo give a good idea of the sort of facilities available for developing knowledge-based systems in a modern knowledge-engineering software environment.

3 Towards the Sixth Generation

The knowledge bases listed in the previous section are unrealistic in size, but realistic in being hand-crafted. That is to say someone (the present author in this case) had to think up the rules. This is one of the weak points of expert systems, and one of the reasons why machine learning is enjoying a revival [7]. If we want truly intelligent machines the issue of machine learning will have to be tackled, and there are signs on the horizon that the effort needed to do so has already begun.

3.1 Beyond 1992

In 1992 the Japanese Fifth Generation Project, which caused great excitement in the computer industry when it was launched a decade earlier, reaches its conclusion. It is already safe to state that it will fail to attain some of its declared objectives. Goals likely to remain unrealized by the 1992 deadline include:

(1) unrestricted machine translation
(2) applied speech understanding
(3) image understanding systems
(4) highly parallel general-purpose inference engines

These, and some other aims, would — we were initially led to believe — come to fruition within the time span of the ten-year project. But their realization has been postponed.

In Europe (and probably North America) such an outcome would no doubt lead to the discrediting of a whole line of research — i.e. to another paradigm shift within AI. The Japanese, however, are not responding in that way: they do not plan to abandon what they have done so far. Instead they intend to build on it by trying harder (with, admittedly, a change of emphasis).

The Fifth Generation project will almost certainly be followed by a Sixth Generation initiative, which will pick up many of the unfulfilled aims of the Fifth Generation as well as adding new goals of its own. The shape of the Sixth Generation is becoming clear, at least in outline, and it is certain that it will be a dominant influence on the course of AI from now till the end of the twentieth century. Just as the centre of AI moved west across America in the 1970s, so now we are witnessing its move, further west, across the Pacific.

The Sixth Generation (6G) is a rather tenuous concept, perhaps even more so than the Fifth Generation before it. But it is a useful term, none the less, for gathering together several disparate strands at the leading edge of AI research. According to Gomi [10], the phrase was first seriously used in a 1985 report from a working group at the Japanese Agency of Science and Technology (JAST). However the Ministry of International Trade and Industry forced JAST to stop using such terminology and in fact suppressed that report, fearing that it would have a negative impact on the Fifth Generation project, which then had more than half its life still to run.

Today, however, many Japanese (and some Americans) are starting to talk more freely about 6G computing and what it would entail. Two groups in particular have taken up the ideas embodied in the lost JAST report, and embellished them some more. These are the the Human Frontier Science Program (HFSP) researchers and the Advanced Telecommunications Research (ATR) group. Their plans for the 6G explicitly call for major advances in

- psychology
- physiology
- linguistics
- logic

as well as computer science and AI. Applications will include:

- machine translation
- intelligent autonomous robots
- real-time expert systems
- analogical and qualitative reasoning

Two specific projects, above all, typify the challenge which these research groups expect to meet:

(1) computerized cars
(2) translating telephones

3.2 Autonomous Automobiles

At present it would be quite absurd to expect a computer-controlled vehicle to travel for more than 25 meters down a busy city road without crashing. Driving is one of those skills that has so far resisted all attempts at automation. Several teams in the USA, largely under military direction, have been working on Autonomous Land

Vehicle (ALV) projects, but — even allowing for military secrecy — they do not appear to have succeeded.

At HFSP (roughly speaking, Japan's answer to the Stanford Research Institute) they believe that the failure of previous efforts to build an ALV can be explained, at least in part, by over reliance on symbolic processing. By integrating the perceptual and learning abilities of large-scale neural nets as subsystems within a modular cognitive architecture, they hope to create, by early next century, an ALV which will not cause panic and danger when let loose in urban traffic.

A successful ALV demands the solution of a high proportion of the outstanding problems at the frontiers of AI. Among other things, it would have to be able to do real-time image processing (possibly supplemented by sonar or radar information); it would have to integrate long-term and short-term planning in a dynamic environment; and, above all, it would have to be adaptive, since its plans would need amendment from minute to minute to deal with the unexpected. The challenge posed by designing an ALV leads us to reflect that a typical truck driver exhibits skills much further beyond the current boundaries of AI than those of, say, a chess grandmaster.

Of course, we should not idealize human abilities: humans are not very good at driving either. In 1987 in the UK, 69418 people were seriously injured in road accidents (of whom 5125 died). Thus there were, on average, 190 serious injuries every day that year on British roads. More concretely, a quick survey outside my house prior of writing this sentence revealed evidence of collision damage on 3 of the 7 vehicles parked in a quiet side street. This is only a tiny sample, but it does show that accidents are relatively normal. That is one reason why robotic transport might be desirable.

3.3 Translating Telephones

Perhaps even more ambitious are the plans of ATR. They have a budget of 615 million US dollar for the first 7.5 years of a 15-year advanced research programme which began in 1986. According to Dr Koichi Yamashita, president of ATR's Kansai Science City laboratory, their main goal is research into what they call HOCS (Human Oriented Communications Systems). A central part of this programme is the development of a telephone system that will understand utterances by parties in foreign languages (e.g. English) and translate them — in real time — into Japanese. Their plan calls for the building of a prototype system, operating between Japan and the United States, by 2001. Less complete prototypes are to be tested earlier, including a major milestone demonstration in 1995.

The system will have to handle continuous speech, from many different speakers, with a large vocabulary, in real time. In addition, it is foreseen that most of the input will be ungrammatical: people do not actually talk in well-formed sentences. Allowing irregular input will result in a high degree of uncertainty in the translation process, making accurate translation extremely difficult.

ATR plans to use an interlingual representation, such that all foreign-language input will be translated into a common internal base (not Japanese but a kind of universal semantic code) which will then be rendered into Japanese, or possibly other languages. This goes well beyond anything currently possible, or even planned, elsewhere in the world.

Even if this particular project is a "glorious failure" it is very probable that its technological spin-off will include a number of inventions that will confirm Japan's status as world leader in telecommunications. And the scientific knowledge gained on the way could lead to a revolution in linguistics.

3.4 A Prognostication

The idea of a telephone exchange that understands enough about human concerns and human communication to perform simultaneous translation on multiple channels is, strictly speaking, fantastic. (Surely an intellect capable of such a feat would be driven insane by being buried beneath Tokyo and compelled to listen to incessant chatter?) I personally would be most surprised if such a device is created within the time scale envisaged. But that does not mean that it is a futile enterprise. On the contrary, the translating telephone, like the ALV, is an excellent focus for 6G research.

In conclusion: the 6G is still little more than a collection of buzz words, but it would be wrong to dismiss it on that account. There is a well-funded, worldwide effort in progress to make a reality of what until recently would have been seen as science fiction. The Japanese, especially, are determined to make the 6G more than just a slogan.

If, by the early years of the 21st century, ordinary folk really can pick up a phone in California and speak fluent English to a monolingual Japanese speaker (and be understood without perceptible delay) or can hail a ride in a computer-driven taxi, then AI will at last have earned its name; and a profound change in the whole character of civilization will have taken place.

If such things do not come to pass, AI will once again have promised more than it can deliver, and the search for a new paradigm will begin all over again.

References

[1]   I. Aleksander & P. Burnett, *Reinventing Man*, Pelican Books, Middlesex, 1984.

[2]   B. Buchanan & E. Feigenbaum, "DENDRAL and Meta-DENDRAL: their Applications Dimension", *Artificial Intelligence*, **Vol-11**, pp 5-24, 1978.

[3]   Creative Logic Ltd, *Leonardo : the Manual*, Creative Logic Ltd, Uxbridge, 1988.

[4]   R. Davis & D. Lenat, *Knowledge based Systems in Artificial Intelligence*, McGraw-Hill, New York, 1982.

[5]   G.W. Ernst & A. Newell, *GPS : a Case Study in Generality* and *Problem Solving*, Academic Press, New York, 1969.

[6]   R. Fikes & N. Nilsson, "STRIPS: a New Approach to the Application of Theorem Proving to Problem Solving", *Artificial Intelligence*, **Vol-2**, pp 189-208, 1971.

[7]   R. Forsyth, *Machine Learning : Principles and Techniques*, Chapman & Hall, London, 1989.

[8]   R. Forsyth & R. Rada, *Machine Learning*, Ellis Horwood, Chichester, 1986.

[9]   J. Gasching, "Prospector: an Expert System for Mineral Exploration", in *Introduction Readings in Expert Systems*, D. Michie (ed.), Gordon & Breach, New York, 1982.

[10] T. Gomi, "Sixth Generation Computing by the Year 2001", *Proc. 2nd International Symposium on Artificial Intelligence and Expert Systems*, BCEEP, Berlin, pp 213-312, 1988.

[11] K. Haase, "Automated Discovery", in *Machine Learning: Principles and Techniques*, R. Forsyth (ed.), Chapman & Hall, London, 1989.

[12] A. Hart, *Knowledge Acquisition for Expert Systems*, Kogan Page, London, 1986.

[13] J. Holland, *Adaptation in Natural and Artificial Systems*, University of Michigan Press, Ann Arbor, 1975.

[14] ISI Ltd, *Expert Systems with Egeria*, Intelligent Systems International Ltd, Redhill, 1989.

[15] A. Kidd, *Knowledge Acquisition for Expert Systems*, Plenum Press, New York, 1987.

[16] D. Lenat, "Eurisko: a Program that learns new Heuristics and Domain Concepts", *Artificial Intelligence*, **Vol-21**, pp 61-98, 1983.

[17] R. Michalski & R.L. Chilausky, "Knowledge Acquisition by Encoding Expert Rules versus Computer Induction from Examples: a Case Study Involving Soybean Pathology", *Int. J. Man-Machine Studies*, **Vol-12**, pp 63-87, 1980.

[18] D. Michie & R. Johnston, *The Creative Computer*, Pelican Books, Middlesex, 1985.

[19] M. Minsky & S. Papert, *Perceptrons: an Introduction to Computational Geometry*, MIT Press, Cambridge Mass, 1969.

[20] A. Newell & H. Simon, *Human Problem Solving*, Prentice-Hall, Englewood Cliffs, 1972.

[21] J.R. Quinlan, "Induction of Decision Trees", *Machine Learning*, **Vol-1**, pp 81-106, 1986.

[22] F. Rosenblatt, "The Perceptron, a Perceiving and Recognizing Automaton", *Cornell Aeronautical Lab Report* 85-460-1, Cornell University, New York, 1957.

[23] F. Rosenblatt, *Principles of Neurodynamics*, Spartan Books, New York, 1962.

[24] D. Rumelhart & J. McClelland (eds.), *Parallel Distributed Processing*, **Vols-1 & 2**, MIT Press, Cambridge, Mass, 1989.

[25] E. Sacerdoti, "Planning in a Hierarchy of Abstraction Spaces", *Artificial Intelligence*, **Vol-5**, pp 115-135, 1974.

[26] T. Sejnowksi & C.R. Rosenberg, "Parallel Networks that Learn to Pronounce English Text", *Complex Systems*, **Vol-1**, pp 145-168, 1987.

[27] O. Selfridge, "Pattern Recognition and Modern Computers", *Proc. Western Joint Computer Conference*, Los Angeles, March 1955.

[28] O. Selfridge, "Pandemonium: a Paradigm for Learning", in *Mechanization of Thought Processes*, HMSO, London, 1959.

[29] M. Shelley, *Frankenstein: or, the Modern Prometheus*, Bantam Books, New York, 1981.

[30] E. Shortliffe, *Computer-based Medical Consultations: MYCIN*, Elsevier, New York, 1976.

[31] A. Turing, "Computing Machinery and Intelligence", *Mind*, 59, 256, pp 433-460, 1950.

[32] J. Von Neumann, *The Computer and the Brain*, Yale University Press, New Haven, 1958.

[33] B. Widrow & M. Hoff, "Adaptive Switching Circuits", *Inst. Radio Engineers*, Western Electronics Convention Record, **part 4**, pp 96-104, 1960.

[34] T. Winograd, *Understanding Natural Language*, Edinburgh University Press, Edinburgh, 1972.

[35] L. Zadeh, "Fuzzy Sets", *Information and Control*, **Vol-8**, pp338-353, 1965.

Chapter 2

Blackboard Architectures and Systems

J. Hallam

1 Introduction

Blackboard systems have been widely used in many different applications. They have been implemented in different languages, have exploited different processor configurations and machine architectures, and their applications have laid stress on different features of their design or use.

This chapter does not set out to review existing blackboard systems or to describe in detail how to implement them. Excellent reviews of blackboard systems exist already (e.g. [6]). Rather, it tries to present an introduction to the essential ideas in a way that does not presuppose a great deal of background knowledge of artificial intelligence or knowledge-based systems. The aim is to provide an introduction to the prolific technical literature on blackboard systems and assist application designers in deciding whether the blackboard architecture is the appropriate one for their problem. Readers interested in a fuller explanation of blackboards, their applications, and their attendant folklore, are referred to the excellent book by Engelmore and Morgan [1] which collects together many classic and several new papers on the blackboard model and its applications.

To motivate our thinking, we begin with a brief look at intelligent problem solving. We then turn to an extended description of the blackboard model and architecture, using a hypothetical jigsaw puzzle solving program as the principal motivating example. We examine a modern blackboard shell, look at some of the problems associated with maintaining a consistent blackboard state, and conclude by considering some open directions for further research into blackboard systems.

2 Why Blackboards?

In attempting to solve any problem, a series of problem-solving actions must be performed. Possible actions at any stage depend on the current state of the problem-solving process, and at each stage a variety of actions may be possible. Correct choice of problem-solving steps will frequently be crucial to the performance of the problem solver; the determination of which actions to perform in what order is the control problem in problem-solving.

Hayes-Roth and Hewett [2] argue that a solution to this control problem is fundamental to intelligent behaviour. In resolving this issue a system determines the sorts of problems it will attempt to solve, the knowledge it will employ, the strategies it is prepared to use, the value it will assign to alternative approaches, and under what circumstances it will re-prioritize its activities.

Despite considerable advances in problem-solving knowledge and heuristics, many problem-solving systems built in and outside artificial intelligence use relatively unsophisticated strategies. Their response to the control problem is hard-wired or minimally flexible. In contrast, human problem solving shows great versatility, flexibility and many variations of strategy.

There is no shortage of hard problems. Most problems involving the interpretation of noisy signals — speech understanding, sonar interpretation, analogue circuit diagnosis, nuclear reactor control, etc. — fall into this category. Not only is the input data complex, partial, frequently erroneous, ambiguous and prolific, but the systems solving such problems are often required to operate under tight resource constraints. For such problems, the effective deployment of knowledge is of great benefit, as experience with the HASP/SIAP blackboard system shows:

> In signal processing applications, involving large amounts of data with poor signal-to-noise ratio, it is possible to reduce computation costs by several orders of magnitude by the use of knowledge-based reasoning rather than brute-force statistical methods. ... Sensor parameters can then be "tuned" to the expected signals and signal directions; not every signal

every signal in every direction need be searched for. (Nii *et al.* [7])

Sophisticated solutions to the control problem, permitting versatility rivalling that of human problem-solving at comparable or substantially greater speed, are necessary if machine assistance or automation is to be realized in solving complex problems. Hayes-Roth and Hewett identify eight key kinds of control behaviour in an intelligent system. Each one is based on assumptions about what makes for effective problem-solving and so should be viewed as necessary, but not sufficient [2]. They are:

(1) To make explicit control decisions that solve the control problem, i.e. the system must explicitly decide what to do and when.

(2) To decide what actions to perform on the basis of independent decisions about the desirability and the feasibility of actions.

(3) To adopt variable grain-size control heuristics in response to the changing problem-solving situation.

(4) To adopt control heuristics that focus on those action attributes useful in the current problem-solving situation.

(5) To adopt and discard individual control heuristics in response to dynamic problem-solving situations.

(6) To decide how to integrate multiple control heuristics of varying importance .

(7) To plan strategic sequences of actions on a dynamic basis.

(8) To reason about the relative priorities of control actions (thinking about problem solving) and domain actions (solving the problem).

These eight kinds of behaviour are expounded in more detail in the paper cited above. For our purposes, it is enough to note that the intelligent problem solver that meets all these constraints will always be adjusting its activities to reflect the current state of the problem-solving process and to take best advantage of the resources available; in other words, it will act opportunistically. It will also be able to reason about its reasoning as well as its actions — it will be able to think about problem solving. Blackboards, of all the tools available in artificial intelligence, offer the most potential for realizing such a system.

3 The Blackboard Model

If blackboard systems show great diversity of application and implementation what, then, are their essential defining characteristics? Blackboard systems embody a particular model of intelligent problem-solving activity, generalized from the techniques used in early systems such as the HEARSAY-II speech-understanding system developed between 1971 and 1976 (e.g. [8,9]). The model, which we shall refer to as the *blackboard model* of problem solving, is both powerful and general, yet sufficiently well defined to permit computational realization. It is this model that defines the blackboard system.

Imagine a group of experts collaborating to solve a complex problem. They have at their disposal their considerable collective expertise, a quiet room, and a large blackboard. Each expert is a specialist whose knowledge may be relevant at some point in the problem-solving process.

The experts agree to maintain a record of their current best partial solution(s) to the problem on the blackboard for all to see. Anyone able to contribute to the current partial solution writes their contribution on the blackboard. The information on the blackboard may also be modified or deleted by experts during problem solving, if, for example, a particular line of reasoning being pursued by the group is recognised by an expert to lead nowhere. Each expert watches the blackboard, looking for the opportunities to contribute to the solution which arise in the course of problem solving as the combination of items on the blackboard fits their particular specialist expertise.

Of course, in real life, things are not as straightforward as this. The interaction of the experts as defined above is somewhat anarchic and the team would need to be well disciplined in order to make the problem-solving process fruitful. At any one time there will typically be a number of experts whose knowledge is applicable to the contents of the blackboard; they cannot all be allowed to modify the information on the blackboard indiscriminately, or chaos will result. Furthermore, not all the contributions will be equally valuable: some may advance the solution a long way, others not at all; some may be relevant to the current point of attack on the problem, others incidental or even irrelevant to the group's activity at the time when they arise. What is needed is an agreed method of evaluating the contributions of the experts and of determining who should be allowed to write on the blackboard at each stage in the problem-solving process.

A second difficulty with the style of problem solving wc are discussing is the constraint that everything be written on the blackboard for all to see. This raises two questions:

(1) is it possible to write down, or represent, the information relevant to the problem-solving process (facts, assumptions, partial solutions, lines of reasoning, plans of attack...) in terms that all the experts can understand — or, at least, in terms comprehensible to and agreed by the experts who need to manipulate particular parts of the blackboard?

(2) is it possible to make the *relevant* information readily accessible to the people who need it — i.e. can the experts easily find the items on which their expertise can most profitably be brought to bear?

Given that scheduling of problem-solving activity can be arranged, and that a consistent, accessible method of representation for the information required by the problem-solving process can be found, the style of problem solving adopted by our team of experts has a number of advantages, as we shall see. In particular,

-    it allows expertise to be brought to bear on the problem in a manner and order determined by the progress of the problem-solving process and the expertise available, i.e. problem solving proceeds opportunistically;

-    it is easy to add new experts, even during the problem-solving process, since all the information required by the experts can be found on the blackboard;

-    different aspects of the problem can be considered simultaneously by different groups of experts using different areas of blackboard;

-    since all interactions between experts take place through the blackboard, complete control of the problem-solving process can be exercised solely by determining the experts' order of access.

It is now time to leave our analogy of collaborative problem solving by a team of experts and consider the blackboard model more formally. In essence, the blackboard model is just the abstraction of the desirable features of the problem-solving activity of the experts: a highly structured special case of opportunistic, distributed problem-solving. The blackboard model prescribes the organization of all the information relevant to the problem-solving process — input data, partial and complete solutions, hypotheses, plans, etc. — and determines the application and organization of knowledge used during problem solving.

4 What's in a Blackboard System?

The blackboard model, then, comprises three major components (Figure 2.1): *knowledge sources,* analogous to the experts, comprising the knowledge necessary for solving the task problems; a structured global database, analogous to and also named *the blackboard,* through which the knowledge sources interact and in which the state of the problem-solving process is recorded; and *a control or scheduling regime* which determines the order of problem-solving activity.

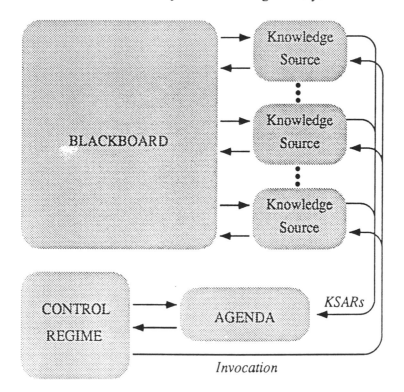

Figure 2.1- Components of a blackboard system.

In order to examine these in more detail, we shall use another analogy — that of solving jigsaw puzzles. The analogy is a good one, since these puzzles provide considerable scope for variety in problem-solving strategy, they share considerable common ground with the signal interpretation problems for which blackboard systems are frequently employed, and they are accessible to almost everyone. Even those who have never seriously played with jigsaws have definite views on the right way of tackling them! We shall take it rather further than most, however, and describe a putative design for a blackboard system to solve jigsaw puzzles.

Suppose, then, that we have the task of designing a system to solve jigsaw-puzzles automatically. The system will be presented with a large box of pieces comprising a number of different jigsaws muddled together; it has access to the pictures on the original boxes and so knows what the completed jigsaws look like; it can describe the shape and patterns of pieces chosen from the box; and it can manipulate the pieces as required to assemble the puzzles. (In fact, the sensor and effector assumptions would probably be the hardest to validate in a real system; however, we shall neglect this extra complexity for the sake of brevity.) We shall consider each of the major components of the blackboard model in turn and see how they might be realized in our jigsaw puzzle solver.

4.1 The Blackboard

As we have seen, the blackboard is a globally accessible structured database in which all information relevant to the problem-solving process is recorded. Knowledge sources change the contents of the blackboard as a result of their reasoning, and all communication between knowledge sources passes through the blackboard.

In the jigsaw puzzle solver, the blackboard contents comprise the set of pieces currently under consideration, their properties (shape, connectivity and pattern), the partial solutions achieved so far — assemblies of pieces — and perhaps control information. This information recorded in the blackboard is structured into a number of layers of abstraction organized hierarchically. For example, we could partition the blackboard into *panels* as shown in Figure 2.2:

The Picture Panel holds the information contained in the picture from a jigsaw box; there is one of these for each puzzle to be solved.

The Jigsaw Panel holds the current partial solution to a single jigsaw; there will also be one of these panels for each jigsaw.

The Assembly Panel holds representations of all the current partial assemblies of pieces; this is a common area, since at this level it is not known to which jigsaw a given assembly belongs.

The Pieces Panel holds descriptions of individual pieces that the system has encountered and processed, is waiting to process, or is seeking.

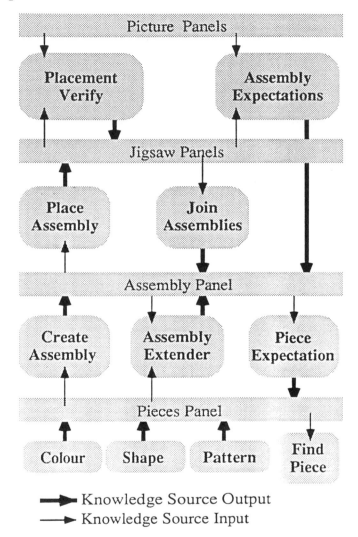

Figure 2.2- The jigsaw puzzle solver blackboard.

The objects present in each panel are described in a vocabulary appropriate to their level of abstraction. For example, the jigsaw panel records the relative placement of the partial assemblies in the complete puzzle, while the pieces panel records the properties (shape, connectivity and pattern) of individual pieces. The information in a blackboard panel is typically represented as object-attribute-value records. Relationships between objects are represented by named links which may connect objects within a panel (e.g. *assembly_*1 [is] **south_west** [of] *assembly_*2) or in different panels (e.g. *assembly_*1 **comprises** *piece_*276).

Note that whatever representation we use for recording the information in the blackboard panels, it is vital that it be able to cope with partial information. For instance, we may at some point need to search for bright blue pieces (to complete the sky, for example) without knowing their shape or connectivity; we will certainly wish to place assemblies in their respective jigsaw frames without knowing precisely where they go. Thus, the blackboard panels record not only the proven facts connected with a problem solution, but also hypotheses and expectations.

4.2 The Knowledge Sources

Information associated with the description at one level of abstraction forms the input to knowledge sources that modify the same or other panels of the blackboard. Thus knowledge sources will mediate the construction of assemblies from pieces, the placement of assemblies in the jigsaws, comparison of jigsaws with pictures, and so on.

These knowledge sources contain the expertise necessary to the problem-solving process. Their objective is to contribute information leading toward a solution to the problem. For our jigsaw puzzle solver, and in general, they fall into three categories:

Constructive Knowledge Sources, which collect together objects at one level of abstraction and generate objects at a higher level (e.g. assemblies from pieces);

Predictive Knowledge Sources, which generate expectations of objects on lower levels of abstraction on the basis of partially complete instances of objects at higher levels (e.g. the colours of pieces needed to extend an assembly);

Strategic Knowledge Sources, which influence the control of problem-solving activity on the basis of the current constructs and expectations on each blackboard panel (e.g. should we focus on trying to extend an existing assembly, or collect and describe more pieces?).

Each knowledge source examines the blackboard for combinations of its input objects that allow it to generate new conclusions. Knowledge sources, like the experts, are held responsible for knowing under what conditions their expertise may be applied. This information is generally split into two components: *trigger conditions,* which signify that the knowledge source may be able to contribute; and *preconditions* which must be met by items in the blackboard before the knowledge source can legitimately be activated.

As an example, consider the knowledge source which handles searches for expected pieces in the jigsaw solver (See Figure 2.3). This knows how to match new pieces to expectations, generated from an assembly, of pieces that would extend the cluster. Its task is to locate such pieces and join them to the existing assembly. The trigger conditions for this knowledge source are two: *either* a new expected piece has been generated from an assembly, *or* a new actual piece has been described by the sensor knowledge sources. Its precondition, on the other hand, is that an actual piece match a particular expected piece; its action is to attach the matching piece appropriately to the assembly.

Note that the precondition may be quite expensive to compute. In our example, when a new actual piece is recorded it should be checked against all existing expectations for compatibility, and conversely when a new expectation is proposed. Only when the precondition has been met can a piece be inserted in an assembly. The separation of trigger conditions and preconditions allows the identification of knowledge sources that might be appropriate without immediate commitment to the effort of verifying their appropriateness.

Because all communication between knowledge sources is routed through the blackboard, the knowledge sources are effectively isolated from one another. This has several consequences.

First, the knowledge sources can be developed and implemented independently, since their interface is defined by the vocabulary and organization of the blackboard. This allows the construction of a complete system to be partitioned into independent modules. However, it also assumes that the problem-solving knowledge required by the system can be partitioned cleanly into independent specialities.

Second, the knowledge sources may be implemented in different ways depending on the type of knowledge they contain. For example, the knowledge sources able to describe jigsaw pieces on the basis of sensory inspection might be coded as procedures in a language such as C or FORTRAN, allowing them to execute the requisite signal processing algorithms at reasonable speed. Knowledge conveniently encoded as rules (e.g. "if the current assembly is blue, try to add blue pieces to it") can be represented in that way. Taxonomic knowledge of objects, their relationships and properties, can be encoded using frame-based methods. Because the interface is defined, internal details of the knowledge sources can be hidden.

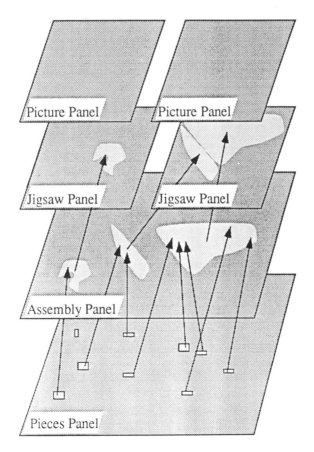

Figure 2.3- Some of the jigsaw puzzle solver knowledge sources.

All steps in the problem-solving process are explicit, being made by some knowledge source and resulting in some change to the blackboard. Thus they are visible to any knowledge source that might be able to use them. This is important from the control point of view, since scheduling decisions are based on the state of the problem and on the recent activity of the problem solver.

4.3 The Control Regime

Anyone who has watched a small child learn to do jigsaws will be aware that, once they have grasped the idea, the principal limit on their ability to do complex jigsaws is the strategy they employ. With a limited attention span, if the strategy does not result in a timely completion of the puzzle they become disillusioned and move on to some other activity.

The same is true of problem solving by machine: ultimately what limits the applicability of a given set of techniques is the effectiveness of the strategy they encapsulate for problems of interest. The constraints may be physical, such as space and time resource limitations imposed by a particular computer system; informational, in that the problem may not be soluble in terms of the sensory information directly available to the problem solver (knowledge is needed); or economic, in that only a certain expenditure of effort or resource can be permitted for solving the problem.

One of the main attractions of the blackboard model for complex problem solving in time-limited or resource-limited applications is the flexibility it affords. The model specifies precisely the interaction between the knowledge sources and that the problem-solving knowledge is to be partitioned into independent modules, but it allows considerable freedom of choice in the deployment of the knowledge and the exploitation of opportunities that arise during problem solving.

For example, when faced with a jigsaw puzzle of some complexity, a standard strategy (one which small children are not good at without practice) is to subdivide the problem into manageable chunks. We might first sort out the edge pieces of the puzzle and try to assemble the complete frame. Brightly coloured or recognisably patterned assemblies form the next likely candidates for work. Towards the end of the process, and at times during the middle, much of the activity involves detailed shape and colour matching. A good puzzle solver will know how to organize these different activities (strategic decomposition, search, detailed inspection...) in response to the size and nature of the particular puzzle and the order in which pieces come to hand.

Further, at different times during the problem-solving process we may reason in quite different ways. When constructing an assembly (e.g. the sky) out of a sizeable collection of appropriate pieces we operate in a data-driven manner, matching pieces together. When collecting the pieces, we are working in an expectation-driven way. Orthogonally to this distinction, we may wish to work with particular pieces of the puzzle (object-centred activity), or to apply particular types of knowledge (knowledge-centred activity). The blackboard model allows these different problem-solving styles to be interleaved appropriately at will, just as they are in intelligent human reasoning.

The blackboard model includes, then, a control regime which monitors the blackboard and determines what actions to take at each stage. It directs the current focus of attention of the problem solver, which may be a knowledge source to apply (knowledge-centred activity) or a set of blackboard objects to process (object-centred activity), or a combination of both. The solution to the problem is built up one step at a time, and any type of reasoning step (data-driven, goal-driven, expectation-driven, etc.) can be applied at each stage. The control regime is thus able to adapt the invocation and application of knowledge dynamically as problem solving unfolds.

The blackboard model specifies that problem-solving activity is an iterative process:

(1)   A knowledge source changes the blackboard in some way. A record of these changes is made (perhaps on a panel of the blackboard dedicated to the control regime) in a global data structure.

(2)   Each knowledge source indicates the contribution it can make given the new state of the blackboard. Typically, knowledge sources will be polled on the basis of the changes that have been made — the relationship between changes made and interested knowledge sources can either be specified by the application designer, computed dynamically or a mixture of the two. Each proposed contribution, representing a bid for work, is stored in an agenda as a Knowledge Source Activation Record (KSAR) which forms part of the information accessible to the control regime.

(3)   On the basis of change and agenda information, a focus of attention is selected by the control regime.

(4)   The selected KSAR is prepared for execution by the control regime:

-    if the focus of attention is a knowledge source then it will be necessary to determine the set of blackboard objects it should deal with (equivalent to evaluation of its preconditions);

-    if the focus of attention is a blackboard object then the control module will choose a knowledge source to process it;

-    if the focus of attention comprises both a knowledge source and an object then the selected KSAR can be executed.

The problem solver must be supplied with criteria which indicate when the solution process should terminate. This may be because an acceptable solution has been found or because the system can proceed no further. Often the termination conditions will be supplied by one of the knowledge sources.

The control information on which scheduling decisions are based may include, in general, not only the set of KSARs, representing possible actions, but also estimates of the resource implications of each bid for work, the expected benefits of that activity, the current resource constraints under which the system is operating, and strategic plans for solving the problem (encoded by the application designer or generated by the system).

As a final remark in this section, note that the control of problem-solving activity is itself an interesting problem. The blackboard model, by its flexibility, allows considerable versatility to be built into a problem-solving system. The control regime of a blackboard system can be (and, as we shall see, has been) provided by a collection of control knowledge sources which act on a control blackboard wherein the agenda and control information resides. This puts knowledge about problem solving in the abstract on an equal footing with knowledge about the particular task and domain in which the problem solver is to operate. The control knowledge sources are scheduled with the task knowledge sources by a knowledge-free scheduler whose decision parameters are set by the former. The system is then free to evaluate the potential benefits and costs of each choice for a particular step of problem-solving activity on whatever basis is appropriate at the time, and can interleave task problem solving and strategic reasoning as required.

4.4 Summary

To summarize what we have said so far, the blackboard model is a special case of opportunistic problem solving. Its basic approach is to partition the problem into loosely coupled subtasks which can be thought of as areas of specialization. For a particular application, the designer defines the sorts of information necessary for constructing solutions to the problem, selects a set of appropriate analysis levels corresponding to various degrees of partial or intermediate solution, and defines a vocabulary suitable for expressing the relevant information at each level. The domain knowledge is divided into specialist modules that typically map between the levels of representation, using objects present at one level to construct objects on other levels. The decision to employ a particular knowledge source or to focus on a particular set of blackboard objects is made dynamically on the basis of the current state of the problem-solving process recorded explicitly in the blackboard.

The blackboard model is flexible and powerful, both conceptually and computationally. It has been made to work well in many diverse application areas. There is one important caveat, however: the way in which the problem is partitioned into subproblems will crucially affect the clarity of the resulting system, the resources required, the time taken to compute solutions, and indeed the ability of the system to solve problems at all.

5 The BB1 Blackboard Shell

At this point, it is appropriate to consider the facilities offered by a modern blackboard system. We shall look at the BB1 blackboard shell [2], which offers a substructure on which a variety of blackboard applications may be constructed. Although there are other shells available, BB1 is arguably the most general from the point of view of control regime, having been designed with the necessity of solving the control problem firmly in mind. For a more detailed view of BB1, the reader should consult the paper cited, on which this section is based.

BB1 is a particularly uniform implementation of the blackboard model. It comprises instances of four conceptually distinct categories of blackboard:

Problem Blackboards record the problems that the system must solve. Their organization and content is specified by the application designer.

Solution Blackboards record the state of problem solving, in particular the data, hypotheses, partial and complete solutions associated with the task in hand. There may be multiple solution blackboards corresponding to different views of the task or to different tasks to be tackled concurrently. Once again, the organization and content is chosen by the application designer.

Knowledge Blackboards record the relatively static knowledge needed by the system for problem solving. Essentially, the system's knowledge sources are stored here. An application may have several knowledge blackboards corresponding to different views of its knowledge base. The knowledge blackboards may be modified during the system's operation if learning knowledge sources are provided.

The Control Blackboard is BB1's explicit recognition of the control problem. It records information allowing the system to evaluate, reason about, and prioritize its own feasible and desirable actions. It records a control plan for the activity of the system structured in terms of time and abstraction. Control knowledge sources record focus decisions in the control blackboard which are used by a relatively knowledge-free scheduler to determine which action to execute next. Its decisions are also recorded on the control blackboard.

In addition to the four types of blackboard, BB1 distinguishes three types of knowledge source. These are *task* knowledge sources, which represent task domain knowledge needed for solving problems and which act on the solution blackboards; *control* knowledge sources, which collaborate to solve the control problem, and act on the control blackboard; and *learning* knowledge sources, which add to or modify the system's knowledge recorded in the knowledge blackboards. Knowledge sources specify their triggering conditions, preconditions, obviation conditions (i.e. states of the blackboard that render the proposed action obsolete), and the actions they will perform. A number of generic control knowledge sources are provided to permit the implementation of simple strategies such as action sequences.

The BB1 system is a moderately large LISP system, comprising the blackboard management kernel and various editing and display utilities. Its extreme uniformity of representation is both a source of great generality and also its principal weakness, since it leaves so much to the application builder. However, front-end specializations that tailor the generic system to particular application classes are becoming available (e.g. the ACCORD framework [10]).

6 What Goes On in the Blackboard?

We have, so far, described the blackboard as if it were a structured, but passive, global database. Information recorded on the blackboard constitutes the current state of the problem-solving process. For some applications, this is a fair view of things. However, it leaves open one important question: how do we know that the contents of the blackboard represent a consistent solution or partial solution to the problem?

If the reasoning performed by the knowledge sources in solving the problem is monotonic, and we make no mistakes in coding the knowledge sources, then a simple database is sufficient. Monotonic reasoning means that the system acquires new facts as a result of its activity, but never has cause to alter its belief about old ones. Thus, provided knowledge sources are truth-preserving, all the facts recorded in the blackboard are true and consistent — if they were inconsistent with the blackboard contents at the time of their addition, the truth-preserving knowledge sources could not have deduced them; the fact that the information is present in the blackboard implies that it was held to be true at some time, and by monotonicity, it is therefore still true.

Unfortunately, things are rarely this easy. Even in the jigsaw puzzle domain, we occasionally have to strip down assemblies that turn out to be incorrect. In more complex problems, we may have to indulge in probabilistic reasoning if the input information is uncertain; we may have to make assumptions, in the absence of input, which will later turn out to be partly or wholly false; we may have to maintain a number of mutually inconsistent partial solutions to a problem, themselves internally consistent, until it is possible to identify the true solution on the basis of the available evidence. Furthermore, there are as yet no general techniques for ensuring the internal consistency of large collections of knowledge, so even if problem solving can proceed monotonically, there is the possibility of accidental non-monotonicity in the knowledge sources rendering the system's behaviour incorrect.

A full discussion of the problems implicit in these types of reasoning is beyond the scope of this chapter. However, we shall consider their implications for blackboard systems and look at two methods of addressing the issues (though not entirely solving the problem, which remains an open research question).

6.1 Consistency of the Blackboard

As we have seen, it is vital that a blackboard system maintains the internal consistency of its partial solutions to the problem it is solving. This issue, discussed rarely in the research literature, is often handled by keeping a record of how items of information come to be recorded in the blackboard — a *justification* for each fact. This may be stored in the form of a blackboard relationship such as "*fact* 1 **supports** *fact* 2" [11] or may be stored non-transparently in appropriate indexing structures. The advantage of maintaining transparent support relationships is, of course, that it is possible for the system to reason explicitly about them if necessary.

All items in the blackboard, then, have a justification. Either this is a set of other items in the blackboard — the premises on the basis of which item was deduced — or they are identified as axiomatic, self-evident *a priori* assumptions (the external inputs to the system may well possess justifications of this type). This network of relationships makes it possible to investigate the internal consistency of the information recorded in the blackboard. Unfortunately, it does not solve the problems, but merely exposes them!

The central difficulty concerns, as we have seen, non-monotonic inference. In terms of the blackboard this expresses itself as a need to modify or retract items of information recorded there. However, between the assertion of some datum and its subsequent modification or retraction other inferences will have been drawn, some of which may depend on the item as originally asserted. What happens to them when the item is modified?

To explore the scope of the difficulty,

(1) Suppose the system makes an assumption which later proves to be false. In the meantime, information dependent on that assumption has been accumulating; the retraction of the assumption implies the retraction of all the items that logically depend on it.

(2) Suppose the system is reasoning probabilistically and decides that an assumption has now become more probable in the light of additional justifying evidence. All the information which depends on that assumption must be reviewed: should the system repeat the derivations of each item, or merely recalculate the confidences it places in those deductions?

(3)   Suppose that the system makes an assumption as above, later retracts it, and then has good grounds for assuming it once more. In principle, the system may have to re-derive all the blackboard entries based on that assumption.

(4)   Finally, suppose that the reasoning performed by the knowledge sources results in circular justifications, i.e. assumptions or facts that, possibly indirectly, support themselves. Should the system permit this?

A more interesting and serious instance of this example arises if we maintain justifications for the KSARs on the system agenda. This is actually a very good idea, since the justification mechanism can then keep track of whether a bid for work is still valid — if retraction of an item invalidates its preconditions, the KSAR will no longer have a valid justification and so can be removed. Unfortunately, it then becomes possible for a paradoxical circular justification to occur. A KSAR may bid to delete an essential item of its own support.

The potential for complication in maintaining the internal consistency of the blackboard database in non-monotonic systems is clearly large. It is somewhat surprising, therefore, that few papers on blackboard systems devote any space to the topic; evidently, few problems of this sort have so far been experienced in practice. However, the difficulties do need to be addressed in any system whose behaviour is to be guaranteed in some way.

There are two readily accessible methods of maintaining blackboard consistency of which one can easily find working examples — the idea of maintaining multiple contexts, and the idea of using a truth maintenance system. We shall consider each in turn below.

6.2 Contexts and Consistency

The most obvious way of ensuring consistency is to maintain a current problem-solving context within which all assumptions, facts and derivations are assumed (and, preferably, proven) mutually consistent. If a change to the blackboard would violate the consistency of its contents, a new context is constructed containing only those entries consistent with the new one. Examples of this system include the PROLOG Blackboard Shell constructed at Edinburgh [11] and the HEARSAY-III system [12].

The former is actually a single context system, but we can think of it as a multiple context system with the proviso that the new context *replaces* the old. When an entry is to be made in the blackboard, all entries inconsistent with it are deleted. This results in a new context containing only those facts consistent with the new inference. An entry which is incompatible with itself (because it is inconsistent with the supports of the KSAR making it) is not inserted. Although this is a single context system, it could be made multi-contextual in a straightforward manner.

The HEARSAY-III system implements multiple contexts, organized hierarchically, corresponding to explicit choices made by knowledge sources. The contexts are defined by the collection of such choices encountered so far in the problem-solving process. In making a choice, HEARSAY-III allows the knowledge source two options: it can create a subcontext of the current context, or it can overlay the current context with the new. The former option allows the system to return to the parent context if the reasoning that led to the subcontext proves unfruitful, and avoids the duplication of effort that follows from overlaying a successful context during an inappropriate choice.

6.3 Assumption-based Truth Maintenance

The second method of maintaining consistency that we shall consider is to use an assumption-based truth maintenance system. Such a system not only manipulates the justifications of entries in the blackboard but, in addition, maintains the sets of assumptions on which the entries are based. In consequence, it becomes possible to explore many mutually incompatible partial solutions to a problem in an efficient manner. Contextual maintenance is free, and retraction of blackboard entries is avoided.

Work on assumption-based truth maintenance originated with Johan de Kleer [3] and has been taken up widely since its emergence. We shall consider one application of this technology to a blackboard system, the Edinburgh Designer System (EDS), which is part of the Alvey Large Scale Demonstrator "Design to Product". The goal of EDS is to assist human designers and support the various kinds of knowledge-based activity in which they engage. To this end it comprises (for our purposes; see Figure 2.4):

> a number of general purpose support systems (specialists in algebraic manipulation, kinematic reasoning, geometric display and reasoning, and tabular data management are resident in the

current system);

- a large declarative knowledge base of design information (engineering, physical and mathematical information is encoded);

- a record of the design process — the design description document, the DDD, (which resides in the system blackboard);

- an assumption-based truth maintenance system (ATMS) which maintains consistency in the DDD;

- and system management, control and interface components.

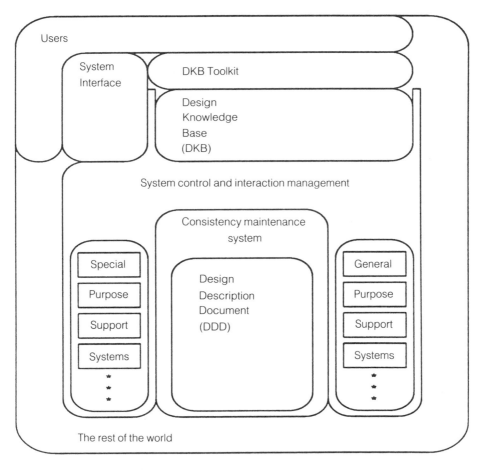

Figure 2.4- The Edinburgh Designer System (EDS).

The ATMS is used here since design is seen as an exploratory process. The designer makes assumptions and explores their consequences in the course of trying to find both a satisfactory specification for the object being designed and a consistent set of design requirements (the set of requirements with which the designer begins is typically incomplete and may also be inconsistent). A number of mutually incompatible designs will be investigated by the designer and it is vital, not only that the system maintain the various contexts required by the user, but also that it be possible to switch between contexts without penalty. The ATMS allows the system to infer the creation of new contexts for itself, since it always knows which sets of assumptions made by the designer are mutually consistent, and it also maintains all the contexts in simultaneous existence.

We do not have space to describe in detail the operation of the ATMS, for which the interested reader is referred to de Kleer's work [3,4]. However, we can illustrate the behaviour of a system like EDS informally with an example, a schematic representation of which is shown in Figure 2.5. The figures show graphically the state of the blackboard as inference proceeds.

Initially, we assume the conjunction $\{x^2-x-6=0 \cap x \geq 0\}$, denoted by $\{A\&B\}$ in Figure 2.5a. A knowledge source bids to work on this item, and after its execution, introduces two new items justified by the conjunction. These are the two components of the conjunct (Figure 2.5b). Now it is possible for an algebraic specialist knowledge source to solve the quadratic equation generating the disjunction $\{x=3 \cup x=-2\}$ shown in Figure 2.5c as $\{CorD\}$. The system can now assume each side of the disjunct in turn and invoke a knowledge source to perform inequality reasoning between the new assumptions and the $\{x \geq 0\}$ fact derived from the original conjunction. When the incompatibility of $\{x=-2\}$ and $\{x \geq 0\}$ is observed by that knowledge source (Figure 2.5d), the ATMS ensures that all the consequences of that incompatibility (including the fact that the original conjunction is not consistent with the $\{x=-2\}$ assumption) are available.

This example gives something of the flavour of the interaction between the ATMS and the knowledge sources in a system like EDS. Notice that the KSARs, represented by the circles in the figures, are managed by the ATMS on the same footing as derived facts and assumptions and mark the growth points of the ATMS dependency network. When the assumption set of a KSAR is shown to be inconsistent, the KSAR is automatically labelled so by the ATMS. The control mechanism therefore does not have to worry about the validity

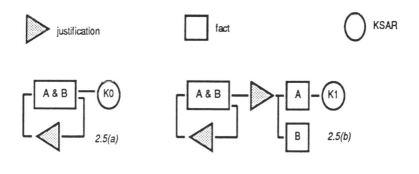

justification   fact   KSAR

2.5(a)   2.5(b)

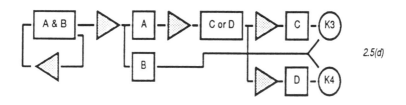

2.5(c)

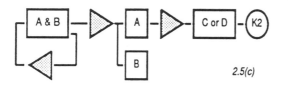

2.5(d)

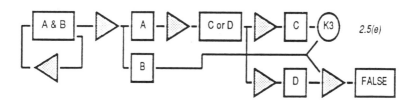

2.5(e)

$$A = \{x^2 - x - 6 = 0\} \qquad B = \{x \geq 0\}$$

$$C = \{x = 3\} \qquad D = \{x = -2\}$$

Figure 2.5- Constructing a dependency network.

of bids for work provided only justified KSAR nodes are considered for execution. However, the system does have to maintain records of bids for work dependent on items that have been derived but cannot currently be justified, since the system may discover a justification at a later time (or the designer may explicitly assume the item in question).

There are a number of respects in which EDS differs from other blackboard systems, principally because of its domain of application. As we have remarked, design is an exploratory process and this prohibits the use of the single-context system style commonly applied. The use of an ATMS to support multiple contexts efficiently has certain consequences, of which the principal one is that EDS does not (at present) make any use of deletion (or its close relative, amendment, which implies deletion) of items in the DDD. (KSARs are of course deleted from the agenda when they have been executed.) This is because it is not yet well understood how deletion ought to interact with the ATMS. Deletion of an item always occurs within some context; to remove an item completely from the blackboard may have consequences for other contexts in which the system is not currently reasoning.

7 An Alternative to Blackboards — Active Chart Parsing

Not every problem requires the full flexibility of a blackboard system. It is thus reasonable to ask whether there are any alternative approaches that retain some of the flexibility while avoiding some of the complexity. One candidate worth considering, particularly for applications which can be thought of in terms of construction and filtering of partial sequences, is the active chart parser.

Chart parsing is a non-deterministic parsing technique in which the process of assigning grammatical structure to a sequence of lexical tokens is modelled in terms of the construction of a chart. Vertices in the chart are used to represent the start and end points of components of the sequence while arcs, or edges, denote complete or partial sentences and their associated grammatical structures. Although it originated in work on the understanding of language, the chart parser is basically a universal sequence analysis tool and has been used as the fundamental architectural concept in the construction of a speech-driven word processor [13].

A chart consists of a collection of vertices (one more than the number of lexical tokens in the sequence to be parsed — they represent the *gaps* between the tokens) and a number of edges. Each edge must record its initial and terminal vertex, the grammar rule responsible for its existence, and the conditions to be met before it can be extended. Edges fall into two classes: inactive, or complete, edges, which record a complete sub-sequence corresponding to some structural element specified by the grammar; and active, or incomplete, edges, which correspond to structural elements for which search is in progress and record the sub-sequence of tokens matched so far. The initial sequence of tokens is represented by a collection of complete edges giving the lexical type of each item. Some initial active edges denoting the grammatical structures being sought must also be placed in the initial chart.

The basic operation in the chart parser is the insertion of new edges and this is possible wherever an active edge meets an inactive one which satisfies some of the needs of the active edge (I shall call such a place a "growth point"). When this occurs a new edge spanning the original two can be inserted. This combination process is called the *fundamental rule* of active chart parsing. The new, more complete, edge has the same grammatical category as the active edge and other properties computed from those of its two constituents. It is complete if the inactive edge meets all the needs of the active edge, otherwise it is incomplete (i.e. active). Note that the original edges remain — the new edge is added without deleting those it spans. This enables the parser to accommodate ambiguous token sequences as well as to pursue multiple hypotheses in parallel without knowing in advance which will prove successful. A more complete introduction to chart parsing together with the code of a parser can be found in [14].

In a practical system there are two issues that must be resolved. First, the set of possible growth points must be identified; and, second, the next growth point to be expanded must be chosen. The first issue can be addressed by maintaining an agenda of pending edges to be added to the chart. Whenever the fundamental rule is applied the new edge generated is added to the agenda of pending edges. Whenever an edge is inserted into the chart, all possible applications of the fundamental rule are enumerated and the new edges generated are inserted in the agenda, which thus continues to contain the current set of growth points.

Selection of a growth point to expand is achieved by choosing one of the edges in the current agenda and inserting it into the chart. The order in which edges are selected from the agenda implements the control strategy of the system — an emphasis on active edge insertions results in an expectation-driven system (since active edges represent search in progress) whereas an emphasis on complete edges results in a data-driven strategy (since complete edges represent recognized structure).

As in blackboard systems, opportunistic control regimes can be implemented using the chart parser. Pending edges in the agenda can be used to record potential contributions from knowledge sources, while the fundamental rule corresponds (loosely) to knowledge source invocation. Different levels of abstraction on the blackboard correspond to different charts, and the grammars parsed encode the knowledge sources operating at each level. However, unlike the blackboard architecture, it is harder to see how the control knowledge for an active chart parser might be encoded in a chart. Nevertheless, the framework is particularly suitable for applications like the speech-driven word processor [13], where hypotheses can be generated and then selectively filtered at various abstraction levels. It is also readily amenable to distributed implementation.

8 Open Research Issues

There are a number of open research issues connected with blackboard and other knowledge-based problem-solving methodologies. We consider a number of them below.

Consistency Maintenance, as we have seen, remains an open issue. The integration of truth-maintenance and blackboard systems and the maintenance of multiple contexts are areas in which further research is required. Where the context tree is generated explicitly by the user, there is the possibility of recording not only the choices which cause context forking but also the user's reasons for making those choices. The same approach could be taken with system-generated contexts as well. As usual, making this information explicit allows the system to reason about the relationships between the contexts and between items in the blackboard and the context(s) to which they belong.

Knowledge Source Consistency is also an issue of importance. In a system of realistic complexity, the question of whether knowledge-sources are internally and mutually consistent and the reasoning of the system correct looms large. Proving the correctness of knowledge, especially if elicited from experts, is at least very hard and probably intractable with present computational technology; we are frequently forced to fall back on disciplined coding practices. There is considerable scope for work on knowledge source consistency analysis and display tools.

Distributed Blackboards also pose some interesting problems. Issues of how to distribute the contents of the blackboard over several processing systems, how to extend the blackboard model to permit concurrent problem-solving steps, how to maintain the consistency of a distributed blackboard, and how to couple disparate hardware in a distributed blackboard are all active research areas.

Real-time Systems comprise another area of considerable challenge. We may define real-time systems as those for which time affects meaning — they have input processing and output generation deadlines that must be met. Many systems that address complex signal interpretation and decision problems, for which the blackboard model is eminently suitable, must overcome considerable engineering difficulties to obtain adequate throughput for real-time operation. Often the solution is to use a distributed blackboard (e.g. the real-time autonomous vehicle control system of Harmon [5]), and this brings its own complexity.

9 Conclusions

We have examined the blackboard model, looked at a modern blackboard system shell, and examined some of the difficulties associated with maintaining one or more consistent partial solutions to the problem about which the system is reasoning. We have also seen, briefly, one alternative approach to the full blackboard model. In conclusion, we make a few comparative comments illustrating the advantages and disadvantages of blackboard systems over more rigid models of problem-solving performance.

(1) The use of modular knowledge sources provides a mechanism for structuring the knowledge required for problem solving and for differentiating different kinds of knowledge about the problem.

(2) The explicit focus on control makes it possible to include general knowledge about problem solving with specific knowledge about the task problems, for the system to reason about both and to interleave task and control reasoning in a flexible way.

(3)   The use of the blackboard as the central medium of interaction frees the knowledge-source designer from the task of managing the interaction of the knowledge sources. It allows the use of diverse knowledge representation mechanisms appropriate to the type of knowledge being coded, and affords the possibility of incremental system engineering.

(4)   Using the blackboard and knowledge sources as a repository for control information constitutes a more structured approach to meta-level reasoning than is typically found in logic programming approaches and is more convincing as a model of human problem-solving activity.

(5)   There remain a number of open issues, particularly concerning real-time performance, contextual consistency in the blackboard, and the distribution of blackboard and reasoning over several or many similar or disparate processing systems.

Although the blackboard model is the most convincing model of intelligent problem-solving skills available in artificial intelligence today, evidenced by its widespread application in many diverse domains, it is still the case that the construction of a blackboard system is not something to be undertaken lightly. Straightforward application building can indeed be moderately straightforward with appropriate tools such as BB1 or other blackboard shells (other exemplars may be found in the book by Engelmore and Morgan [1]). However, the use of a blackboard for real-time control, for complex exploratory processes, or in situations where it is necessary to guarantee system behaviour, is still a substantial research undertaking.

References

[1] R. Engelmore & T. Morgan (eds.), *Blackboard Systems*, Addison-Wesley, 1988.

[2] B. Hayes-Roth & M. Hewett, "BB1: An Implementation of the Blackboard Control Architecture", in *Blackboard Systems*, Engelmore & Morgan (eds.), Addison-Wesley, 1988.

[3] J. de Kleer, "Choices Without Backtracking", *Proc. AAAI-84*, pp 79-85, 1984.

[4] J. de Kleer, "An Assumption-Based TMS", *Artificial Intelligence*, **28, (2)**, 1986.

[5] S.Y. Harmon, "Practical Implementation of Autonomous Systems: Problems and Solutions", in *Proceedings of the Intelligent Autonomous Systems Conference*, Hertzberger (ed.), Elsevier Science Publishers, 1987.

[6] H.P. Nii, "Blackboard Systems: The Blackboard Model of Problem Solving and the Evolution of Blackboard Architectures", *The A.I. Magazine*, **7**, pp 38-53, 1986.

[7] H.P. Nii, J.J. Anton, E.A. Feigenbaum & A.J. Rockmore, "Signal-to-Symbol Transformation: HASP/SIAP Case Study", in *Blackboard Systems*, Engelmore & Morgan (eds.), Addison-Wesley, 1988.

[8] D.R. Reddy, L.D. Erman & R.B. Neely, "A Model and a System for Machine Recognition of Speech" *IEEE Transactions on Audio and Electroaccoustics*, **AU-21**, pp 229-238, 1973.

[9] V.R. Lesser, R.D. Fennell, L.D. Erman & D.R. Reddy, "Organization of the HEARSAY-II Speech Understanding System", *IEEE Symposium on Speech Recognition*, pp 11-M2 to 21-M2, 1974.

[10] B. Hayes-Roth, M.V. Johnson, A. Garvey & M. Hewett, "Building Systems in the BB* Environment", in *Blackboard Systems*, Engelmore & Morgan (eds.), Addison-Wesley, 1988.

[11] J. Jones, M. Millington & P. Ross, "A Blackboard Shell in PROLOG", in *Blackboard Systems*, Engelmore & Morgan (eds.), Addison-Wesley, 1988.

[12] L.D. Erman, P.E. London & F.S. Fickas, "The Design and an Example Use of HEARSAY-III", in *Blackboard Systems*, Engelmore & Morgan (eds.), Addison-Wesley, 1988.

[13] H.S. Thompson & J.D. Laver, "The Alvey Speech Demonstrator Architecture, Methodology and Progress to Date" *Proceedings of SpeechTech-87*, New York, 1987.

[14] H.S. Thompson & G.D. Ritchie, "Techniques for Parsing Natural Language: Two Examples", in *Artificial Intelligence: Tools, Techniques and Applications*, Eisenstadt & O'Shea (eds.), Harper and Row, London, 1984.

Chapter 3

Machine Learning: Techniques and Recent Developments

P. Clark

1 Introduction

1.1 The Role of Machine Learning

The use of expert systems is becoming more and more widespread. A survey in 1988 reported the number of deployed systems had risen sharply from around 50 in the previous year to 1400, and the number under development increased from 2500 to 8500 [32]. Expert systems are characterized by the use of a particular programming methodology in which domain-specific knowledge is clearly separated from the more general inference machinery within the system. This methodology has several advantages, including easier inspection and modification of the knowledge which the system is using, and the generation of explanations by the system describing how it arrived at its conclusions.

As a result of this expansion, issues concerning the incorporation and refinement of knowledge within such systems have risen in importance. The difficulty of manually acquiring knowledge from an expert (sometimes referred to as the "Feigenbaum Bottleneck") is now well recognized and hence systems for automatically learning in ways more sophisticated than simply by being told are being more widely used.

In addition to assisting in the knowledge acquisition task, there are other motivational factors for developing machines which can learn for themselves. Firstly, the ability to learn is a primary characteristic of intelligence and hence is an essential area of study in the quest for developing artificially intelligent systems. Secondly, there exists the goal of building machines which can acquire knowledge and form theories which were previously unknown, and then communicate this knowledge to people. In this way, machines may enhance the global body of scientific and other knowledge. Michie has referred to this phenomenon as "superarticulacy" and it has already been demonstrated in limited domains of application [17].

One particular form of learning, that of inducing classification rules from a set of training examples, has received substantial attention within the machine learning field and represents the learning method most frequently and successfully used in expert system applications (e.g. [20]). Because of its relative success in applications we focus on this technique in this chapter, first describing two algorithms for rule induction which form the basis of many rule induction systems, and then reporting on recent developments in this area, seeking to extend their applicability and overcome the difficulties presented by real-world applications. Following this, we examine some of the more fundamental limitations of this approach and briefly survey some of the other methods currently being developed which strive towards producing more powerful and flexible learning machines.

1.2 The Nature of Machine Learning

An adaptive system must have, by definition, the capacity to perform a task in more than one way. Consequently the system must make choices about the most appropriate course of action to take, and if the system is adaptive it should be able to modify its choice-making behaviour should a choice turn out to be inappropriate.

In order to make choices it is necessary to predict the likely outcomes of making them, requiring some kind of internal model of the world. An adaptive system can be viewed as performing two processes involving this model: firstly, to use it to respond most appropriately to the environment, and secondly to continuously extend and correct such a model in the light of success or failure, keeping it up-to-date and efficient.

This process of self-analysis and modification can usefully be viewed as a special kind of problem-solving task — one in which the problem to be solved is that of self-diagnosis and improvement rather than the diagnosis of something external to the system. Thus it follows that many of the problem-solving techniques used in "non-learning" systems are also important in learning systems. A learning system can be viewed as performing a search, not for a solution to some external problem, but for an improved representation of knowledge within itself. Inductive leaps and generalization by a machine at one level can be regarded as the result of this special type of problem-solving search at a higher level.

This paradigm of learning as search is of central importance to machine learning, and many systems operate by searching a space of representations to find that which best fits known observations. Two examples of algorithms which do this are the ID3 and AQ algorithms, described in detail later. However, these algorithms use a fairly limited representation language requiring careful formulation of the learning task by the user in order to permit effective learning.

To move forward from such systems brings the designer face to face with a serious dilemma, concerning the trade-off between flexibility and tractability of learning. Allowing the system greater flexibility to learn by introducing a more powerful representation language for embodying learned knowledge immediately creates a major search problem, which can easily become computationally infeasible to perform. Methods for handling this trade-off are a major focus of current research, and we review some of these developments later.

1.3 Michie's Criteria

Before embarking on more detailed descriptions of learning algorithms, we make some more general comments concerning types of machine learning. Recently, alternative paradigms of machine learning besides the traditional AI type, symbolic learning, have received substantial attention. In particular, the increasing power of computers is enabling connectionist and genetic techniques to become feasible areas of study, although their status as artificial intelligence research remains controversial.

Michie [16] presents three criteria for machine learning. The *weak criterion* states that machine learning occurs when a "system uses sample data to generate an updated basis for improved performance on subsequent data". This definition assumes that all that is important is problem-solving performance, and ignores other desirable properties of an intelligent learning system such as an ability to explain its reasoning. Statistical, genetic and connectionist methods of learning also fall within this criterion.

Michie's *strong criterion* of machine learning states that the system must additionally be able to "communicate its internal updates in explicit symbolic form", and thus be able to explain in an understandable way what it has learned. The *ultra-strong criterion* goes one step further in insisting that internal updates be communicated in "operationally effective" as well as explicit form, i.e. in a form which additionally allows the expert to improve his or her own performance as well as to understand the machine's behaviour.

We have drawn on these different criteria to highlight the distinction between different forms of machine learning. In this chapter we are concerned with the strong and ultra-strong type of learning, requiring comprehensibility as well as performance, and thus we focus on systems learning structured, symbolic representations of the world.

2 The Inductive Rule-learning Methodology

2.1 Introduction

There are a wide variety of techniques used for machine learning — however the technique which has perhaps received the most attention and has been most commercially successful to date (e.g. [20]) has been the paradigm of learning classification rules from a set of training examples. In this paradigm the learning system searches a space of rules to find those which "best" classify the training examples, where "best" is defined in terms of accuracy and comprehensibility. The rules represent generalizations of the training examples with which the system was presented.

In this section we first describe two algorithms for learning such rules, namely the ID3 and AQ algorithms. These algorithms have been used as the basis of several machine-learning systems, for example ID3 in ASSISTANT-86 [3] and C4 [31] and the AQ algorithm in AQ11 [13], AQR [8] and AQ15 [11]. An example of the form of the inputs and outputs which these algorithms receive and produce is shown in Figure 3.1. Each training example is described by giving *values* for a fixed number of (user-selected) *attributes*, plus the corresponding *class* of which the example is a member.

The inductive rule-learning paradigm used in the AQ and ID3 algorithms (as well as others) is based on a simple pattern-recognition model of learning, in which correlations between observable features and some final classification are sought for.

Training Examples Input to Rule Induction Algorithms

Attributes			Class
Furry?	Age?	Size?	
furry	old	large	lion
not furry	young	large	not lion
furry	young	medium	lion
furry	old	small	not lion
furry	young	small	not lion
furry	young	large	lion
not furry	young	small	not lion
not furry	old	large	not lion

Decision Tree Output by ID3

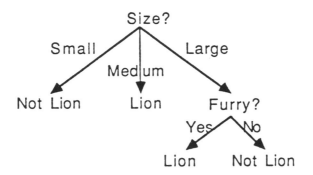

Decision Rules Output by AQ

```
if      furry=yes
and     size=large
then    class=lion.

if      size=medium
then    class=lion.

if      furry=no
then    class=not lion.

if      size=small
then    class=not lion.
```

Figure 3.1- Examples of rule induction

The initial features used to describe examples are chosen manually, and classification is made into one of a fixed number of user-defined classes. Clancey refers to this as a task of "heuristic classification" [4]. The systems do not make use of any other domain-specific information beyond that of the training examples themselves.

The rules which ID3 and AQ produce constitute a simple "model" of the world, automatically generated from the observations with which they have been presented. Although the structure of this model is simple, the operations they perform in generalizing, compressing and organizing data are fundamental to learning. Later in this chapter we discuss the possibilities and problems of extending these learning systems to acquire and refine more complex, structured representations of the world.

2.2 The ID3 Algorithm

2.2.1 Knowledge Representation

The ID3 algorithm [29] is a descendant of Hunt *et al* Concept Learning System [10]. The "rules" which ID3 learns are represented as *decision trees*. A decision tree is like a flow chart, in which a node of the tree represents a test on an attribute and each outgoing branch corresponds to a possible result of this test. Each leaf node represents a classification to be assigned to an example, as shown in Figure 3.1.

To classify a new example, a path from the root of the decision tree to a leaf node is traced. At each internal node reached, the branch corresponding to the value of the attribute tested at that node is followed. The class at the leaf node represents the class prediction for that example.

2.2.2 The Learning Algorithm

A decision tree is generated or "grown" in stages. The tree starts as a single node, containing all the training examples. ID3 looks to see if all these examples are of the same class. If they are not, it needs to grow branches from that node which will test an attribute of the examples, and sort them into groups corresponding to the different values of that attribute. An attribute is a good test to use if it sorts the examples into classes well, i.e. when most examples with the same attribute value also have the same class value. ID3 uses a function called *entropy* to measure how well an attribute test sorts examples into classes (the lower the entropy, the better the sorting). ID3 places the attribute test yielding minimum entropy at the node being expanded, and attaches branches to the node corresponding to the different values of that attribute.

Each of the leaf nodes in the new tree is now examined. If all the examples at a leaf node are found to be of the same class, then this node is finished, and this class assigned to that node. If there are examples of more than one class, then ID3 must grow the tree further at this node to sort them apart. To do this, the same procedure is used (consider all attribute tests — choose the best — expand the node by adding branches representing results of this test).

When there are no nodes left to expand, the procedure is finished. Figure 3.2 summarises this algorithm.

```
let examples = a set of training examples
let atts = the set of all attributes

procedure id3(examples,atts):
if    examples are all in a single class c
thenreturn a leaf node labelled 'predict class c'
else  for each attribute a in atts
          sort examples according to their values vᵢ of attribute a
          calculate the entropy of the sorted examples
      endfor
      select abest, the attribute which yielded the lowest entropy
      for each value vᵢ of attribute abest
          select examples eᵢ from examples for which abest = vᵢ
          generate subtreeᵢ using id3(eᵢ,atts)
      endfor
      return a node which tests abest and has subtrees subtreeᵢ
          attached
```

Figure 3.2- The ID3 algorithm.

2.2.3 Heuristic Functions

The entropy measure which ID3 uses to select the best attribute test is defined as follows:

$$Entropy = \sum_i w_i E_i$$

where w_i is the weight of the i'th branch defined as the number of examples in branch i divided by the total number of examples at the parent node, and E_i is the entropy of the i'th branch given by:

$$E_i = -\sum_j p_j \log_2 p_j$$

p_j is the probability of the j'th class in this branch, estimated from the training data.

For example, consider evaluating the entropy of placing a test on the attribute *furry* at the root of the tree, using the data in Figure 3.1. If we placed the test, the examples would be sorted at this node into two groups as follows:

furry = yes: 3 lions, 2 non-lions
furry = no: 0 lions, 3 non-lions

Hence, to calculate the entropy (a measure of how well the test sorts the examples into classes) for the attribute test *furry*:

$$Entropy_{LeftBranch} = -(0.6\log_2 0.6 + 0.4\log_2 0.4)$$

$$Entropy_{RightBranch} = -(1.0\log_2 1.0 + 0.0\log_2 0.0)$$

$$Entropy_{Total} = 0.625 \times E_{Left} + 0.375 \times E_{Right} = 0.607$$

Similarly, the entropy for tests on attributes *age* and *size* are 0.955 and 0.500 respectively. As a result, *size* is chosen for the test at the node, as it has the lowest entropy.

2.2.4 Summary

(1)   A decision tree is produced in stages, each stage being achived by adding an attribute test and branches to a leaf node in the tree.

(2) To choose which attribute test to use, consider what the new tree would look like for each possible attribute, and choose the best.

(3) "Best" is decided by applying the evaluation function *entropy* to each of the possible expansions of the node — this function returns a number which is a measure of how well the attribute test has sorted the examples at the node.

(4) If all the examples at a leaf node are of the same class, this node does not need to be expanded further. If it contains more than one class, it must be expanded further.

(5) The procedure continues expanding the unfinished nodes until no more need expanding.

2.3 The AQ Algorithm

2.3.1 Knowledge Representation

Unlike ID3, the AQ algorithm outputs a set of "if...then..." classification rules rather than a decision tree. This is useful for expert system applications based on the production-rule paradigm, and is often a more comprehensible representation than a decision tree, especially when the decision tree produced by ID3 is large.

We deviate from the terminology introduced by Michalski [11] in order to maintain continuity with the description of ID3 above. Each decision rule which AQ induces is of the form "if <condition> then predict <class>", where <condition> is a conjunct of attribute tests. There may be more than one rule for each *class*[*]. For simplicity, we use "test" to refer to an attribute test (e.g. "*furry* = *yes*") and "conjunct" to refer to a conjunct of attribute tests. A test or conjunct of tests is said to *cover* an example if all the tests are satisfied by the example.

In AQ, a new example is classified by finding which of the induced rules have their conditions satisfied by the example. If the example satisfies only one rule, then the class predicted by that rule is assigned to the example. If the example satisfies more than one rule, the most common class of training examples that were covered by those rules is predicted. If the example is not covered by any rule, then it is

---

[*] In other descriptions of AQ, the <condition> is sometimes referred to as a "complex" and rules for each class are sometimes combined into a single rule whose <condition> is a disjunct of the complexes, sometimes referred to as a "cover".

assigned by default to the class that occurred most frequently in the training examples.

2.3.2 The Learning Algorithm

AQ generates decision rules for each class in turn. This generation occurs in stages; each stage generates a single rule, and then removes the examples the rule covers from the training set. This step is repeated until enough rules are found to cover all the examples of the chosen class. This whole process is repeated for each class.

To generate a single rule, AQ first selects a "seed" example for the rule to cover and starts with the most general rule "*if* true *then* predict class c" (i.e. "all examples are class c"), where c is the class of the seed. Specialisations of this rule are then repeatedly generated and explored until a rule which covers only examples of class c and no examples of other classes has been found. Figure 3.3 summarizes the AQ algorithm.

Several "best specializations-so-far" are retained and explored in parallel, thus AQ conducts a variation on a beam search of the space. This set of solutions being explored is called a *star*. The search is shown schematically in Figure 3.4. Note that AQ is guaranteed to return rules completely consistent with the training data (if such rules exist). This is a desirable property in noiseless domains, but, as we see later, is undesirable when there is noise in the training data.

2.3.3 Heuristic Functions

AQ uses a heuristic function to decide which <condition>s in the star are "best". This function is used to decide,

(1)   which <condition>s to throw out of the star should its size exceed the user-defined maximum size, and

(2)   which is the best <condition> in the final star to use for a new rule.

The particular heuristic function used by the AQ algorithm varies from implementation to implementation. One example is to "sum of positive examples covered and negative examples excluded" and prefer <condition>s with highest score. In the case of a tie for either heuristic, the system prefers <condition>s with fewer attribute tests. Seeds are chosen at random and negative examples are chosen according to their distance from the seed (nearest ones are picked first, where distance is the number of attributes with different values in the seed and negative example).

```
let examples = a set of training examples
let classes = the set of all classes

procedure aq(examples, classes):
let allrules = {}
for each class c in classes:
    sort examples into pos (members of c) and neg (the rest)
    generate rules by aqrules(pos,neg,c)
    add rules to allrules
endfor
return allrules.

procedure aqrules(pos,neg,c):
let rules = {}
for each member of pos (each 'seed') not covered by any rule in rules:
    call aqrule(seed,neg,c) to generate a rule covering seed
    add rule to rules
endfor
return rules

procedure aqrule(seed.neg,c):
let mgc = the most general <condition> ('true')
let star initially contain only the mgc
for each negative example n in neg:
    for each <condition> c in star:
        if    c covers n
        then remove c from star
            & generate all specialisations of c which still cover seed
                but no longer cover n by adding an extra attribute test to c
                ('c' becomes 'c & test' for each test true of seed and false
                of n)
            & add them all to star.
        if    size of star > maxstar (a user-defined constant)
        then remove worst <condition>s in star
                until size of star = maxstar.
    endfor
endfor
select the best <condition> bestcond in star
return the rule 'if bestcond then predict c'
```

Figure 3.3- The AQ algorithm.

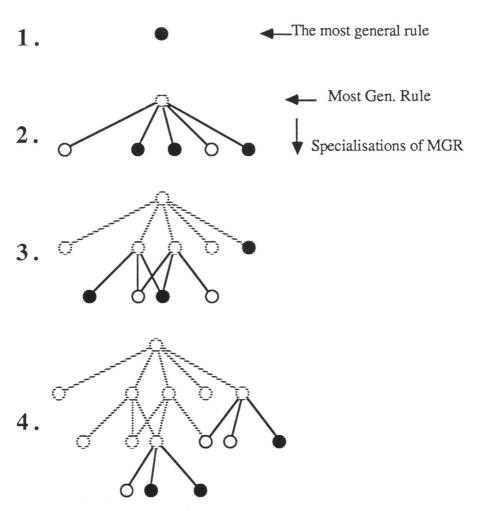

1. ●   ←—The most general rule

2. ←— Most Gen. Rule

↓ Specialisations of MGR

3.

4.

A set or `star' of current best nodes is maintained.
At each step, a different negative example is considered.
Only nodes inconsistent with the negative example are specialised.
Only specialisations which reachieve consistency are considered.
On completion of the search, the best node in the star is returned.

●   The \<n\> best nodes at each stage are stored in the `beam'
    (or `star'), where \<n\> =\< maximum star size (here it's 3).
    All other nodes are discarded.

○   Nodes explored and rejected in the current iteration of search.

○   Discarded nodes.

Figure 3.4- Schematic representation of the AQ search.

The AQ algorithm can be efficiently implemented using the Incidence Calculus methods of Bundy [2], whereby a bit-string for each attribute test is constructed, each bit representing a different example ("1" if the test is passed and "0" if it is not). Thus, calculation of the coverage of a conjunct is simply performed by the ANDing of the bit-strings for each test in the conjunct and then summing the "1"s in the resultant bit-string.

2.3.4 Summary

(1) AQ induces a set of "if...then..." rules rather than a decision tree.

(2) Each rule is generated in turn, using a variation of a *beam search* of the space of rules.

(3) A size-limited set called the *star* of best conditions-so-far is maintained during the search for a rule.

(4) The algorithm locates rules which are *completely consistent* with the training data.

2.4 Current Developments

2.4.1 Limitations

There are two classes of limitation with the AQ and ID3 algorithms presented above. Firstly, there are a number of deficiencies with the mechanisms they use which can be overcome by refining the algorithms. Considerable effort has been devoted by the machine learning community towards such improvements in recent years, and we review the major developments in this area below. Secondly, there are restrictions imposed not by the particular algorithms themselves but by the whole paradigm of rule induction from examples. These restrictions are caused by the inherent limitation of learning rules with such a simple structure (simply looking for input-output correlations). To move beyond this paradigm a more radical change of approach is required, and we discuss the possibilities and difficulties of creating more powerful learning systems of this form later.

The algorithms described above make several limiting assumptions as follows:

(1)   There is no noise in the training data.

(2)   The features used to describe examples are *adequate*, i.e. correct classification rules can be formed by boolean combinations of tests on an example's features.

(3)   The number of training examples is small enough for the algorithms to run to completion in acceptable time.

These assumptions reduce the applicability of these algorithms to many real-world applications. Indeed, these basic algorithms are rarely used on their own. We now describe some of the recent developments in work to overcome these limitations and widen their applicability.

2.4.2 Noise Tolerance

One of the most serious limitations of the above algorithms is the "noiseless domain" assumption which they make, namely that any genuine regularity in the data will be perfect (i.e. without counter-examples). Consequently the systems will return only rules which are completely consistent with the training examples. By searching for the most general, consistent rules, these systems locate regularities which involve large numbers of training examples and hence are statistically unlikely to be due to chance choice of the training examples. Instead, they reflect genuine correlations between attributes and classes in the domain and consequently perform well.

However, in most real-world domains genuine correlations are rarely perfect and there are often a few counter-examples in the training data. Such counter-examples arise due to the presence of noise and an inadequate description language for representing the domain. Searching only the space of consistent rules does not find such regularities and instead more specific rules based on only a few training examples tend to be selected. Although these rules perform perfectly on the training examples, their predictive accuracy on future test examples is often lower because rules formed on the basis of small numbers of examples are susceptible to noise. The small trends they reflect are more likely to be due to chance choice of training set compared with other rules found reflecting major correlations, but rejected due to the presence of counter-examples in the data. As a consequence, the rule set is both large and not of the highest predictive power. This is sometimes referred to as an *overfitting* of the rules to the data.

There are several techniques which have been developed for coping with this problem, and we briefly review these here.

Data Filtering

One technique is to perform induction using only *representative* training examples, as selected by the expert or automatically. This technique was used in AQ11's application to the task of soya bean diagnosis, where the ESEL system [14] was first used to select representative training examples.

Pruned general-to-specific search

One of the most common techniques for filtering out noisy components of data is to perform the search for a generalized description of observations in a general-to-specific manner, and then to halt the search before complete consistency with the training examples is reached. Such halting occurs when the number of examples supporting the current hypothesis falls too low. The general-to-specific search acts as a "covers lots of examples"-to-"covers few examples" search, which can be seen as a reliable-to-unreliable search that can be prematurely halted should a specified level of unreliability be passed.

The ID3 algorithm lends itself to easy modification due to the nature of its general-to-specific search. Tree pruning techniques (e.g. [30,24]), as used for example in the systems C4 [31] and ASSISTANT-86 [3], have proved to be effective methods of avoiding overfitting. These use statistical methods to assess confidence in the correlations the decision tree branches represent.

The AQ algorithm, however, is less easy to modify due to its dependence on specific training examples during its search. There are two possibilities of remedy here. Firstly, the basic algorithm can be left intact and noisy data can be dealt with by using pre-processing (e.g. data filtering, mentioned above) or post-processing techniques (e.g. post-pruning, see below). Existing implementations (e.g. AQ11 [13] and AQ15 [11]) have adopted this approach. A second approach is to modify the algorithm itself, removing its dependence on specific examples and increasing the space of rules searched. This approach was taken in the CN2 system [8], where instead of conducting a beam search of rules covering a seed but excluding negative examples, the beam search explores (in a general-to-specific manner) the space of all rules, and uses a statistical significance test to prevent statistically insignificant specializations being made, as illustrated in Figure 3.5.

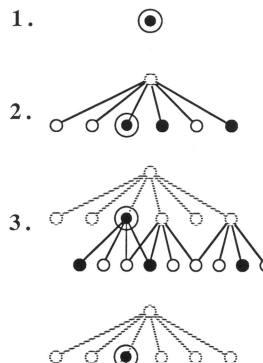

1. ← The most general rule

2. ← Most Gen. Rule

↓ Specialisations of MGR

3.

4.

A set or `star' of current best nodes is maintained.
At each step all nodes in the star are specialised.
All specialisations are considered.
A record of the best, statistically significant node is maintained.
On completion of the search, this best node is returned.

● The <n> best new nodes at each stage are stored in the `beam'
(or `star'), where <n> =< maximum star size (here it's 3).
All other nodes are discarded.

○ Nodes explored and rejected in the current iteration of search.

◌ Discarded nodes.

◉ The best, statistically significant node found so far.

Figure 3.5- Schematic representation of the CN2 search.

Post-Pruning

An alternative to prematurely halting a general-to-specific search is to allow it to run to completion (i.e. form a rule set completely *consistent** with observation) then to remove components from ("post-prune") the final rules which are deemed unreliable. The advantage of this is that the quality of pruned and unpruned versions of a rule set can be directly compared rather than having to estimate the latter's quality during search.

Again, in rule induction systems, this technique is common, for example in the most recent ID3 descendants C4 [31], ASSISTANT-86 [3] and by Niblett and Bratko [25]. Niblett [24] gives a review of pre- and post-pruning techniques used for decision trees. AQ15 [11] employs a post-pruning technique for production rules (termed "rule truncation"). The use of post-pruning of decision tree branches to generate production rules has been used by Quinlan [28].

Corroborative Rule Application

Another technique to prevent unreliable rules degrading performance is to allow all rules to contribute in some way during classification, with different weights attached to their decisions. (This requires rules which "nearly" fire to also contribute towards the final class prediction). This avoids heavy reliance on a specific, possibly unreliable, part of the system, allowing noisy effects to be over-ridden and smoothed out by other components, but also degrades the comprehensibility of the rule set. Statistical methods such as Bayesian techniques (e.g. chapter 4 of [15]) can be employed. AQ15 [11] performs weighted rule application in this way, and Quinlan [26] suggests how decision tree application can be made less brittle by introducing a degree of corroboration between decision tree branches.

2.4.3 Probabilistic Classification

Another limitation with simple rule induction methods is that no degree of certainty is attached to the classification they give. Degrees of certainty are often required for applications (most expert systems use some measure of uncertainty as part of their problem-solving strategy).

In fact probabilities and measures of certainty are easily attached to classifications, as probabilities can easily be calculated by examining

---

* Or as nearly consistent as possible if complete consistency is impossible.

the performance of the rules on the training data. This technique has been demonstrated in recent systems based on ID3 (e.g. [26]) and AQ (e.g. [11]).

2.4.4 Large Data Sets

As computers increase their speed and memory capacity, larger and larger data sets can be handled. However, with data sets containing millions of examples there may still be too much data for induction to be feasible within time and memory constraints of application machines.

One technique for handling large data sets is the method of *windowing*. We describe it here as applied to ID3, but it can be applied also to other induction algorithms. First, a subset or "window" of the training examples is selected at random (the window size defined by the user) and ID3 generates a decision tree. Then the tree is tested on the whole data set and misclassified examples are used to replace other examples in the window. The examples displaced from the window are chosen as those least essential for the tree; examples from leaves covering a large number of examples are prime candidates, whereas the example from a leaf covering only that one example is important to retain in the window, as it is singularly responsible for the presence of that leaf. ID3 is then re-run on the new window, and the process iterated until the number of classification errors of subsequent trees reaches a minimum. This technique is described in more detail in [27].

2.4.5 Incremental Learning

Another constraint sometimes cited against rule induction systems is their non-incremental nature. The algorithms as described above do not permit modification of existing rule sets/decision trees, but require them to be grown again from scratch.

It should be noted that the problem of non-incrementality is one of efficiency rather than of rule quality. Recently, incremental versions of both ID3 and AQ have been proposed which will refine decision trees or rules given new training data rather than re-induce them from scratch. The resulting updated trees or rules are (usually) those which re-induction would have produced anyway, but found more efficiently.

ID3 can be easily modified to act incrementally by storing the counts of examples at each node in the tree, and updating them as new examples arrive. Should a new example "tip the balance" so that the existing attribute test at a node is no longer the best, this triggers ID3 to change the attribute test and re-induce the subtrees which are attached to the node. This technique is described and evaluated by Utgoff in the ID5 system [36].

AQ can similarly be modified to act incrementally. Given a new training example, existing rules which are inconsistent with it are deleted and the AQ algorithm re-run to cover all those examples now without rules covering them. This technique is described by Michalski [12] and used, for example, by Mozetic [21].

3 Beyond Rule Induction

3.1 Increasing Representational Power

Algorithms such as ID3 and AQ can be seen as forming "theories" about the world using data with which they have been presented. However, these theories are of a very simple form, with minimal structure. Observations are linked to predictions by a single inference step, and there is no attempt to learn more structured representations explaining observations.

Unfortunately, reasoning in most real-world domains is substantially more complicated than simply applying input-output correlations, as reflected by the degree of structure in most expert systems where many intermediate concepts are used to solve problems. The introduction of intermediate concepts (sometimes referred to as "new terms") and more structured representations can have a profound effect on a learning system's ability to acquire knowledge. The reason for this can be understood as follows:

(1) Generalization is essential if old information is to be applied to new, previously unseen problems.

(2) The process of generalization involves a search to sift out relevant from irrelevant information. This is a *semantic* aim of generalization (i.e. an aim concerning the *meaning* of generalizations rather than their particular syntactic form).

(3) Generalization in a learning system is defined in terms of *syntactic operations* (e.g. "delete part of the <condition> of this rule") on a representation.

(4) For a generalization to be effective, the representation must be in a form in which the syntactic operations of generalization can achieve the semantic aims. In other words, we can easily exclude irrelevant information by simple syntactic changes to the representation.

(5) The introduction of intermediate terms and structure can dramatically improve this coupling of syntactic operations to semantic form.

A simple example of how introducing terms can profoundly affect learning is that of learning the concept of *parity* from examples, for instance as shown in Table 3.1. Here, ID3 and AQ will be unable to learn a good classification rule for classifying numbers as being "even parity" or "odd parity", because the generalization operations of removing attribute tests always remove important information. However by introducing new terms, for example as shown in Table 3.2, the problem becomes solvable because syntactic operations now allow essential information to be retained. Rules such as "if A7=2 then parity=even" are now present in the search space.

Thus, the role of a representational scheme in a machine-learning system is a dual one:

(1) As "program" to perform the application task for which the system has been designed.

(2) As "data" to be manipulated by the learning component of the system.

No.	Attributes				Parity (= Class Value)
	A1 2^3	A2 2^2	A3 2^1	A4 2^0	
9	1	0	0	1	even
7	0	1	1	1	odd
8	1	0	0	0	odd
2	0	0	1	0	odd
5	0	1	0	1	even

Table 3.1- Examples of binary numbers and their associated parity.

No.	Attributes							Parity (= Class Value)
	A1 2^3	A2 2^2	A3 2^1	A4 2^0	A5,= A1+A2	A6,= A3+A4	A7,= A5+A6	
9	1	0	0	1	1	1	2	even
7	0	1	1	1	1	2	3	odd
8	1	0	0	0	1	0	1	odd
2	0	0	1	0	0	1	1	odd
5	0	1	0	1	1	1	2	even

Table 3.2- Examples of binary numbers and their associated
parity with new attributes introduced.

In order to learn effectively, there must be correspondence between these two roles. The represented knowledge must interact appropriately not only with the inference machinery during a performance task but also with the machinery for learning. Introducing intermediate terms and additional structure can greatly assist in creating a good correspondence.

However, allowing a system greater representational power immediately results in a vastly expanded search of possible "theories" which can account for observations. Controlling this search is a major problem. Some of the most common methods which are used for controlling the search are as follows:

(1) Use of representations at *multiple levels of abstraction* (e.g. [21]). Here a representation at a coarse level of detail is first acquired, then a more detailed representation is formed. The abstract (coarse) level serves to constrain search at the more detailed level.

(2) Use of an *oracle* (e.g. [23,22]). Here, the user is asked to verify the system's operation at each step.

(3) Assuming *no noise* (e.g.[34]. By making this assumption, any learned knowledge for which counter-examples exist can immediately be rejected, greatly reducing the search space.

3.2 Constructive Induction

We have argued that more structured representations are to be aimed for in order to allow the system to acquire more complex knowledge. Many learning systems (e.g. those just cited) can make intermediate inferences as well as the restricted "if <inputs> then <output>" inferences permitted by ID3 and AQ, but the majority are constrained to use only concepts and terms supplied by the user.

To go beyond this, ideally the learning system itself should automatically introduce "new" concepts, as functions of already known concepts, if it would prove beneficial to structuring knowledge. This automatic introduction of terms is sometimes referred to as "constructive induction". An analysis of the importance of constructive induction in the learning of certain classes of concepts is made by Rendell [33]. The importance of structuring problems in this way has also been investigated by Shapiro [35]. Research in this area is fairly new; the system CIGOL [23] is one example of recent work, using the principle of inverse resolution to introduce new terms in logic programs.

3.3 Using Additional Domain Knowledge

Another limitation of inductive approaches as used in the ID3 and AQ algorithms is that no additional domain-specific knowledge is employed to control search beyond that of the training examples themselves. Although additional domain knowledge has been applied manually by the expert before the induction program is run (in the form of his or her selection of appropriate attributes and classes for the system), this extra knowledge is not available for the system to use during learning.

The class of problem which ID3 and AQ deal with — namely those with a large number of training examples and where no additional domain knowledge is available — is perhaps not typical of the majority of real-world applications. More commonly, problems are characterized by the availability of:

(1) only a small number of examples of problem solving, too few to perform reliable induction with on their own, and

(2) a large amount of available domain knowledge, but not precise or certain enough to reliably solve problems with alone.

In this case, a system using both previous examples and available domain knowledge is required, a hybrid of "pure" expert system and rule induction methods. This raises complex issues of both how to represent uncertain domain knowledge and how to integrate and modify it as new evidence appears.

3.4 Case-Based Reasoning

One approach to integrating the use of domain knowledge and examples is that of "case-based" or "exemplar-based" reasoning. Case-based approaches are characterized by retaining examples of previously solving problems in memory, and then new problems solved by first retrieving a solution to a similar old problem and secondly modifying it to solve the new problem. In this way, old solutions act as "anchor points", providing islands of reliable information, and domain knowledge has a reduced role of relating a new problem to an old problem rather than solving the entire new problem from scratch. This technique allows uncertain domain knowledge to be used in conjunction with examples to solve problems, and the accumulation of new solutions over time results in improved performance. Additionally, this technique models the behaviour of much human problem solving and thus contributes towards its psychological validity and comprehensibility by an expert. Examples of recent work in case-based reasoning are Chef [9], Protos [1] and by Clark [6,7]. A comparison of this approach with rule induction approaches is given in [5]. While case-based approaches are rising in popularity, it should be noted that many remain rather *ad hoc* with little theoretical underpinning.

3.5 Knowledge Compilation

In addition to learning "new" knowledge (knowledge which does not follow deductively from what is already known), some work in machine learning has been devoted to making existing knowledge more efficient. The area of explanation-based learning (EBL) covers a variety of techniques, most working with some first-order logic variant such as Horn clauses or production rules as a representational language. The most common technique, explanation-based generalization (EBG), involves generating and storing a general solution to a problem [19]. Solving a problem often involves instantiating and applying a number of operators or "rules" — explanation-based "generalization" ("re-generalization" is perhaps more appropriate) collects and simplifies the uninstantiated operator sequence, storing it for later use. EBG can in fact be viewed as selectively applying the logic programming method of partial evaluation [37].

EBG improves efficiency when the cost of generating, storing and retrieving these learned solution sequences is outweighed by the improved speed they give (a learned solution sequence no longer needs to be recalculated and therefore can be applied immediately). Early work assumed generalizing solutions to old problems would yield such an overall benefit (thus assuming new problems will be similar to old problems). However, this is not necessarily the case — Minton [18] has recently conducted more detailed analyses of the criteria for deciding which generalizations to store in order to achieve an increase in the system's performance.

4 Conclusion

Machine learning is becoming an increasingly important area of study within the field of artificial intelligence. Despite its simplicity, the technology of rule induction from examples is rapidly becoming an important area of application of machine learning and we have described two systems for this task in detail in this chapter. If we are to progress beyond rule induction to systems capable of learning more complex knowledge about the world, there are still major problems of search, knowledge representation and knowledge integration which must be addressed and we have surveyed some of the recent work in this area targeted at these problems.

References

[1]   E. R. Bareiss, B. W. Porter, and C. C. Wier, "PROTOS: An Exemplar-based Learning Apprentice," in *Proc. 4th International Workshop on Machine Learning*, P. Langley (ed.), Kaufmann, California, 1987.

[2]   A. Bundy, "Incidence Calculus: a Mechanism for Probabilistic Reasoning," *Journal of Automated Reasoning*, **Vol-1**, No-3, pp 263-283, 1985.

[3]   B. Cestnik, I. Kononenko, and I. Bratko, "Assistant 86: a Knowledge-elicitation Tool for Sophisticated Users," in *Progress in Machine Learning (proceedings of the 2nd European Working Session on Learning)*, I. Bratko and N. Lavrac (eds.), Sigma Wilmslow, UK, pp 31-45, 1987.

[4]   W. J. Clancey, "Classification Problem Solving," in *AAAI-84*, pp 49-55, 1984.

[5]   P. Clark, "A Comparison of Rule and Exemplar-based Learning Systems," in *International workshop on Machine Learning, Meta-reasoning and Logics*, P. Brazdil (ed.), Portugal: Faculdade de Economia, Univ. Porto, pp 69-81, February 1988. (Proceedings to be published in book form in 1989).

[6]   P. Clark, "Exemplar-based Reasoning in Geological Prospect Appraisal," TIRM 034, Turing Institute, Glasgow, UK, 1988.

[7]   P. Clark, "Representing Arguments as Background Knowledge for Constraining Generalization," in *Proc. Third European Working Session on Learning (EWSL-88)*, D. Sleeman (ed.), Pitman, London, pp 37-44, October 1988.

[8]   P. Clark and T. Niblett, "The CN2 Induction Algorithm," *Machine Learning Journal*, **Vol-3**, No-4, pp 261-283, 1989.

[9] K. Hammond, "CHEF: a Model of Case-based planning," in *AAAI-86*, 1986.

[10] E. B. Hunt, J. Marin, and P. T. Stone, *Experiments in Induction*, Academic Press, New York, 1966.

[11] R. Michalski, I. Mozetic, J. Hong, and N. Lavrac, "The Multipurpose Incremental Learning System AQ15 and its Testing Application to Three Medical Domains," in *AAAI-86*, Kaufmann, California, pp 1041-1045, 1986.

[12] R. S. Michalski, "Knowledge Repair Mechanisms: Evolution vs. Revolution," ISG 85-15, Dept. of Computer Science, Univ. of Illinois at Urbana-Champaign, Urbana, 1985.

[13] R. S. Michalski and J. Larson, "Incremental Generation of VL1 Hypotheses: the Underlying Methodology and the Description of Program AQ11," ISG 83-5, Dept. of Computer Science, Univ. of Illinois at Urbana-Champaign, Urbana, 1983.

[14] R. S. Michalski and J. Larson, "Selection of Most Representative Training Examples and Incremental Generation of VL1 Hypotheses: the Underlying Methodology and the Description of Programs ESEL and AQ11," UIUCDCS-R 78-867, Dept. of Computer Science, Univ. of Illinois at Urbana-Champaign, Urbana, 1978.

[15] D. Michie, *Machine Intelligence and Related Topics: an Information Scientist's Weekend Book*, Gordon & Breach, New York, 1982.

[16] D. Michie, "Machine Learning in the Next Five Years," in *Proc. Third European Working Session on Learning (EWSL-88)*, D. Sleeman (ed.), Pitman, London, pp 107-122, 1988.

[17] D. Michie, "The Superarticulacy Phenomenon in the Context of Software Manufacture," in *Proceedings of the Royal Society (Series A)*, pp 185-212, 1986. Also available as internal report TIRM-85-13, Turing Institute, Glasgow, UK).

[18] S. Minton, "Quantitative Results Concerning the Utility of Explanation-based Learning," in *AAAI-88*, Kaufman, California pp 564-569, August 1988.

[19] T. M. Mitchell, R. M. Keller, and S. T. Kedar-Cabelli, "Explanation-based Generalization: a Unifying View," *Machine Learning Journal*, **Vol-1**, No-1, pp 47-80, 1986.

[20] P. Mowforth, "Some applications with inductive expert system shells," TIOP 86-002, Turing Institute, Glasgow, UK, 1986.

[21] I. Mozetic, "The Role of Abstractions in Learning Qualitative Models," in *Proc. 4th International Workshop on Machine Learning*, P. Langley (ed.), Kaufmann, California, 1987.

[22] S. Muggleton, "Duce: an Oracle-based Approach to Constructive Induction," in *IJCAI-87*, J. McDermott (ed.), Kaufmann, California, pp 287-292, 1987.

[23] S. Muggleton and W. Buntine, "Machine Invention of First-order Predicates by Inverting Resolution," in *Proc. 5th Int. Conf. on Machine Learning*, J. Laird (ed.), Kaufmann, California, pp 339-352, 1988.

[24] T. Niblett, "Constructing Decision Trees in Noisy Domains," in *Progress in Machine Learning (proceedings of the 2nd European Working Session on Learning)*, I. Bratko and N. Lavrac (eds.), Sigma Wilmslow, UK, pp 67-78, 1987.

[25] T. Niblett and I. Bratko, "Learning Decision Rules in Noisy Domains," in *Expert Systems 86, Brighton, UK*, M.A. Bramer (ed.), 1986.

[26] J. R. Quinlan, "Decision Trees as Probabilistic Classifiers," in *Proc. 4th International Workshop on Machine Learning*, P. Langley (ed.), Kaufmann, California, pp 31-37, 1987.

[27] J. R. Quinlan, "Discovering Rules by Induction from Large Collections of Examples," in *Expert Systems in the Micro-Electronic Age*, D. Michie (ed.), Edinburgh Univ. Press, UK, pp 168-201, 1979.

[28] J. R. Quinlan, "Generating Production Rules from Decision Trees," in *IJCAI-87*, J. McDermott (ed.), Kaufmann, California, pp 304-307, 1987.

[29] J. R. Quinlan, "Learning Efficient Classification Procedures and their Application to chess endgames," in *Machine Learning*, **Vol-1**, (J. G. Carbonell, R. S. Michalski, and T. M. Mitchell, eds.), Tioga Palo Alto, Tioga, California, 1983.

[30] J. R. Quinlan, "Simplifying Decision Trees," *Int. Journal of Man-Machine Studies*, **Vol-27**, pp 221-234, September 1987.

[31] J. R. Quinlan, P. J. Compton, K. A. Horn, and L. Lazarus, "Inductive Knowledge Acquisition: a Case Study," in *Applications of Expert Systems*, Addison-Wesley Wokingham, UK, pp 157-173, 1987.

[32] R. Reddy, "Foundations and Grand Challenges of Artificial Intelligence," *AI Magazine*, **Vol-9**, No-4, pp 9-21, 1988.

[33] L. Rendell, "Learning Hard Concepts," in *Proc. Third European Working Session on Learning (EWSL-88)*, D. Sleeman (ed.), Pitman, London, pp 177-200, 1988.

[34] C. Sammut and R. Banerji, "Learning Concepts by Asking Questions," in *Machine Learning*, **Vol-2**, (J. G. Carbonell, R. S. Michalski, and T. M. Mitchell, eds.), Palo Alto, Tioga, California, 1986.

[35] A. D. Shapiro, *Structured Induction in Expert Systems*, Turing Inst. Press, in association with Addison-Wesley Wokingham, UK, 1987.

[36] P. E. Utgoff, "ID5: an Incremental ID3," in *Proc. 5th Int. Conf. on Machine Learning*, J. Laird (ed.), Kaufmann, California, pp 107-120, June 1988.

[37] F. VanHarmelen and A. Bundy, "Explanation-based Generalization = Partial Evaluation," *Artificial Intelligence*, **Vol-36**, pp 401-412, October 1988.

Chapter 4

Concept Learning

with a Multi-Layer Perceptron

A. Hart

1 Introduction

Machine learning has been an important aspect of artificial intelligence research. As is the case with other aspects of AI work, there have been some encouraging results, and other tasks which have proved more difficult than might at first have been envisaged. The problems with machine learning have some similarities with those associated with expert systems or knowledge-based systems. General methods tend to be restrictive, and it is often beneficial to have some domain knowledge in order to be able to learn more about a domain.

Before the recent revival of interest in neurocomputing, or neural networks, AI research was based on psychological theories. That is, the models have been based on conscious and goal-directed learning and behaviour. Such models are rationalizations of how we might think, and there have been many criticisms about the underlying assumptions of this approach (for example see [17,4,18]). In fact many of the tasks at which we excel almost defy logical explanation. For many complex pattern-recognition tasks we just "see" the solution, and any retrospective rationalization appears to provide highly inadequate explanations for the actual performance.

In contrast, neurocomputing is based on a biological metaphor, drawing the analogy from the physiology of the brain. There are about 10^{11} neurons in the brain, and there is a very high connectivity: any neuron can be connected to up to 10^5 other neurons. The activity is highly parallel, and it is the parallel distributed nature of the processing which appears to give it its power. As with AI in general, there are two streams of interest in neural networks. First, some researchers try to model the brain and thereby to explain cognitive behaviour. Others draw on the principles, and aim to construct useful "computers", that is powerful machines which can carry out useful computations. People within the second group have no objective of "constructing brains", they merely extract what seem to be the salient features from the physiology of the brain and then use these principles to build effective machines. In terms of real-world problems of classification or pattern recognition it is this second class of research which is of interest.

2 Neural Networks

Neural networks consist of very simple processing units analogous to the brain's neurons. These elements are usually termed nodes, and they are interconnected by links. Figure 4.1 illustrates this principle.

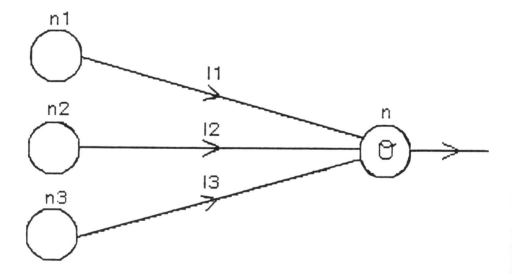

Figure 4.1- A node is connected to several other nodes. Its output, or state, depends on the values of the other nodes and of the connective strengths and thresholds.

The power of a network lies not in the processing power of an individual unit, but in the systemic behaviour of a configuration of connected units. The units operate as follows. Any node has a number of other nodes feeding into it. It also feeds into other nodes in a similar manner. Each connection has a strength associated with it, analogous to the synaptic strength in a brain. In general a positive connection will mean that the two nodes connected will tend to be in similar states, for example "high" or "low". A negative connection will mean that those nodes tend to be in opposite states. Nodes commonly take real values in the range [0,1], although some people prefer to use the range [−1,+1], and others allow only a pair of discrete values. A node also has a threshold value, θ, which represents its bias towards an "on" or "off" state. The state of a node is therefore determined by θ and the states of all the nodes which feed into it. Thus

$$n = f\left(\Sigma n_i l_i + \theta\right) \tag{2.1}$$

where θ is the threshold value for the node, the n_i's are the states of the nodes which feed in, and l_i values represent the links between nodes.

The function $f(x)$ can take several forms. If it is a strict step function then the nodes will behave like simple binary devices. A more common function is a sigmoidal function, e.g.

$$f(x) = \frac{1}{1 + e^{-x}} \tag{2.2}$$

This is often described as being a continuous and differentiable approximation to a step function. It is, however, more subtle than that, and turns out to be a powerful function which can result in highly complex network behaviour.

At any point in time the nodes will have particular values. This particular state of the network corresponds to short-term memory. The possible states are determined by the values of the thresholds and the connecting strengths. In neurocomputing, learning involves modifying these values for the strengths and thresholds until the network can perform a designated task. The "knowledge" of the network is thus in the weights and corresponds more to long-term memory. It is important to realize that the knowledge is essentially different from the explicit symbolic knowledge of traditional AI. It is distributed in the weights, and in general it is not easy to predict the behaviour of the network by looking at the values of the weights.

The surge of interest during the past few years has resulted in a plethora of papers. The principal texts are by Rumelhart and McClelland [16] and, in Europe, by Aleksander [1] and Kohonen [10]. The primary areas of application are in pattern recognition and pattern completion. Networks have also been used to solve complicated constraint-based mathematical problems. This chapter examines one particular neural network architecture and discusses its place in machine learning.

3 Inductive Learning

Induction involves learning generalizations from a set of specific examples. (See also chapter 3 of this volume.) Induction is by its nature not a strictly logical process, and so the results cannot be proven. Inductive learning generates rules or patterns which appear to explain a set of training examples, and it is hoped that these principles also have some general application. This is usually tested by applying the rules to a new set of examples called the test set. The power of any inductive method is dictated by two aspects. First there is the ability of the method to *represent* the concept of interest. Secondly there is the ability of the method to *learn* an optimal representation from the examples. It is perfectly possible to have a powerful representation which is undermined by a weak learning method. A severe problem with many inductive methods has been that they are very sensitive to the way in which the examples are presented, that is to say the characteristics which are used to describe those examples. Thus, for example, using one characteristic (X and Y) as opposed to two characteristics X and Y can have a great effect on the usefulness of the results. For a simple discussion of this see [8].

It is a truism that any inductive results will rely on the quality of the training examples. The induced results will usually be those which are the simplest possible within the representational power of the method, as consistent with the input examples. Stated simply, if a concept is not fully represented in the training set then one cannot hope to find it in the results. This can usually be viewed as a problem with extrapolation. Interpolation is usually relatively safe, but extrapolation can be dangerous. It is worth illustrating this point. Figure 4.2 shows a set of data which belong to two classes. The aim is to learn how to classify a data point (as O or X) given its coordinates. In fact in the training set each data point had five real values , i.e. the examples were of the form ($x1, x2, x3, x4, x5, D$) where D was O or X.

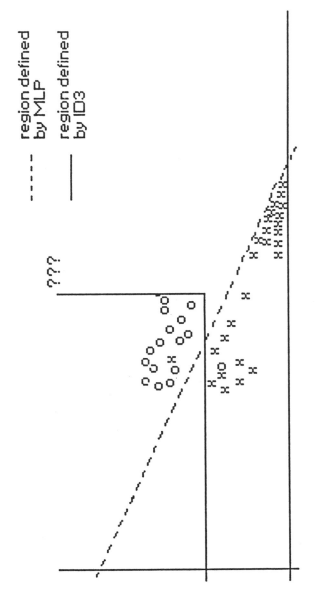

Figure 4.2.- This scatter diagram shows points in two classes. Decision regions have been generated by two machine learning methods, as shown. In the test set there were some points far away from the training data; it is unfair to expect the induced results to classify these correctly.

An inductive method ID3 [14,15], based on information theory, was used to generate a decision tree for this task, and a neural network of the type described later in this chapter was used on the same data. An examination of the output from each method suggested that only 2 of the 5 variables were important in classifying the data items. The scatter diagram uses these two variables.

Also shown in the figure are the two decision regions as generated by each of the methods. Notice how two of the examples are misclassified, but this is a small proportion of the whole data set. The test set, however, contained examples which appear in the top region of the scatter diagram, as indicated by question marks. These points are a long way away from the other points, and so using the induced results amounts to extrapolation. One set of results predicts X whereas the other predicts O for these points. Given no other information about the problem it is impossible to say which is correct. In fact the results from the ID3 algorithm were correct, although an informal test on a handful of human subjects suggested that people would perceive the neural network answer to be more "natural". The point is that it is hardly the fault of the inductive method that its results might fail if the examples in the test set are essentially different in some respect from those in the training set. Also in this unpublished study the test set contained a number of examples which lay very close to those which were misclassified in the training set, and were similarly misclassified in the test run. This problem is similar to extrapolation. It means that the decision region is not as simple as that suggested by the training examples, and that a refinement is needed to account for the misclassified cases. It would, however, be dangerous to draw definite conclusions from the isolated cases which were present in the training data. It is therefore important that the examples presented to the inductive method adequately cover all the types of cases which are likely to be encountered.

4 Multi-Layer Perceptrons

Although neurocomputing is conceptually rather different from conventional computing, and the intention of many researchers is to build neurocomputers, it is possible to simulate networks on conventional computers. This is what many people do at present. The architecture for a multi-layer perceptron (MLP) (sometimes referred to as a backward propagation model) is shown in Figure 4.3. There is a layer of input nodes consisting of one for each characteristic of the examples. These nodes feed forward into another layer of nodes, which can feed into either the output nodes which describe the classes of the problem, or into another layer which then feeds into the output nodes. The intermediate layers which are not part of the original examples are usually termed hidden nodes. Without these hidden nodes the network could have limited knowledge-representational capabilities.

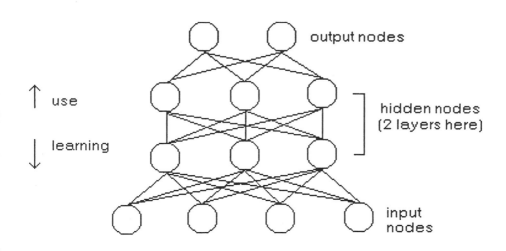

Figure 4.3- A MLP is used for supervised learning where the classifications are known. The input layer reads in the characteristics which describe the examples. These nodes feed forward into one or more layers of hidden nodes which then feed into the output nodes. The output nodes describe the class for a particular example. Training involves modifying the parameters in the network until the observed values on the output nodes generated from the values on the input nodes are the "correct" ones.

It is useful to view classification problems as dividing n-dimensional space into regions corresponding to the various classes. Many classification methods have difficulties with intermeshed regions, as exemplified in Figure 4.4.

A multi-layer perceptron with a sigmoidal activation rule has extremely powerful representational capabilities. A mathematical result of Kolmogorov based on Hilbert's 13th problem is concerned with the representation of a function of n variables as combinations of simpler functions of fewer variables [11]. The results show that, given certain conditions concerning the range of values taken by the input variables (they must lie in some bounded interval) and the continuity, range and differentiability of the function, then a multi-layer perceptron with up to 2 hidden layers is capable in principle of approximating that function. Given that a classification problem can be modelled by a suitable smooth and well-behaved function it follows that the MLP model can be extremely powerful. Of course, the mathematical results do not prescribe how the parameters can be chosen to achieve such a model. Furthermore, the number of parameters which are needed to achieve an adequate model may be very large.

The strengths and thresholds are the parameters of the model, and they have to be learnt. For any example, the output can be viewed as a function of the input values and the strengths, or parameters, of the model. Learning is effected as an optimization process whereby an error function is minimized by selecting an optimum set of parameter values. The error function is

$$E = \frac{1}{2} \sum_{all\ examples} \sum_{i} (E_i - O_i)^2 \tag{4.1}$$

where the summation is over each of the output nodes for all the examples in the training set, E_i is the Expected value of a node, and O_i is the Observed value. Clearly, if this total error value is zero then all the differences are zero, and for each example the network will produce the correct output values from the input values. The method which is generally used is gradient descent, which is well known as a standard but limited method in numerical optimization. The method calculates the partial derivatives, $\frac{\partial E}{\partial p}$ where p is a parameter, and then adjusts each parameter by the formula

$$\delta p = -\lambda \frac{\partial E}{\partial p} \tag{4.2}$$

where λ is the learning rate (corresponding to "step length" in optimization). For the MLP there is an elegant method of calculating the partial derivatives, making use of the structure of the network [16].

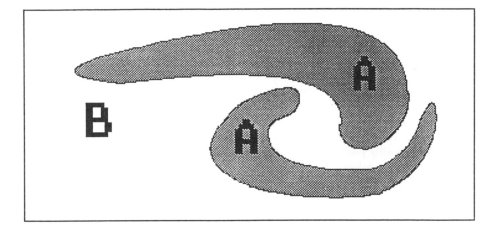

Figure 4.4- A meshed decision region such as this can cause problems for classification methods, especially when the regions are defined in n-dimensional space.

There are well-known problems with gradient descent as a method, and any optimization method works best when starting from a reasonably good approximate solution. Unfortunately, in the case of a MLP one does not normally have a good starting point. Commonly the weights are randomized to some small starting values. Other problems with gradient descent are that the process can converge to a non-optimal minimum; the process can take very many iterations; if the learning rate is too high then the process may fail to converge at all; and if the learning rate is too small then the process may take far too long.

In practice the process involves many passes through the training set. It is not unusual for "many" to mean several thousand. Although the straightforward application of the gradient descent method would mean that the parameters were updated after reading all examples in the training set, in practice most people update after every example, thereby considering the function

$$E^k = \frac{1}{2}\sum_i (E_i - O_i)^2 \qquad (4.3)$$

where $1 \le k \le$ number of examples at any one time. Other authorities prefer to update after reading one of every class of example [2]. In order to smooth the process and avoid unnecessary fluctations (in "ravines" rather than true "valleys") a momentum term can be added to the update function which then becomes:

$$\delta p(k) = -\lambda \frac{\partial E}{\partial p} + \mu \delta p(k-1) \qquad (4.4)$$

where $\delta p(k-1)$ is the change at the *previous* presentation and μ is the momentum constant. In some literature the values 0.1 for learning rate and 0.9 for momentum term are cited as being "standard" following the advice of Rumelhart. However, practitioners do not always follow this advice, and there is an element of heuristic knowledge involved in the selection of valid parameters for a particular run. Other decisions to be made are the numbers of layers and numbers of nodes. For a discussion of some of this folklore see [5].

For a reasonable problem the error function reduces with learning, and a typical graph is shown in Figure 4.5.

It is important to raise the issue of what is meant by a "good" solution. If one could be assured of the quality of the training set then clearly one would require the total error function to be as small as possible. In practice a "better", in the sense of being more generally applicable, solution might be achieved by stopping the learning before the minimum error was reached. Some people prefer to stop training when all output nodes are within 0.5 of their correct value. They hope that this will reduce the effects of overfitting, and note that sometimes further training gave worse results on the test data [2].

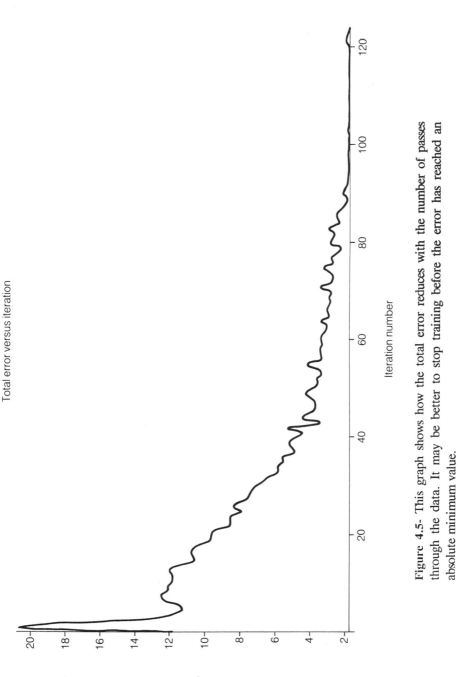

Figure 4.5.- This graph shows how the total error reduces with the number of passes through the data. It may be better to stop training before the error has reached an absolute minimum value.

This strategy may not fully address the problems. Sometimes it is possible to have "solved" the problem apart from a single example which appears to have been misclassified by the network. If the network is left for long enough then usually it will move away from this local minimum to another point where a "better" solution can be achieved. (Informal tests have shown that this can take ten times as long as that for the initial "convergence"). If this point is a genuine one then the later solution may well be better; if the point is spurious then the earlier solution may be more general. In other words, the network could have detected an outlier in the data. The ways in which outliers are joined to other regions in the decision space cannot be guaranteed to be optimal owing to the paucity of information. The problem is compounded if the network settles to a solution where a few examples have not converged. These could all be distinct outliers, or they could be a cluster of points which will eventually redefine the decision space in an sensible manner. Interestingly, it is the power of the network, in being able to represent complex mappings, which causes these dilemmas.

5 Learning the Concept of Right-angled Triangle

These principles are illustrated in an artificial but interesting example. The task was to learn the concept of "right-angled triangle" given the three real values representing the sides of a valid triangle. The training set therefore comprised examples of the form $(X1, X2, X3, D)$ where the X's are real values and D takes the value 1 if and only if

$$X1^2 + X2^2 = X3^2 \quad or \quad |X1^2 + X2^2 - X3^2| < \epsilon \qquad (5.1)$$

where ϵ is very small. $X1$ and $X2$ were constrained to lie in the interval $[0,1]$. The examples in the training set were generated randomly such that half of them represented right-angled triangles, and half did not. An independent test set of 500 examples was also generated. For simplicity $X3$ was always the largest of the X values. Clearly, the region of space represented by the decision function is non-trivial to learn, given that the data are presented in the form X rather than X^2.

Table 4.1 shows the results obtained from different models with various numbers of examples in the training set. Figure 4.6 illustrates some of these data.

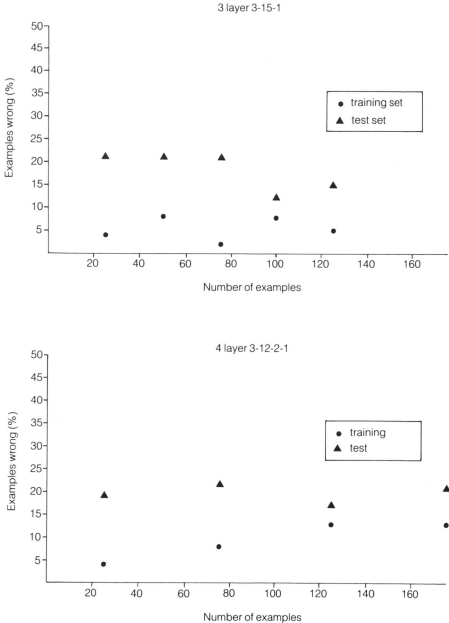

Figure 4.6- These graphs show the accuracy of MLP's with one and two hidden layers trained on different numbers of examples. In each case there were 6000 passes through the data.

Network Structure	training examples	No. of passes through data	%incorrect in training set	%incorrect in test set	G value
3-15-1	25	6000	4	21	0.10
	50	6000	8	21	0.21
	75	6000	2	21	0.18
	100	6000	8	12	7.48
	125	6000	15	15	6.39
	150	12000	4	13	3.47
	175	12000	6	14	6.64
3-2-3-1	25	6000	16	30	0.15
	50	6000	13	32	2.40
	75	6000	17	38	2.69
	100	6000	10	31	2.78
	125	6000	15	16	0.64
	150	6000	14	16	2.63
	175	6000	22	25	7.29
3-12-2-1	25	6000	4	19	0.09
	75	6000	8	22	0.55
	125	6000	13	17	9.25
	175	6000	13	21	5.78

Table 4.1- Accuracy of MLP's trained on various numbers of examples, and tested on 500 further examples.

The gradient measure, G, is given by

$$G = \sum_{all\ examples} \sum_{all\ parameters} (\frac{\partial E}{\partial p})^2 \qquad (5.2)$$

and is an indication of how "flat" the solution point is, that is how much scope there is for reduction of the total error in the vicinity of the current solution. Although not widely cited, the author finds this a very good diagnostic statistic to output during training together with the total error. Note how the performance on the test set improves with the number of training examples, but that a very large number of examples might be needed to get a very good performance.

In this case the fact that the data were generated to lie uniformly in each region meant that the performance on the test set, although predictably worse, is of the same order of magnitude as that on the training set. Also the task is made relatively easy by the fact that there are equal numbers of examples in each class. Notice also the performance of the networks after a large number of passes through 175 examples.

6 Real Problems

In practice one would not have a uniform distribution of examples, and one might have very little idea as to how representative the training data were. This is not the case if there is a potentially infinite set of training examples. Speech recognition or sensor data for control are cases where one might not be concerned about difficulties in generating enough data. (For applications of MLP for speech recognition see chapter 9 of this volume.) For classical discrimination problems, such as diagnosis from medical data, this is not the case. Furthermore, unlike the case of the triangle data, one might not have the insight into the problem to know which input variales are important, or how many decision regions there are, and so one might easily over-estimate the number of nodes in the model.

Nonetheless, favourable results have been reported for the analysis of data concerned with diagnosing back pain [2]. MLP networks were trained on 25 examples of each of 4 classes of problem, and achieved an overall performance of 80% on the test set , and within the four classes the results were better than those of three groups of clinicians.

In contrast a study of data on patients with chest pain proved very much more complex. The data were collected from patients complaining of chest pain who attended a chest clinic. There were essentially two classes of diagnosis, namely High Risk Cardiac cases (HRC) and No Risk Cases (NC). The work is reported in detail elsewhere [9]. The training set comprised 174 examples of which only 34 were HRC. Several multi-layer perceptron models were used; for example a three layer model with 14 hidden nodes and one output node, and a four layer model with 8 and 4 hidden nodes respectively. As is often the case with medical data (including that described for the back pain problem) some data values were missing, and these had to be estimated in some way. Various methods were tried which involved attempting to simulate the distribution of that variable as indicated in the remainder of the examples. Training was effected with a fairly high learning rate which was varied interactively during the run (in general starting high and then reduced) and no momentum term. With the exception of one or two examples which appeared to behave as outliers, the model converged to a very good approximation to the training examples in about 400 to 600 passes through the training set.

The test set comprised 143 examples of which 34 were HRC. In any medical application it is extremely likely that it is the risk associated with the decision-making process which is important, and not just the accuracy. That is to say it is more important to minimize the overall risk than to maximize the probability of "being right". In this case a false negative diagnosis (i.e. HRC coded as NC) is more serious than a false positive. For this reason it was decided not to use the obvious rule of coding the diagnosis as HRC if the output was greater than 0.5 and NC otherwise. A suitable cut-off point for such a decision was chosen by running the first 70 of the test examples through the network, and by examining the resultant performance. This is shown in Table 4.2. From this a cut-off value of 0.3 was chosen.

Results from first 70 test cases of which 12 were HRC

Threshold	0.1	0.2	0.3	0.4	0.5	0.6	0.7	0.8	0.9
True +ve	0.67	0.67	0.58	0.58	0.58	0.50	0.50	0.50	0.50
False +ve	0.34	0.31	0.24	0.22	0.21	0.17	0.14	0.10	0.09

Table 4.2- Performance of network with one hidden layer on 73 test cases. From this a threshold value of 0.3 was chosen.

The final results on the remainder of the test set are shown in Table 4.3.

True +ve	False +ve	Accuracy
0.73	0.31	70%

Table 4.3- Results on 73 new test cases, 22 of which were HRC, with threshold of 0.3.

It is clear from this that the network's performance is very poor on the test examples. There was no significant improvement with a four-layer model. Several modifications have been made to the network architecture and learning process, and none has had a significant positive effect on the results [9].

In the physical situation from which these data were collected it would have been feasible to have had an effective black box classifier. There is an expert system in daily use by nurses at the hospital [19]. They tend to ignore explanation facilities and concentrate wholly on the recommendation in conjunction with their own intuitions. The results from this study are unacceptable for routine use.

It is worth noting that a parallel and independent study was carried out on the same chest pain data using logistic discrimination. Very similar results were obtained. In fact, the logistic results were slightly better overall, but worse at diagnosing HRC cases. This is highly suggestive of the data being defective. The neural network appears to be able to provide a reasonable result without requiring the user to go through the tedium of selecting variables by hand and tailoring the model. In other words it achieves a very good result with minimal effort.

It is hardly surprising that the full complexity of diagnosing heart attacks cannot be described in a set of 174 examples. Many clinicians have pointed out that diagnosing heart attack cases is one of the most difficult judgements they have to make. It is nonetheless instructive to study the performance of the network on such data. Certainly these results compared with those from the triangle data would suggest that a phenomenal number of examples might be needed to get anything like a clinically acceptable level of performance. This is especially true in light of the fact that the MLP model would be validated in terms of its performance alone, that is without recourse to medical principles (as would be the case with rules in an expert system).

As a simple comparison Table 4.4 shows the results from the triangle data where the X values were coded in random order, i.e. the longest side was equally likely to be represented by $X1$, $X2$ or $X3$. It is perfectly possible to construct a four-layer network based on the combination of three three-layer networks learnt from the early runs. The problem is, therefore, well within the representational capabilities of a MLP. The performance after learning on 175 examples of this form is, however, much worse. Learning with unordered data is much harder than with ordered data.

3-30-1 nodes	
21/175 wrong from training set	(12%)
164/500 wrong in test set	(33%)
3-25-3-1 nodes	
10/175 wrong from training set	(6%)
160/500 wrong in test set	(32%)

Table 4.4- Sample results from networks learning on unordered data, after 15000 passes through the training data of 175 examples.

7 General Comments.

The outcome of getting a good performance on training data followed by a much worse performance on test data is not unusual. It needs to be emphasized that machine learning should not be expected to replace an understanding of the domain and problem. Indeed people are now reporting methods of refining the inputs to neural networks in an attempt to improve the learning capabilities. For example Namatame and Kimata [13] suggest the use of Chebychev polynomials. An alternative approach is to use some knowledge about the domain in the design of a network architecture. This can be difficult given the mathematical and sometimes obscure behaviour of the networks, but work in this area is reported by Gallant [6], and the use of networks as analogous to causal or probabilistic models is reported by Deleu and Beuscart [3]. Giles and Maxwell [7] report the use of higher order networks designed to recognize higher order correlations in data with reasonable computational effort. General comments on the capabilities of MLP's, and a critique of computational problems in learning is given in the classic text by Minsky and Papert [12]. (See also [20].)

8 Conclusion.

This chapter has given an overview of the rationale for neural networks, and described the potential of one commonly used model. It has shown that the multi-layer percpetron can represent very complex mathematical functions, but that a good training set of examples is necessary. It has concentrated on supervised learning, where the "answer" is known and the network is tuned to that answer. Unsupervised learning is used to detect features or patterns in data [10]. Many of the principles outlined here apply to connectionist models in general. In particular there is the need for an understanding of the real capabilities of networks, and of the problems on which they are used "in anger". Methods of validation and testing need to be developed for such "intelligent black boxes".

References.

[1] I. Aleksander (ed.), *Neural Computing Architectures*, North Oxford Academic Publishers, London, 1989.

[2] D.G. Bounds and P. Lloyd, "A Multi Layer Perceptron for the Diagnosis of Low Back Pain", *Proc. San Diego Conference on Neural Networks*, July 1988.

[3] J. Deleu and R. Beuscart, "Bayesian Networks and Medical Diagnosis", *International workshop on Neural Networks and their Applications*, Nimes, pp95-103, French, 1988.

[4] H. Dreyfus and S. Dreyfus, *Mind over Machine*, Free Press, New York, 1986.

[5] L.B. Eliot and F. Holliday, "Expert Systems and Neural Networks; an Experimental Study of Methodological Expertise", *The international journal of Neural Networks Research and Applications*, **Vol-1**, No-2, pp96-106, 1989.

[6] S.I. Gallant, "Connectionist Expert Systems", *Comm. ACM*, Vol-31, pp152-166, 1988.

[7] C. Giles and T. Maxwell, "Learning Invariance and Generalization in Higher-order Neural Networks", *Applied Optics*, **Vol-26**, No-23, pp4972-4978, 1987.

[8] A. Hart, "Machine Induction as a Form of Knowledge Acquisition in Knowledge Engineering", in *Machine Learning principles and techniques*, R. Forsyth (ed.), Chapman and Hall, pp23-38, London, 1988.

[9] A. Hart and J. Wyatt, "Connectionist Models in Medicine: an Investigation of Their Potential", *Proc. AIME 89*, Springer Verlag, 1989.

[10] T. Kohonen, *Self-organization and Associative Memory*, Springer Verlag, Heidelberg, 1988.

[11] A.N. Kolmogorov, "On the Representation of Continuous Functions of Several Variables by Superposition of Continuous Functions of Smaller Number of Variables", *Dokl. Akad. SSSR 108*, pp179 - 182, 1959.

[12] M.L. Minsky and S.A. Papert, *Perceptrons*, MIT Press, Cambridge Mass, (expanded edition) 1988.

[13] A. Namatame and Y. Kimata, "Improving the Generalising Capabilities of a Back-propagation Network", *The international Journal of Neural Networks Research and Applications*, **Vol-1**, No-2, pp86-94, 1989.

[14] J.R. Quinlan, "Discovering Rules by Induction From Large Collections of Examples", in *Expert systems in the electronic age*, D. Michie (ed.), Edinburgh: Edinburgh University Press, pp168-201, 1979.

[15] J.R. Quinlan, *Induction of Decision Trees*, Technical Report 85.6, New South Wales Institute of Technology, Australia, 1985.

[16] D.E. Rumelhart and J.L. McClelland, *Parallel Distributed Processing*, **Vols 1 and 2**, MIT Press, Cambridge Mass, 1986.

[17] L.A. Suchman, *Plans and Situated Actions: The Problem of Human Machine Communication*, Cambridge University Press, 1987.

[18] T. Winograd and F. Flores, *Understanding Computers and Cognition: a New Foundation for Design*, Ablex Publishing Co, Norwood N.J, 1986.

[19] J. Wyatt and P. Emerson, "A Pragmatic Approach to Knowledge Engineering with Examples of Use in a Difficult Domain", in *Expert Systems : Human Issues*, D. Berry & A. Hart (eds.), North Oxford Academic Publishers, London, 1989.

[20] W.R. Huang and R.P. Lippman, "Neural Net and Traditional Classifiers", *Proc. of Conf. on Neural Information Processing Systems*, Denver, Colorado, pp 387-396, Nov. 1987.

Chapter 5

Learning Using Pattern Recognition and Signal Processing

A.R. Mirzai, C.F.N. Cowan and T.M. Crawford

1 Introduction

Our interest in learning and the subsequent development of a machine learning system (MLS) described in this chapter grew out of a desire to find a more generic solution to the problems of fault diagnosis and adjustment in electronic systems and devices than that offered by rule-based expert systems (ES). The goal is to produce a tool which can be used with low incremental investment on new applications. Fault diagnosis and adjustment strategies involve relating patterns of symptoms to specific corrective courses of action. Classical ESs acquire these relationships through interrogation of practitioners of the particular art. This is often difficult, costly and time consuming and therefore limited in economic application to problems with high potential payback. Our particular interest centres on areas of application where theoretical relationships between symptoms and faults or corrective actions are impossible or uneconomic to obtain. We can set this class of problems within a wider context by listing classes of problems in descending order as measured by explicitness of our knowledge about cause and effect.

At the top of the list everything is known from the start in the form of explicit logical rules but the combinatorial effects are complicated to follow through. An example of this type of problem might be the assessment of qualifications for social security payments. Next on the scale are problem types where the underlying relationships are not known but empirical rules of thumb are obtainable and combinatorial effects manageable. Examples from medical diagnosis might fit here. At the bottom of the scale is the class of problems where the underlying relationships are not known, many of the variables are continuous in nature and the interactions between the variables are too complex to allow simple rules of thumb to be applied. Good examples of this class can be found in attempts to fault-find or adjust many multi-variable interactive industrial production processes.

The MLS described in the following sections is directed at examples drawn from this last class [10,11]. In practice many real problems will include a whole spectrum of sub-problems with varying degrees of known explicitness in causal relationship encouraging the application of appropriate methods to each sub-problem.

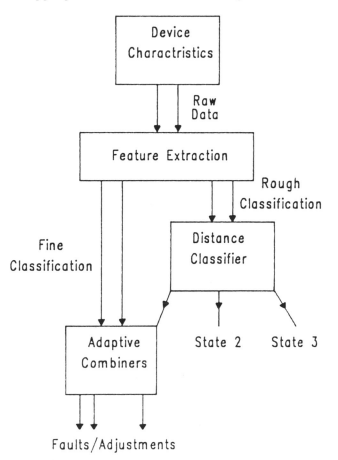

Figure 5.1- Block diagram of the machine learning system (MLS).

Figure 5.1 shows the block representation of the MLS. In this approach, we employ techniques from pattern recognition and adaptive signal processing to form two types of processor, a distance classifier and a set of adaptive combiners. In general, the distance classifier is used for rough classification of the problem while the combiners are used for fine classification. In the following section, we illustrate the application of distance measures in multi-dimensional space for classification. Section 3 describes the principle of the adaptive combiners and illustrates how the recursive least squares (RLS) algorithm, which has been used for many years in communication systems and signal processing, can be employed as a learning strategy for the combiners. In Section 4, the RLS algorithm is manipulated to generate explanations of the relationships between the inputs and the outputs of the device under investigation and finally Section 5 outlines the main features and the limitations of the MLS.

In the next part of the book, the concept of the MLS is applied to two different problem areas. In Chapter 10, the system is used for fault diagnosis of microwave digital radio and in Chapter 11 it is adapted for waveguide filter alignment. Chapter 10 also illustrates the application of a classical ES for the first problem and shows the main features of both approaches. The waveguide filter alignment problem is so complex that the adaptation of a classical ES is not feasible.

2 Classification and Pattern Recognition

The problem of classification may be defined as the assignment of an object to one of a number of predefined groups or clusters. Classification techniques have been used in many disciplines and in some areas of science they form an important basis. It must be mentioned that in different disciplines terms such as "pattern recognition", "discrimination analysis", etc may be used instead of classification but the main principle remains the same. Typical applications of a classification system would include weather forecasting, handprint character classifications, speech recognition, medical signal and image processing, remote sensing and satellite image interpretation. Figure 5.2 illustrates a general configuration for a classification system. The common step in any classification technique, or pattern recognition technique, is to represent physical patterns or objects in a form suitable for classification. This is done using a feature extraction technique as shown in Figure 5.2. The input to the feature extraction block is a set of raw data which has been collected from the object using a suitable tranducer.

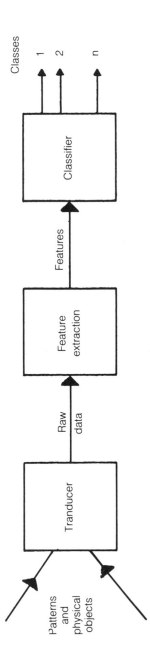

Figure 5.2.- General configuration for a classification system.

In general, it is possible to represent a feature set in vector form as shown below,

$$x = [x_1 x_2 \cdots x_n]^T$$

where n represents the number of features and T denotes the matrix transpose operation. A feature set can then be represented as a point in a feature space. Figure 5.3 illustrates a 2-dimensional feature space with two distance clusters. If n is greater than 3 the feature space can not be represented pictorically. When the feature set is extracted from the raw data it will be fed into the classifier for classification. In the rest of this section, we review some simple distance classification techniques. It is not intended to give a comprehensive view of classification algorithms and readers are referred to [1,2] for further details.

2.1 Measuring Distance in Multi-dimentional Space

To start our discusion of measuring distances, first consider a 2-dimensional feature space. Figure 5.3 shows the feature space with two clusters. The distance between any two points, (x_{1i}, x_{2i}) and (x_{1j}, x_{2j}), in the feature space is given from *Pythagoras'* theorem as,

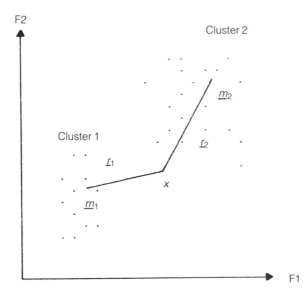

Figure 5.3- Geometric representation of the Euclidean distance in a two dimensional feature space.

$$r = \sqrt{[(x_{1i} - x_{1j})^2 + (x_{2i} - x_{2j})^2]} \tag{2.1}$$

where x_{ki} represents the ith value on the kth feature axis. and is refered to as the *Euclidean* distance. Now if a new point, x, has been introduced in the feature space then the simplest form of classification consists of finding the means of the two clusters, m_1 and m_2, and then calculating the *Euclidean* distances between the new point and the mean of the clusters. In a multi-dimensional feature space, this distance is given as,

$$r_i = \sum_{k=1}^{n} (x_k - m_{ik})^2 \tag{2.2}$$

where r_i represents the distance between the new point x from the ith cluster and m_{ik} is the kth element in the mean vector for the cluster i. For our example in Figure 5.3, $r_1 < r_2$ therefore point x will be classified in cluster 1. A simple visual inspection of the points in the clusters shows that this is most likely an erroneous result since the points in cluster 2 come much closer to x than in cluster 1. A refinement of equation 2.2 would be to take into account the distribution of the points in each cluster and *weight* the distance on each axis by the variance along that axis. This would result in the *weighted Euclidean* distance and is given as,

$$r_i = \frac{\sum_{k=1}^{n} (x_k - m_{ik})^2}{\sigma_{ik}^2} \tag{2.3}$$

where σ_{ik} represent the variance of cluster i in direction k. In this case the clusters will be represented by their equal probability lines as shown in Figure 5.4. As such, it is obvious that x is more likely to be classified in cluster 2 rather than cluster 1.

The *weighted Euclidean* distance will fail to give a correct measure of the distance if the main diagonal axis of the clusters are not perpendicular to the feature axis, i.e. correlation between the features is not equal to zero. Here a more general form of the *Euclidean* distance known as the *Mahalonobis* distance can be used. In this case, the variance along each axis is replaced by the covariance matrix. When the points in a cluster contain correlated features then by the use of the covariance matrix the cluster would become ellipsoidal and its orientation would indicate how the features are correlated (see Figure 5.5).

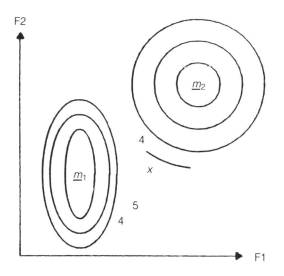

Figure 5.4- Geometric representation of the weighted Euclidean distance.

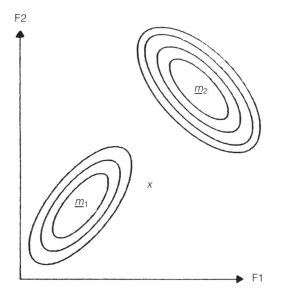

Figure 5.5- Geometric representation of the Mahalanobis distance.

In terms of the covariance matrix, the correlation between the features is expressed by non-zero terms in the non-diagonal elements of the matrix. The *Mahalonobis* distance between point $\underline{x}$ to the ith cluster in a n-dimentional feature space is given by,

$$r_1^2 = (\underline{x} - \underline{m}_i)^T C_i^{-1}(\underline{x} - \underline{m}_i) \tag{2.4}$$

where

$$\underline{m}_i = \frac{1}{n}\sum_{k=1}^{n} \underline{x}_{ik} \tag{2.5}$$

$$\underline{C}_i = \frac{1}{n}\sum_{k=1}^{n} (\underline{x}_{ik} \cdot \underline{x}_{ik}^T) - (\underline{m}_i \cdot \underline{m}_i^T) \tag{2.6}$$

and $\underline{C}_i$ is the covariance matrix of the ith cluster. A simple example is used to illustrate the application of the *Mahalonobis* distance in a 2-dimensional feature space.

2.2 Example

In order to visualize the feature space, a 2-dimensional classification problem will be considered. Given a number of feature sets for two clusters, it is required to classify new points by measuring the *Mahalonobis* distances between the points to the pre-defined clusters. The cluster points are shown in Figure 5.6 and tabulated in Table 5.1. The first step is to calculate the means and the covariance matrices of the clusters using equations (2.5) and (2.6) respectively. The means of the clusters are given as,

$$\underline{m}_1 = \frac{1}{5}\sum_{i=1}^{5} \underline{x}_{1i} = \frac{1}{5}\begin{bmatrix} 10 \\ 11 \end{bmatrix}$$

and

$$\underline{m}_2 = \frac{1}{5}\sum_{i=1}^{5} \underline{x}_{2i} = \frac{1}{5}\begin{bmatrix} 36 \\ 44 \end{bmatrix}$$

Cluster 1	(1,1)	(2,1)	(3,2)	(1,3)	(3,4)
Cluster 2	(6,8)	(8,9)	(7,9)	(9,9)	(6,9)

Table 5.1

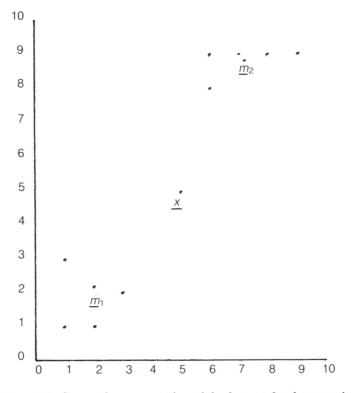

Figure 5.6- Geometric representation of the features for the example.

The covariance matrices for the clusters are given as follows,

$$\underline{C}_1 = \frac{1}{5}\sum_{i=1}^{5}(\underline{x}_{1i}\cdot\underline{x}_{1i}{}^T)-(\underline{m}_1\cdot\underline{m}_1{}^T)$$

$$\underline{C}_2 = \frac{1}{5}\sum_{i=1}^{5}(\underline{x}_{2i}\cdot\underline{x}_{2i}{}^T)-(\underline{m}_2\cdot\underline{m}_2{}^T)$$

Using the mean and the data points for each of the clusters the covariance matrices can be calculated and are given below,

$$\underline{C}_1 = \frac{1}{25}\begin{bmatrix} 20 & -5 \\ -5 & 19 \end{bmatrix} \qquad \underline{C}_2 = \frac{1}{25}\begin{bmatrix} 34 & 6 \\ 6 & 4 \end{bmatrix}$$

and finally, the inverse of the covariance matrices are,

$$C_1^{-1} = \frac{5}{71} \begin{bmatrix} 19 & 5 \\ 5 & 20 \end{bmatrix} \quad C_2^{-1} = \frac{1}{4} \begin{bmatrix} 4 & -6 \\ -6 & 34 \end{bmatrix}$$

Now we can apply equation (2.4) to any new points in the feature space for classification. If we now assume that the coordinates of the new point are,

$$x = [5 \quad 5]^T$$

then, the distance between x to the clusters will be,

$$r_1^2 = (x - m_1)^T C_1^{-1} (x - m_1) = 17.17$$

$$r_2^2 = (x - m_2)^T C_2^{-1} (x - m_2) = 152.66$$

In this case $r_1 < r_2$ which means point x would be classified in cluster 1.

3 Adaptive Signal Processing

Adaptive signal processing is a large area of research which encompasses areas where incomplete *apriori* knowledge about signal environment is available or this signal environment is time variant. This section will be restricted to looking at the basic adaptive learning algorithms applied to a restricted class of adaptive processor.

3.1 Adaptive Combiners

The class of processor which is investigated here is restricted to the case where the data field available is finite in extent and the processor used provides an output which is a linear weighted combination of these inputs. Such a processor is shown schematically in Figure 5.7, the so-called linear combiner [3]. The output, $\hat{y}(n)$, of this linear combiner is given by the expression,

$$\hat{y}(n) = \sum_{i=0}^{N-1} x_i(n) w_i(n) \tag{3.1}$$

where $x_i(n)$ is the ith data input at time n, and where $w_i(n)$ is the ith combiner coefficient at time n. This expression may be rewritten as,

$$\hat{y}(n) = x^T(n) w(n) \tag{3.2}$$

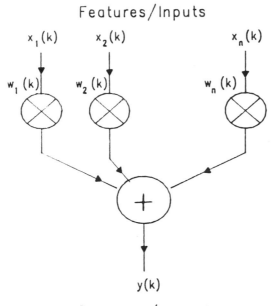

Features/Inputs

$x_1(k)$ $x_2(k)$ $x_n(k)$

$w_1(k)$ $w_2(k)$ $w_n(k)$

$y(k)$

Outcome/output

Figure 5.7- Linear combiner structure.

Features/Inputs

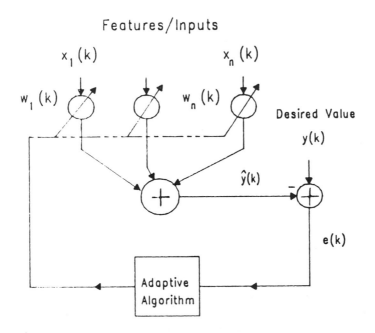

$x_1(k)$ $x_n(k)$

$w_1(k)$ $w_n(k)$

Desired Value

$y(k)$

$\hat{y}(k)$

$e(k)$

Adaptive
Algorithm

Figure 5.8- Schematic diagram of the adaptive linear combiner.

where $\underline{x}(n)$ and $\underline{w}(n)$ are (Nx1) column vectors of the N data elements $x_i(n)$ and coefficients, $w_i(n)$ respectively. The superscript, T, denotes the operation of matrix transposition.

The combiner structure is adaptive when the coefficient vector $\underline{w}(n)$ is time variant and determined recursively in order to minimize some predetermined cost function. Hence the vector has the time index indicated in (3.1). The cost function minimized usually relates to the error in the combiner output (Figure 5.8),

$$e(n)=y(n)-\hat{y}(n) \tag{3.3}$$

where $y(n)$ is some desired target function. Any function of this error which is always increasing for non-zero error may be used but the function normally used is the mean squared error,

$$\epsilon^2(n)=E[(y(n)-\hat{y}(n))^2] \tag{3.4}$$

where $E[\,]$ is the statistical expectation operator. Substituting for $\hat{y}(n)$ from (3.2) yields,

$$\epsilon^2(n)=E[(y(n)-\underline{x}^T(n)\underline{w}(n))^2]$$

$$=E[y^2(n)-2y(n)\underline{x}^T(n)\underline{w}(n)+\underline{w}^T(n)\underline{x}(n)\underline{x}^T(n)\underline{w}(n)]$$

$$=E[y^2(n)]-2\underline{\phi}_{yx}E[\underline{w}(n)]+E[\underline{w}^T(n)]\,\underline{\phi}_{xx}E[\underline{w}(n)] \tag{3.5}$$

where

$$\underline{\phi}_{yx}=E[y(n)\underline{x}(n)]$$

$$\underline{\phi}_{xx}=E[\underline{x}(n)\underline{x}^T(n)]$$

and the assumption made in the last line is that the data field $\underline{x}(n)$ and the coefficient vector $\underline{w}(n)$ are uncorrelated.

The function described in (3.5) is useful in that it is quadratic with respect to the coefficient vector. Therefore it represents a parabaloid in N dimensions with a single unique minimum corresponding to the optimum (in a least squares sense) set of coefficients. The task of the adaptive algorithm is to make use of this error function (or some derivative of it) in order to determine $\underline{w}(n)$, see Figure 5.8.

3.2 Adaptive Algorithms

The optimum value of the coefficient vector is found quite easily by differentiating (3.5) with respect to each coefficient and setting the resulting gradient equal to zero. This yields the Wiener [5] result given by,

$$\underline{w}_{opt} = \underline{\phi}_{xx}^{-1} \underline{\phi}_{xy}$$

This result is not directly usable in the adaptive context since it depends on quantities derived using the expectation operator. That is the quantities $\underline{\phi}_{xx}$ and $\underline{\phi}_{xy}$ are not normally available. However a similar result may be derived by using all the data available up to the present time interval to specify the least squares cost function [4],

$$\xi^2(n) = \sum_{i=0}^{N} (y(n-i) - \hat{y}(n-i))^2 \tag{3.7}$$

Minimizing (3.7) yields the result,

$$\underline{w}_{opt}(n) = \underline{r}_{xx}^{-1}(n)\underline{r}_{xy}(n) \tag{3.8}$$

where

$$\underline{r}_{xx}(n) = \sum_{k=0}^{n} \underline{x}(k)\underline{x}^T(k)$$

and

$$\underline{r}_{xy}(n) = \sum_{k=0}^{n} \underline{x}(k)y(k)$$

This result may be used to derive the so-called recursive least squares algorithm [4] which defines an iterative algorithm for $\underline{w}(n)$,

$$\underline{w}(n) = \underline{w}(n-1) + \underline{r}_{xx}^{-1}(n)\underline{x}(n)e(n) \tag{3.9}$$

and the inverse $\underline{r}_{xx}^{-1}(n)$ may be defined directly from the Sherman Morrison recursion,

$$\underline{r}_{xx}^{-1}(n) = \underline{r}_{xx}^{-1}(n-1) - \frac{\underline{r}_{xx}^{-1}(n-1)\underline{x}(n)\underline{x}^T(n)\underline{r}_{xx}^{-1}(n-1)}{1 + \underline{x}^T(n)\underline{r}_{xx}^{-1}(n-1)\underline{x}(n)} \tag{3.10}$$

Although this does yield a viable adaptive structure it suffers from the problem that the error is weighted equally for all time. This causes difficulty should the required result not be stationary. In this case the error must be weighted towards the more recent data samples. This is commonly done using an exponential window which modifies (3.10) to,

$$\underline{r}_{xx}^{-1}(n) = \frac{1}{\lambda}(\underline{r}_{xx}^{-1}(n-1) - \frac{\underline{r}_{xx}^{-1}(n-1)\underline{x}(n)\underline{x}^T(n)\underline{r}_{xx}^{-1}(n-1)}{\lambda + \underline{x}^T(n)\underline{r}_{xx}^{-1}(n-1)\underline{x}(n)}) \qquad (3.11)$$

where $\lambda < 1$ and usually lies in the range $0.9 < \lambda < 1$. Algorithms of this type offer optimum performance in terms of initial adaptation rate. In the case of relatively noise free signals adaptation to the noise floor should occur within $2N$ iterations (N is the combiner order). However they do suffer from a high degree of computational complexity (order N^2 as this case). In the restricted case where the combiner is applied to the output of a tapped delay line (i.e. temporal filtering) a reduction in complexity to order (N) is possible by using fast Kalman algorithms [6,7].

Other, more computationally efficient algorithms may be derived by using gradient search techniques [3]. In these algorithms the coefficient vector is updated according to an estimate of the error surface gradient,

$$\underline{w}(n) = \underline{w}(n-1) - \mu\hat{\nabla}\epsilon^2(n) \qquad (3.12)$$

where μ is a constant smaller than 1. A frequently used approximation for the gradient uses a single value of error rather than the mean square,

$$\hat{\nabla}\epsilon^2(n) = \frac{\delta}{\delta(\underline{w}(n))}e^2(n) \qquad (3.13)$$

Use of this approximation, which is unbiased, leads to the stochastic gradient search algorithm,

$$w(n) = \underline{w}(n-1) + 2\mu\underline{x}(n)e(n) \qquad (3.14)$$

where μ is bounded by the largest eigenvalue of the input autocorrelation matrix $\underline{\phi}_{xx}$ [8];

$$0 < \mu < \frac{1}{\lambda_{max}} \tag{3.15}$$

This algorithm provides a computationally efficient and numerically robust algorithm. It does however suffer from slow initial convergence and convergence speed is also dependent on the eigenvalues of the input autocorrelation matrix. That is, a highly coloured input signal can lead to extremely slow convergence which is dominated by the lowest valued eigenvalue λ_{min}.

This dependence on input signal colouration may be removed by the use of self-orthogonalizing algorithms [9],

$$\underline{w}(n) = \underline{w}(n-1) + \mu \underline{\phi}_{xx}^{-1} \underline{x}(n) e(n) \tag{3.15}$$

With this algorithm type input colouration effects are removed but it is still slower, in terms of initial adaptation, than the RLS.

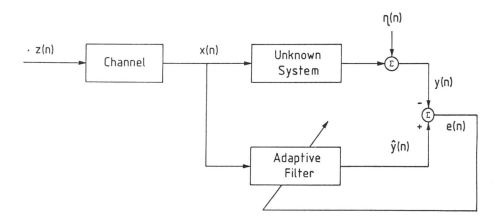

Figure 5.9- Schematic diagram of system configuration used in computer simulations for the adaptive algorithms.

3.3 Performance Comparisons

The performance comparisons presented in this section were obtained using the adaptive combiner as a time series filter. The actual test system is shown schematically in Figure 5.9. The input signal $z(n)$ is random and zero mean with the purpose of the "channel" being to introduce controlled colouration to the input signal, $x(n)$. The performance index used is the coefficient error norm,

$$P(n) = E((\underline{w}(n) - \underline{w}_{opt})^T (\underline{w}(n) - \underline{w}_{opt})) \qquad (3.16)$$

The three sets of curves shown in Figures 5.10-12 demonstrate the convergence of a 16-tap adaptive filter with LMS, RLS and self-orthogonalizing algorithms. The additive noise on the training input is at -60 dB, so the first feature we may examine is the convergence time to the 60 dB noise floor. Features below this level are discussed later.

The result in Figure 5.10 shows convergence when the input signal to the adaptive filter is white (autocorrelation eigenvalue ratio is unity). Here the RLS algorithm converges to the noise floor in about 30 iterations. The LMS and self-orthogonalizing algorithms are identical in this case and both converge to the noise floor in about 300 iterations. Figure 5.11 shows the comparison when the input signal is slightly coloured (eigenvalue ration 11). The convergence of the RLS to the noise floor here is still about 30 iterations, the LMS convergence time is increased to about 700 iterations and the self-orthogonalizing algorithms still converges in 400 iterations. The result shown in Figure 5.12 is for an input signal eigenvalue ratio of 68 (severe colouration). Here we do see slight degradation in the RLS adaptation time to about 70 iterations. The LMS adaptation time has increased to between 2000 and 3000 iterations. The self-orthogonalizing algorithm maintains convergence in about 400 iterations.

At this stage we may draw some interim conclusions regarding algorithm performance in low-noise conditions. First, the RLS algorithm consistently achieves the fastest convergence rates with minimal dependence on input signal colouration. The LMS algorithm behaves worst with variable input signal colouration, and can have extremely long convergence times for heavy signal colouration. The self-orthogonalizing algorithm convergence to the noise floor is completely independent of input colouration, and always converges along the line of an LMS algorithm with white input signal. Set against this is the difficulty in actually implementing the algorithms.

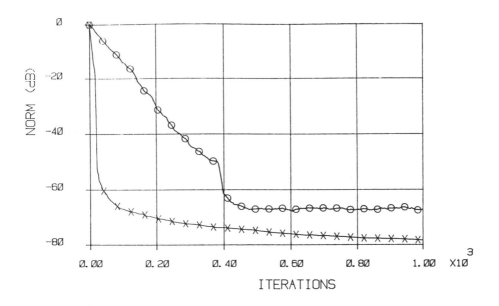

Figure 5.10- Convergence of the three adaptive algorithms when the input signal is white. In all the cases the adaptive noise is at -60 dBs and the filter order is 16. Key: (a) LMS, (b) Self-orthogonalizing and (c) RLS algorithm.

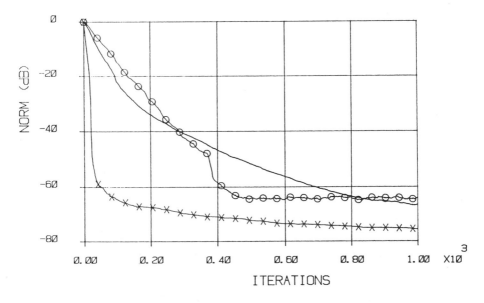

Figure 5.11- Convergence of the three adaptive algorithms when the input signal has an eigenvalue ratio of 11. Key: as in Figure 5.10.

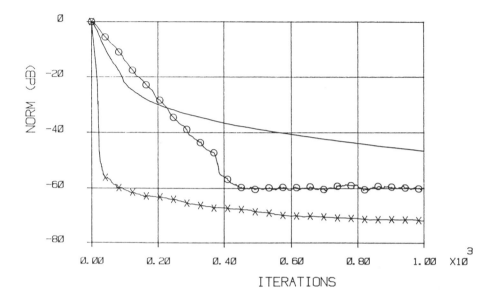

Figure 5.12- Convergence of the three adaptive algorithms when the input signal has an eigenvalue ratio of 68. Key: as in Figure 5.10.

4 Mathematical Feature Analysis

The characteristics and the adaptation of the machine learning system (MLS) described in this chapter depend on the nature of the problem considered and also on the selection of the salient features. The choice of a feature set depends on the characteristics of the problem and the MLS does not provide any information on how to select the features. The feature set is usually chosen by investigating the relationships between the parameters (causes) and the outcomes (effects). Also, when we finally decide on a set of features it is not guaranteed that the features are suitable to the arithmetic architecture of the MLS or that they sufficiently describe the problem.

In the following sections of this chapter, a data analysis program (DAP) is developed. The program is provided with the weight and the correlation matrices and generates explanations on how the combiners are behaving to the selected feature set.

4.1 Feature Manipulation and Analysis

Figure 5.13 illustrates the overall structure of the DAP. The following matrix definitions and parameters will be used throughout the rest of this section,

n : number of features.

m : number of training examples.

l : number of outcomes.

$\underline{w}_i$: weight matrix, $(n,1)$, for the ith combiner.

$\underline{X}$: (n,m) matrix of training features.

$\underline{Y}$: (m,l) matrix of desired values/outcomes.

$\underline{r}_{xx}$: (n,n) matrix approximating the auto-correlation of $\underline{x}$.

$\underline{r}_{xy_i}$: $(n,1)$ matrix approximating the cross-correlation of $\underline{x}$ with outcome y_i.

It is assumed that a set of salient features has been chosen, $\underline{x}$, and also these features have been generated to form $\underline{X}$ in the training mode. At the end of the training mode, the weight matrix for the ith combiner is given by the Wiener solution (See Section 3) as,

$$\underline{w}_i = \underline{r}_{xx}^{-1} \underline{r}_{xy_i} \quad or \quad \underline{r}_{xx} \underline{w}_i = \underline{r}_{xy_i} \tag{4.1}$$

At this stage, the auto-correlation matrix is divided into two parts, $\underline{r}_{xx}^+$ and $\underline{r}_{xx}^0$. $\underline{r}_{xx}^+$ is defined as the positive auto-correlation matrix which contains all the feature sets which have resulted in the outcome, y_i, to be not equal to zero and similarly r_{xx}^0 is defined as the zero auto-correlation matrix. We can now redefine (4.1b) as follows,

$$(\underline{r}_{xx}^+ + \underline{r}_{xx}^0)\underline{w}_i = \underline{r}_{xy_i} \tag{4.2}$$

This decomposition of the correlation matrix allows us to distinguish between the features which contribute towards a particular fault. The significant of the features for the ith outcome may be obtained by further dividing the cross-correlation matrix into two parts,

$$\underline{r}_{xy_i}^+ = \underline{r}_{xx}^+ \underline{w}_i \tag{4.3a}$$

and

$$\underline{r}_{xy_i}^0 = \underline{r}_{xx}^0 \underline{w}_i \tag{4.3b}$$

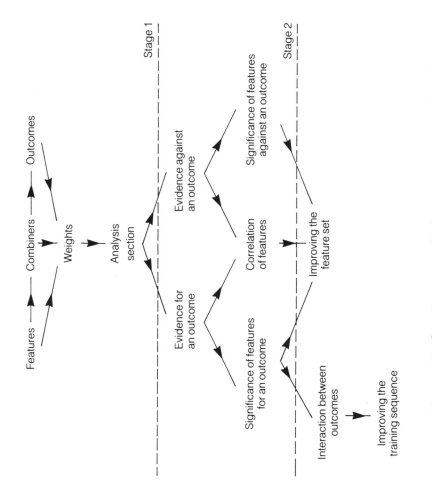

Figure 5.13- Overall structure of the data analysis program (DAP).

where $r_{xy_i}^+$ matrix contains the contribution of each feature towards the ith outcome, i.e. the +ve cross-correlation, and $r_{xy_i}^0$ is defined as the zero cross-correlation matrix.

The +ve cross-correlation matrix should be obtained for all the outcomes to form r_{xy}^+ which would be a (n,l) matrix given as,

$$r_{xy}^+ = [r_{xy_1}^+, r_{xy_2}^+, \cdots, r_{xy_l}^+]$$ (4.4)

where each column in r_{xy}^+ contains the level of significance of each feature towards one outcome. It is then possible to construct an interaction matrix, I_{yy}, which indicates the level of interaction between the outcomes using r_{xy}^+ as shown belove,

$$I_{yy} = (r_{xy}^+)^T (r_{xy}^+)$$ (4.5)

All the matrices, r_{xx}^+, r_{xy}^+ and I_{yy} are normalized and applied to a rule-based expert system which performs the decision functions for evaluating the level of correlation between the features, the significance of the features and the interaction between the outcomes.

4.2 Normalization Techniques

There are two types of normalization required. The first type is applied to the correlation matrices by normalizing every element in the matrix to the diagonal elements using the following,

If (i=j)   Then $\qquad r_{ij} = 1;$

Else $\qquad r_{ij} = \dfrac{r_{ij}^2}{r_{ii} r_{jj}}$

This would remove the contribution of each individual diagonal element from the correlation between the elements of the matrix. The diagonal elements of the normalized matrix will be equal to one and all the other elements will be in the range $0 < r_{ij} < 1$. This type of normalization is applied to the auto-correlation and the interaction matrices.

The second type of normalization is applied to the cross-correlation matrix to indicate the level of significance of the features. In this case, every element in the matrix is normalized to the largest element resulting in values in the range $0 < r_{ij} < 1$. Thresholding is then applied to the normalized matrices to decide on the level of significance, correlation and interaction.

4.3 Thresholding Expert System

When the correlation and the interaction matrices are obtained and normalized, a classical expert system approach, Figure 5.14, is used to decide on the level of correlation, significance and interaction. These decisions are based on some predefined thresholds which can be the same or different for each of the matrices. Here, three values have been used to decide between strong, weak and no correlation or interaction. Thus, the expert system in this case takes the form of three IF THEN statements. The output of the expert system is in the form of tables as shown in Figure 5.16. The larger table contains the level of significance/dependency of each individual feature to each of the outcomes. The '*' indicates strong significance, the '+' indicates weak significance and the '-' indicates no significance of the features to each of the outcome. The other table illustrates the level of interactions between the outcomes. The interaction matrix, L_{yy}, is symmetrical and therefore the expert system only displays one half of the matrix.

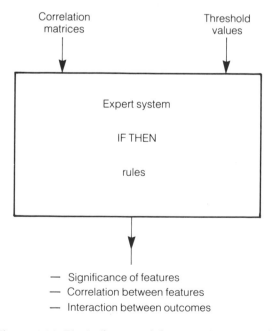

Figure 5.14- Block diagram of the expert system used.

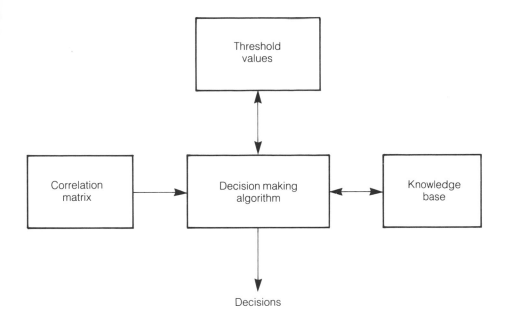

Figure 5.15- Block structure of the expert system with a knowledge base.

The matrices r_{xx} and r_{xy} are only approximations to the true correlation matrices. Therefore the results generated by the analysis section can only be treated as a set of rough decisions. These decisions can be improved by using more training sequences in the system. Therefore, it will be necessary to incorporate some form of memory within the expert system so that the new decisions are not only based on the present inputs but also on the previous decisions. This can be achieved by introducing a knowledge base within the expert system and updating this knowledge base each time a new set of decisions is made. Figure 5.15 illustrates the complete expert system which must be used with the proposed analysis system. The decision algorithm in Figure 5.15 will be more complex than before since it should weight different thresholds for different matrices and also it needs to store the old decisions in such a form that can be used later.

4.4 Example

The performance and the application of the DAP is tested using a simple example. The DAP has also been used on the features generated for the tuning of waveguide filters and the results are presented in Chapter 11. In this example, we apply the system to the following set of equations,

$$y_1 = \sum_{i=1}^{5} x_i \tag{4.6a}$$

$$y_2 = x_1 + x_2 \tag{4.6b}$$

$$y_3 = x_3 + x_4 \tag{4.6c}$$

$$y_4 = x_5 \tag{4.6d}$$

The outcomes, $\underline{Y}$, are all linear combinations of the features, $\underline{x}$, and from (4.6a-d) the output of the DAP may be easily predicted. 15 feature sets were randomly chosen and fed into the system and Figure 5.16 shows the output of the DAP. As expected, outcome y_1 is dependent on all the features while outcomes y_2 and y_3 are only dependent on features (x_1, x_2) and (x_3, x_4) respectively. Also, outcome y_4 is only dependent on feature x_5. The interaction table suggests weak interaction between y_1 and all the other outcomes and no interaction between the other outcomes, as expected from (4.6a-d).

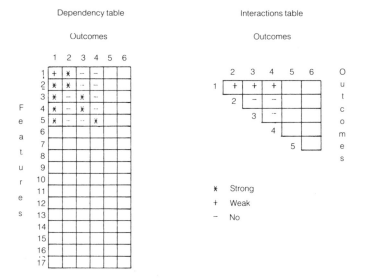

Figure 5.16- The output of the data analysis program (DAP).

5 Conclusion

This chapter has described a combination of well established techniques from pattern recognition and adaptive signal processing applied to machine learning. The limitations of this approach come from the need to partition the particular problem space into linear sub-spaces and choose appropriate salient features. These activities require a higher level of insight into the nature of the problem than is desirable for a generic problem solving tool. That said, the approach has been successful in application and has led to new linkages ([10,11] see also Chapters 10 and 11). The linear combiner structure can be seen as a special case of a one-layer neural network, Chapter 4, and the particular problems addressed by the MLS can now be used as benchmarks for ongoing extensions using neural networks.

Some wider issues have also been brought to the fore. Early success in some applications reinforced the view that the "spacial" recognition of patterns better fitted much of "expert behaviour" than the linguistic representation of classical AI. The combination of both approaches must be a fruitful direction to explore.

References

[1]   B. Sing-Tze, *Pattern Recognition*, Marcel Dekker, New York, 1984.

[2]   B.G. Batchelor, *Practical Approaches to Pattern Classification*, Plenum Books, London, 1974.

[3]   B. Widrow and S.D. Stearns, *Adaptive signal processing*, Prentice-Hall, Englewood Cliffs, N.J., 1985.

[4]   C.F.N. Cowan and P.M. Grant, *Adaptive Filters*, Prentice-Hall, Englewood Cliffs, N.J., 1985.

[5]   N. Wiener, *Extrapolation, interpolation and smoothing of stationary time series*, Wiley, New York, 1949.

[6]   J.M. Cioffi and J. Kailath, "Fast Recursive-least-squares Transversal Filters for Adaptive Filtering", *IEEE Trans., ASSP-32*, pp 304-337, 1984.

[7]   D. Godard, "Channel Equalization Using a Kalman Filter for Fast Data Transmission", *IBM J. R&D*, **Vol-18**, pp 267-273, 1974.

[8]   G. Ungerboeck, "Theory on the Speed of Convergence in Adaptive Equalizers for Digital Communications", *IBM J. R&D*, **Vol-16**, pp 267-273, 1972. pp. 546-555.

[9]   C.F.N. Cowan, "Performance Comparisons of Finite Linear Adaptive Filters", *IEE Proc. Pt-F*, **Vol-134**, pp 211-216, 1987.

[10] A.R. Mirzai, C.F.N. Cowan & T.M. Crawford, "Intelligent Alignment of Waveguide Filters using a Machine Learning Approach", *IEEE Trans. on Microwave Theory and Techniques*, **Vol-37,** pp 166-173, Jan 1989.

[11] K.E. Brown, C.F.N. Cowan, T.M. Crawford and P.M. Grant, "The Application of Knowledge-base System for Fault Diagnosis in Microwave Radio Relay Equipment", *IEEE J. of Selected Areas in Communications*, (Special Issue on Knowledge-Based Systems for Communication), **Vol-6**, June 1988.

Part Two: Applications

Chapter 6

Intelligent Spectral Estimation

B.L.F. Daku and P.M. Grant

1 Introduction

This chapter discusses how artificial intelligence (AI) techniques can be used to enhance traditional signal processing algorithms. This approach is discussed in terms of a spectral estimation application where it is possible to use multiple sources of information to improve a signal processing function. The sources of information of interest in this work are the outputs from multiple signal processing algorithms. In many situations the user must be directly involved to integrate this information, which is undesirable in real-time applications. One potential approach is to integrate the various sources of information with the help of AI techniques. This approach is examined in this chapter, where AI techniques are used to develop and implement a spectral analysis algorithm which uses results of multiple signal processing algorithms. The AI techniques of interest in this problem are expert-system related development tools that can be used to produce a decision-directed intelligent system. The reason for using these AI techniques is to provide a more efficient structure and development environment to produce and refine the enhanced algorithms.

Spectral estimation is typically performed by the robust fast Fourier transform-based (FFT) periodogram [1]. This technique has problems where there are only a small number of samples or if the signal is stationary only over a few samples. For example, the periodogram may not provide the required resolution to differentiate two closely spaced peaks if only a few samples are available.

There are a variety of spectral analysis algorithms [1,2] that could be used to improve upon these results in short data record applications. The difficulty with these algorithms is that they usually require some initial parameters to be specified. This is typically done by trial and error, with the user trying some initial parameters and then checking the results and repeating the process if necessary. It is proposed that AI techniques could be used to determine these initial parameters and thus eliminate the human intervention. A natural extension of this technique is to use a number of spectral analysis algorithms to produce the best spectral estimate for the application. This chapter justifies this concept by developing the AI decision procedures [3] to handle two specific signal processing algorithms, the periodogram and modern autoregressive (AR) parametric spectral analysis methods [1,3].

It would be desirable to develop the AI algorithm so that it could handle any short data record application. This is a rather ambitious goal and in this study the application is restricted to estimating the spectral content of a foetal heart signal, which is a harmonically rich process. At any time frame there is typically only one harmonic sequence in the data. The foetal heart rate measurement application is chosen because the signal is stationary only over short data records [4]. (See also Chapter 7.) Estimation of the spectral content of the foetal heart signal to determine the fundamental component is important for monitoring foetal development and providing diagnosis of medical problems [5,6]. To provide a basis for comparison with other techniques an AI algorithm was developed to estimate the fundamental frequency of the harmonic spectrum automatically. We have specifically concentrated on an application where frequency or heart rate is to be measured and where power level or spectral width is of minor importance.

The chapter is divided into six sections. The first section gives a description of an AI tool, called the blackboard shell, presented in Chapter 2, which is used to simplify the development of the complete system. The second section gives a description of the signal processing algorithms that were used. The third section describes the resulting intelligent algorithm that has been developed to estimate the spectral content of a signal. This is based on a heuristic approach rather than a rigorous theoretical optimization approach, which is most cases does not exist. The fourth section describes the AI algorithm that is used to estimate the fundamental frequency of a harmonic spectrum. The fifth section presents the results obtained by using a number of artificially generated signals and the results from real foetal heart data. The last section presents summary, discussion and conclusions.

2 The Blackboard Shell

The AI system chosen for the development stage is a blackboard shell which is written in Edinburgh Prolog [7]. This particular blackboard shell was developed along the lines of the HEARSAY-II [8] speech recognition system. The blackboard architecture was chosen because it allows a very flexible system. It permits the implementation to be expanded easily. In this project, data is accessed from two signal processing algorithms, but the blackboard could easily be modified to use input from more than two algorithms. Our implementation also allowed the use of C programming language functions through the use of Prolog. This permits a modular transition from the blackboard to a C language implementation when the final algorithm has been determined. The C language can also be used efficiently to implement portions of the program that are very time consuming to run in Prolog such as the AR and FFT routines. The rest of this section briefly describes the blackboard shell.

The architecture for the blackboard consists of three principal items:

        (1) Blackboard
        (2) Knowledge Sources (KS's)
        (3) Scheduler

2.1 Blackboard

The physical organization of the entries or intermediate results is given by the term bb(Tag, Status, Index, Fact, Cf). The system specifies the Tag, which is an integer that uniquely identifies the entry. Status is also specified and used by the system to indicate the state of the entry (for example "in" and "amended" are two possible states). Index, Fact and Cf are user supplied by way of the KS's. The definitions of these three terms are:

Index - Prolog term specifying a user organized blackboard location.
Fact - Term specifing the information to be placed on the blackboard.
Cf   - Term used to indicated the confidence of the entry.

2.2 Knowledge Sources

Knowledge sources implement the knowledge used to create and modify entries. This knowledge is implemented using a set of condition-action rules. The condition part of the rule usually refer to entries on the blackboard. The action part usually adds further entries or amends existing ones. The syntax for the knowledge source rules is:

> If   *Condition*
> then *Goal*
> to   *Effect*
> est   *Estimate*

The *Goal* is a Prolog term that must succeed if the rule is to be carried out. The *Goal* can be used to calculate new values for the entry or perhaps print a message. The *Effect* is the action part of the rule. It is used to add, amend or delete entries and can also be used to execute a Prolog term. The *Estimate* is a way of specifying the usefulness of a rule. The default is an integer, with a smaller integer indicating a more important rule. An example of a rule is:

> If   [fft, hgt_list(L), true]
> and   [fft, n_fft_pks(Npk), true]
> then find_dom_peaks(L,L1,Npk,0.15)
> to   add [dom, dom_peak_list(L1), true]
> est   2

The *Goal* (find_dom_peaks), in this example, calculates a list of the dominant peak heights (L1) from a list of the periodogram peak heights (L). This rule will fire if the two entries in the condition ([fft, hgt_list(L), true] and [fft, n_fft_pks(Npk), true]) are on the blackboard. The result of the rule is an addition to the dominant peak list on the blackboard.

2.3 Scheduler

The scheduler is basically a control mechanism that decides which rule should be executed next. The scheduler execution cycle checks for new entries on the blackboard before evaluating the conditions of the various KS rules to determine which could be executed. This information is displayed on the knowledge source activation record (KSAR) agenda of tasks. (See Chapter 2.) The system orders this agenda according to the *Estimate* before executing the rule associated with the KSAR and subsequently updating the blackboard

2.4 Commands

The blackboard shell provides a variety of commands that can be used to run and refine the rule-based program. The brief command summary in Table 6.1 gives an indication of the tools available to the blackboard user.

Command	Definition
step Mode until Goal	repeatedly carries out a cycle of the system doing a 'show Mode' each time until Goal is true. The system provides a Goal 'entry (Index Fact, Cf)' for the users use. The 'show Mode' can be any one of the show commands listed in the bottom half of this table.
step Mode	does one cycle, and a 'show Mode'
step Number	does Number cycles of the system, and a 'show this' each time
step	equivalent to 'step this'
run	run until the agenda is empty, showing nothing
show this	displays the current cycle
show next	displays a summary of what will happen in the next cycle
show entries	displays all the blackboard
show brief	displays a brief summary of the current cycle
show changes	displays the entries which went into or out of the blackboard
show agenda	displays the current agenda
show nots	displays the 'nots' markers
show supports	displays the supports relationships
show supported by (A)	displays the entries supported by A (integer)
show supports of (A)	displays the supports of the entry A (integer)
show shadow	displays the shadow part of the blackboard
show rule (N)	displays rule number N (N an integer)
show rules	displays all the rules
show N	(N is an integer) prints that blackboard entry
show causes	displays justifications for the user entries

Table 6.1- Blackboard command summary

3 Signal Processing Algorithms

Spectral estimation can be performed by a wide variety of algorithms [1,9]. The two algorithms selected, to test the proposed AI technique, are the periodogram and an autoregressive (AR) technique using the optimum tapered Burg algorithm [1]. The periodogram is a classical spectral estimation method that is implemented using the FFT. It is generally recognized to be the most robust and computationally efficient spectral estimation technique available. However, there are problems related to spectral resolution, sidelobe leakage and stability, which become apparent in short data records. The frequency resolution is proportional to the reciprocal of the data record duration. The implicit windowing due to finite data records results in sidelobe leakage which distorts the spectrum. This distortion can be minimized with window tapering [2], but this is accomplished at the expense of reduced frequency resolution. The final problem relates to statistical stability, to minimize the variance of the spectral estimate it is necessary to do some ensemble averaging.

The periodogram or power spectrum P_p, is calculated using the following equation [10]:

$$P_p = \frac{1}{N^2} |X_m|^2 \tag{3.1}$$

where X_m is the discrete Fourier transform (DFT) and N is the number of data points. It should be noted that the spectral plot produced by this equation is not a true power spectral density (PSD) in the sense that the power is indicated by the peak height not the area under the plot.

The disadvantages of the periodogram for short data records can be overcome by exploiting the advantages of the AR technique. This technique assumes the signal comprises noise which has been spectrally shaped in an AR or recursive generating filter and employs a parametric model or finite impulse response adaptive filter [2] to whiten the received signal, Figure 6.1. For the time series data sequence $x(n)$, the generation model is given by:

$$x(n) = -\sum_{k=1}^{p} a_k x(n-k) + u(n) \tag{3.2}$$

where $u(n)$ is defined as a white noise driving sequence. Note that the model coefficients a_k are not fixed, they can vary both with model order and time.

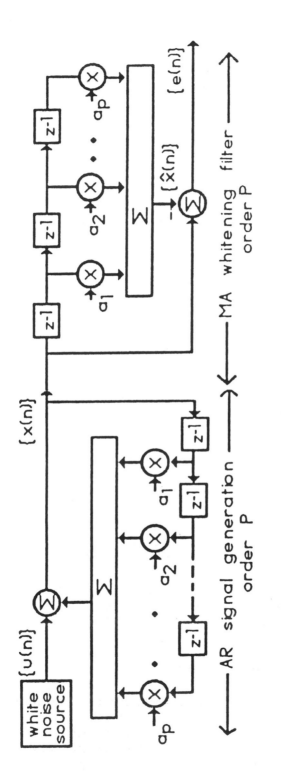

Figure 6.1- Autoregressive (AR) signal generation and whitening filters.

The PSD can be calculated by first estimating the AR coefficients a_k for an assumed order p. These coefficients are then substituted into the following equation which gives the theoretical PSD for the AR model.

$$P_{AR}(f) = \frac{T \rho_w}{\left| 1 + \sum_{k=1}^{p} a_k \exp(-j2\pi f nT) \right|^2} \tag{3.3}$$

where ρ_w is an estimate of the driving noise variance and T is the sampling interval in seconds. The denominator of this equation can be evaluated using the DFT.

The advantage of the AR technique is that it has superior frequency resolution over the periodogram in high signal-to-noise ratio (SNR) environments [10]. Another advantage of the AR method is that it does not suffer from the spectral leakage which is common in the periodogram. The disadvantages of the AR technique are as follows:

(1)   If the model order is too large there can be spurious peaks.

(2)   There can be spectral line splitting, where the PSD sometimes exhibits two close peaks, falsely indicating a second sinusoid.

(3)   The peak location for a sinusoid is dependent on its phase.

(4)   If the SNR is low, the AR resolution is inferior to a FFT.

The disadvantage of point 1 can be reduced by optimizing the AI implementation. The optimum tapered Burg algorithm [9] has been selected to minimize disadvantage 3. In this study the spectral line splitting problem was not addressed, but it appears that it can be easily solved by using a modified covariance method AR technique [1]. Such AR techniques are employed widely in speech signal analysis for linear predictive and other voice coders [2].

4 Spectral Estimation Algorithm

This algorithm is an AI approach to estimating assumed sinusoids from short data records. This attempts to find the best model order for the AR algorithm and then locate the best frequency peaks. The AI algorithm has been optimized for harmonic signals though some rules have been added to make it more general purpose. The algorithm attempts to compensate for the spurious peak problem of the AR technique. The algorithm also produces a confidence rating for each of the peaks selected. Thus in the design of this algorithm the following general guidelines were used:

1. Optimize for harmonic signals.
2. Minimize problem of spurious peaks.
3. Produce a useful confidence rating scheme.

This section is divided into two parts. The first part describes the data features chosen to represent the peaks in the PSD. The second part describes the implementation of the algorithm.

4.1 Data Features

The data features chosen to represent the PSD's must be simple, but they must still contain all the required information. The PSD is basically made up of a series of peaks. Each peak can be represented by three parameters, the location, the height and an indication of the width of the peaks. The location of the peaks can best be given by the centre frequency of each peak and the width of the peak can be easily represented by the half power bandwidth. A fourth parameter is added to give an indication of the relative height of the peaks, this is done by normalizing the peak heights using the peak with the maximum height. This information is represented in the software by the Prolog term *peak* (freq(F),bw(B),height(H),hgt_ratio(HR)). (Note that the symbols starting with capital letters shown represent variables in Prolog.)

The above four parameters, location, width, height and normalized height must be generated for each peak in the periodogram and the AR spectra. The most difficult parameter to estimate is the bandwidth of the peak. This is because the peaks are usually poorly defined. The problem of actually searching for the half-power points was avoided by fitting a curve to the peak and then using an equation to estimate the bandwidth. A parabolic curve was chosen because it is easy to implement and it also produces consistent results. The centre frequency, bandwidth and height of the peaks were all estimated using the parabolic curve. The equation for a parabola, using the conventional x,y axis notation, which opens downwards, with the vertex at point (x_o, y_o) where a is the distance from the vertex to the focus, is

$$(x - x_o)^2 = -4a(y - y_o) \qquad (4.1)$$

This equation is applied to three points about the local maximum, $(-r,y_1)$, $(0,y_2)$ and (r,y_3), where $r = \dfrac{f_s}{tlgth}$ and f_s is the sampling frequency and *tlgth* is the transform length. The resulting equations are

$$(-r-x_o)^2 = -4a(y_1-y_o) \tag{4.2}$$

$$(-x_o)^2 = -4a(y_2-y_o) \tag{4.3}$$

$$(r-x_o)^2 = -4a(y_3-y_o) \tag{4.4}$$

These equations can be solved for a to give

$$a = \frac{r^2}{4y_2-2y_1-2y_3} \tag{4.5}$$

Solving for x_o and y_o gives

$$x_o = \frac{a(y_3-y_1)}{r} \quad \text{and} \quad y_o = \frac{x_o^2}{4a}+y_2 \tag{4.6}$$

The value of x_o gives the frequency and the value of y_o gives the peak height. The bandwidth can be determined by substituting the point $(x_{bw}, \dfrac{y_o}{2})$ into the equation for the parabola. This gives

$$bw = x_{bw}-x_o = \sqrt{(8ay_o)} \tag{4.7}$$

The peaks are then located by a peak searching program, written in C, which simply checks for a local maximum. The bandwidth is chosen as one of the items to represent a peak because it gives a good indication of the quality of the peak. Since the algorithm is looking for assumed sinusoids the closer the peak is to a line spectrum the better. There is a minimum value for the bandwidth since the parabolic interpolation is used. The minimum bandwidth is inversely proportional to the zero padded data record time $(1/r)$, and this minimum value is $\sqrt{2}r$. In the results presented in this chapter $tlgth = (1/128)$ and thus the minimum bandwidth is 0.0110485. All of the bandwidth threshold values used in this chapter are related to this minimum value.

A peak will have a minimum bandwidth when the two outer points, $(-r,0)$ and $(r,0)$, are substituted into equation (4.5), to yield.

$$a = \frac{r^2}{4y_2} \tag{4.8}$$

This value for a is then substituted into equation (4.7) to give

$$bw = \sqrt{(2r^2 \frac{y_o}{y_2})} \tag{4.9}$$

This can be simplified by making the approximation that y_o/y_2 is close to 1 for high frequencies, to yield a minimum bandwidth of $\sqrt{2}r$. This approximation does not apply at lower frequencies, but this is not a problem because the minimum bandwidth will be lower at these frequencies.

4.2 Algorithm

The algorithm comprises five parts each of which is implemented as a knowledge source (KS) on the blackboard shell. The following is a brief summary of the five KS's (the names are indicated in brackets):

(1) Initialize the blackboard (init).
(2) Estimate the dominant periodogram peaks (dom_fft).
(3) Find the AR order where the dominant periodogram peaks match the AR peaks (dom_ar).
(4) Search for stability between six consecutive AR PSD's (ar_ar).
(5) Collect the chosen peaks and assign a confidence value (col).

The first KS, (init), involves reading in the pre-calculated periodogram data, the AR data and the user-specified data. All of this information is placed on the blackboard for future use.

The second KS, (dom_fft), selects the dominant periodogram peaks by choosing all peaks above a certain threshold, whose value is obtained by averaging over all the peaks in the periodogram. This technique provides a good approximation to the human process used when selecting the dominant peaks. A list of the chosen dominant peaks is then placed on the blackboard.

The third KS, (dom_ar), searches out the AR order for a PSD that matches the dominant periodogram peaks in frequency. This gives a good starting AR order since the dominant periodogram peaks are very likely to be real peaks. The implementation consists of the following steps:

(1) Select the initial starting order by examining the number of peaks in AR orders 2, 4 and 6 with a bandwidth below a certain threshold *max_bw*. This is done because it was observed that if there are a large number of harmonically related peaks spaced along the length of the spectrum then the low order AR PSD's have few or no peaks. This can be justified by looking at a pole-zero plot in the z-domain. Initially, when there are only a few poles, the AR algorithm will tend to place the poles in the centre of rather than just inside the unit circle to compensate for all the peaks. This will show up in the AR spectrum as no peaks or a few peaks with very wide bandwidth. The initial orders are chosen as indicated in Table 6.2. Order 6 is checked first, then 4 and 2. These rules only apply if the data record length is greater than or equal to 32.

Order	Peaks (bw < *max_bw*)	Initial Order
2	N	2*N
2	0	10
4	0	16
6	0	20

Table 6.2- Initial order selection for autoregressive analysers

(2) The algorithm starts at this initial order and increments by two until it finds an order with a PSD that contains all of the dominant periodogram peaks (within a tolerance of *peak_tolerance*). If it does not find all of the dominant peaks by order 30, it deletes the problem dominant peaks by removing them from the dominant peak list and starts again at the initial order. Order 30 has been arbitrarily chosen to accommodate a maximum of between 10 and 15 peaks. The problem dominant peaks are deleted because it is very unlikely that they are real peaks. They are probably peaks caused by noise or "spectral leakage" sidelobes.

(3) Once the algorithm has found the correct order it examines each of the AR peaks to make sure it s bandwidth is below *accept_bw*. If any peak has a bandwidth greater than this limit the algorithm increments the order by two and tries to find the dominant peaks with the correct bandwidth. If it reaches an order of 30 it deletes the culprit dominant peaks and starts again at the initial order.

The fourth KS, (ar_ar), begins at the starting order selected in KS 3, and attempts to find a region of stability over six consecutive AR orders. This is done for the following reasons.

(1) Any spurious peaks can be eliminated because they are unlikely to occur at the same frequency over six AR orders.

(2) It has been observed that as the AR order is increased there is a tendency for all the new poles to be assigned to a few prominent peaks. At a higher AR order some of these initial poles may be used to form other peaks. Thus even though one would expect a new peak to appear when the order is increased by two, this does not always occur. Instead there may be a big jump in the number of peaks due to a transfer of poles. If there is a big jump in the number of peaks this indicates that the system is not stable at this AR order and therefore higher orders should be checked.

This KS is implemented in the following steps:

(1) The starting AR order for this KS is the order determined by the previous KS.

(2) The number of peaks over six consecutive orders cannot increase by more than Ns (Ns is a variable that is also used in step 3 and is initially set to one). The AR order is increased until this condition is met. If this condition is not met before the AR order of 30 is reached then Ns is incremented by one and step 2 is repeated. This checks for a large discrepancy in the number of peaks.

(3) The next step is to pick the set of peaks that are common to all of the AR PSD's over six consecutive orders. There cannot be a difference of more than Ns between the number of peaks in the set and the number of peaks in the last order of the six consecutive orders. If the difference is greater than Ns the AR order is increased by two and steps 2 and 3 are repeated. This is continued, if necessary, until AR order 30 at which point Ns is increased by one and a new start is made at step 1. This step eliminates spurious peaks and checks for a stable range of peaks.

(4) The last step is to ensure that at least five of the selected peaks have a bandwidth below *accept_bw*. If these conditions cannot be met the AR order is increased by two and steps 2 and 3 are repeated. If this is still unsatisfactory then the peaks with a bandwidth below *accept_bw* at AR order 30 are taken as the best peaks.

The last KS is used to provide the confidence ranking scheme, Table 6.3, by collecting the best peaks together. The *came_first_peaks* which occur as best peaks in KS 4 (with AR order *Obest*) and also at the AR order of 2/3 times *Obest* have a long range stability and thus are the most confident ones. Stars under the peak classification in Table 6.3 indicate to which category (Best, First, Dom) the peak must belong. The definition of categories is,

Best - The stable peaks selected in KS 4;
First - The peaks selected as *came_first_peaks* in this KS;
Dom - The peaks selected as dominant periodogram peaks in KS 2.

A star in one of the bandwidth columns indicates that the bandwidth of the peak must be less than either *best_bw* or *accept_bw*.

| Confidence | Peak Classification | | | | Bandwidth |
Value	Best	First	Dom	< *best_bw*	< *accept_bw*
1.0	+	+	+	+	
0.95	+	+		+	
0.90	+	+			+
0.80	+		+	+	
0.70	+		+		+
0.65	+			+	
0.60	+				+

•Table 6.3- Confidence values for peak classification

4.3 Implementation Example

This example is presented to give an indication of the procedures required to develop the algorithm. The example concentrates on the KS ar_ar since it is the shortest. The rules for this KS were iteratively developed and refined using the previously described blackboard shell. The blackboard shell provides an organizational structure for the intelligent system and it also provides the necessary tools to refine the rules. This significantly reduces the development complexity compared to a direct implementation in a standard language such as C. The resulting rules are presented in the Appendix. A brief description of the rules is given to indicate their purpose.

The rule-based blackboard structure of the algorithm is a convenient implementation to use during the development process. But this structure is not amenable to the real-time use of the algorithm on a standard computer. Thus to give a reasonable real-time performance the algorithm must be converted to a standard language. In this case the language C has been chosen since all of the signal processing software is written in C.

In a general problem, converting the rules to a C implementation can be a difficult task requiring knowledge of the inference mechanism which defines the inter-relationship of the various rules. This problem has been addressed in some expert system development tools, where it is possible to embed the inference mechanism and the rules directly into another programming environment. For example, the knowledge engineering system (KES) [11], which is written in C, permits the embedding of a frame or rule based system within a C program. This KES system permits a good interface using function calls.

5 Algorithm for the Estimation of the Fundamental Frequency

This algorithm, which is based on AI techniques, is used to estimate the fundamental frequency of a harmonic process. The input to the algorithm consists of the spectrum generated by the algorithm described in Section 4. The algorithm is restricted to a process that has a fundamental frequency in the range of 0.0333 and 0.066 (normalized by the sampling frequency) which is equivalent to a heart rate between 99.9 and 198 beats per minute when sampled at 50 Hz. This algorithm is also implemented using the blackboard shell. The algorithm can be described in the following steps.

(1)   If the total number of peaks in the spectrum is less than four then the fundamental frequency is not estimated for that block of data. Instead a value of 0 is given for the fundamental frequency.

(2)   A check is made to ensure there are no low frequency peaks. Any peaks with a frequency below 0.033 are removed from the peaks under consideration.

(3)   The difference in frequency between each pair of sequential peaks is calculated. The peak frequencies below 0.0999 are also included in this set of difference values. The resulting fundamental values between 0.0333 and 0.066 are identified and placed in another list. The values between 0.066 and 0.0999 are identified as the second harmonics and therefore are divided by 2 and placed in the same list as the previous fundamental

components. This list of values is sorted and an average is calculated around the median to get an initial estimate of the fundamental frequency. If there is an odd number of values the average is done over the three centre values, if even, this is calculated over the two centre values. An average about the median is chosen instead of a complete average to eliminate the potential statistical extremes.

(4)   This initial estimate of the fundamental frequency is then divided into each peak frequency that is greater than this initial estimate. The resulting values are rounded to give a set of integers. These integers give an estimate of the harmonic number for each peak.

(5)   Each of these integers is then divided into the peak frequency that it was derived from to give another set of potential fundamental frequencies. The same median average performed in step 3 is performed on this set of frequencies to produce the final estimate of the fundamental frequency.

6 Results

This section presents the results generated to test the operation of the AI based algorithms. The section is divided into four parts. The first part describes the results from an artificially generated signal consisting of eight harmonically related sinusoids. The second part presents the results from the foetal heart data. The third part presents other results concerned with possible future work. The final part discusses the increased overhead required for the AI implementation.

6.1 Generated Signal

A 32-sample test signal was generated by adding the eight sinusoids described in Table 6.4, with white Gaussian noise. A plot of the analysis results from the above signal is shown in Figure 6.2. The graph shows the periodogram for the signal (when zero padded to 128 samples), as the continuous line plot. It also shows the estimated peak frequencies and the actual peak frequencies as line spectra. The estimated frequencies are indicated by the rectangle at the top of the line, while the actual frequencies are indicated by the cross. Note that the height of the estimated line spectrum indicates confidence value as defined in Table 6.3. The graph in Figure 6.3 shows the results for a signal that is similar to the above signal except all of the SNR's have been decreased by 30 dB.

Freq	0.05	0.1	0.15	0.2	0.25	0.3	0.35	0.4
SNR(dB)	30	29	28	27	26.1	25.2	24.2	23.2

Table 6.4- Sinusoid frequencies for test signal

Figure 6.2 shows that the AI system picked out all of the peaks. The maximum estimation error occurred at frequency 0.030 where the estimated frequency was 0.03039. The AI system clearly produces a better estimate of the peak frequencies than the periodogram because the AR algorithm has a superior resolution. The reduced SNR case of Figure 6.3 shows that the accuracy and confidence of the AI system has decreased significantly as expected. The best AR order chosen in both cases was 22.

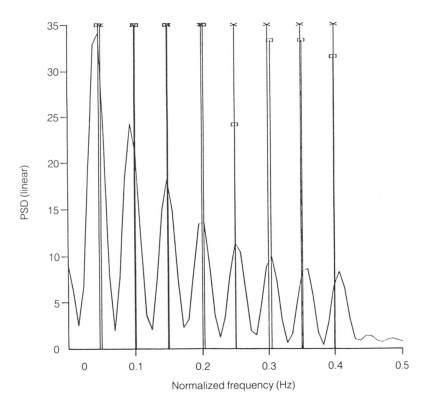

Figure 6.2- Harmonic test signal. Periodogram / continuous line plot. AI estimated peak locations / vertical lines topped by rectangle. Actual peak locations / vertical lines topped by cross.

The fundamental frequency of the above spectra were determined using the AI algorithm of Section 5. The data of Figure 6.2 produced an estimated fundamental frequency of 0.050294 and the data of Figure 6.3 produced a frequency of 0.0510329. This gives a percentage error of 0.59 percent in the first case and 2.1 percent in the second case.

6.2 Foetal Heart Signal

Two sets of foetal heart data have been used to produce the following results. The best set of data is obtained from a direct electrical connection to the scalp of the foetus. The other set of data is obtained using Doppler ultrasound to record the movements of the foetus's heart [12]. The ultrasound data has a lower SNR because it picks up all the movements within the body of both the mother and the foetus. The following results use the scalp data as a reference since it has a high SNR.

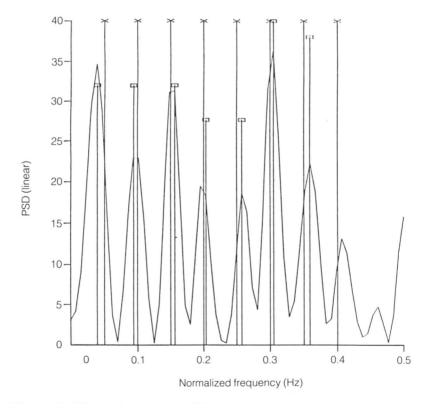

Figure 6.3- Harmonic test signal with reduced SNR. Symbols as in Figure 6.2.

The results will be presented by first giving a few examples of the estimated spectra from a number of different blocks of data. These estimated spectra are then used to determine the fundamental frequency over many blocks of data to give an indication of the robustness of the algorithms. These fundamental frequency results will also be compared with an alternative signal processing technique that is being developed. The data is sampled at 50 Hz and is processed 64 samples at a time to accommodate a minimum heart rate of 100 beats per minute. Thus it is necessary to process at least 1.2 seconds of data to ensure that every block of data will contain at least one complete cycle. The 64 samples (1.28s of data) are zero padded to 128 samples prior to FFT processing.

The scalp is to be used as a reference and thus it is worthwhile to examine a block of scalp data initially. Figure 6.4 shows such a periodogram and AI spectral estimate. This data has been zero padded to 256 samples to improve the resolution of the periodogram so that a better comparison can be made with the estimated spectra. The well defined periodogram indicates that the data has a good SNR and thus should make a good reference signal. The difference between the estimated AI spectra and the periodogram peaks is very small for the majority of the peaks and thus the AI spectra should provide an excellent estimate for this data.

The ultrasound results are examined by presenting the spectra from three blocks of data. The first two examples will present what are considered as poor results and good results dependent on the SNR. The last ultrasound results will examine a problem with the low frequency spectra. Figure 6.5 shows a typical poor result from the ultrasound data. The periodogram is indicated by the continuous line plot. The line spectrum uses the same identification scheme as described earlier. Here, the cross indicates the scalp reference spectra and the rectangle indicates the ultrasound spectra. The scalp and ultrasound spectra are both estimated using the AI algorithm. There is an estimation error for a majority of peaks in the spectrum, as would be expected from this data.

Figure 6.6 shows a good set of results where all but one of the estimates line up, though some peaks were not detected. Figure 6.7 presents some good results except for the lowest frequency. This large error in the low frequency spectra appears frequently in the results. A possible explanation is that there is very little information available to estimate the frequency (i.e. only one cycle). Thus in the lower SNR environment of the ultrasound data it may result in a greater error.

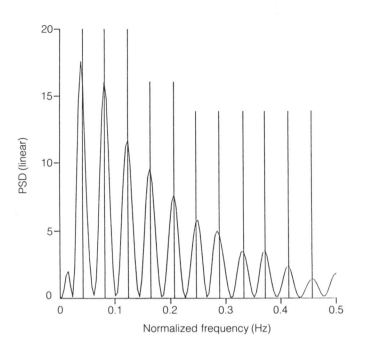

Figure 6.4- Reference plot of foetal heart scalp data zero padded to 256 samples. Periodogram / continuous line plot. AI estimated peak locations / vertical lines.

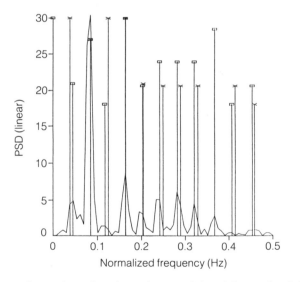

Figure 6.5- Comparison of results when ultrasound foetal heart signal has poor SNR. Periodogram / continuous line plot. AI estimated of ultrasound spectra / vertical lines topped by rectangle. AI estimated of scalp spectra (reference) / vertical lines topped by cross.

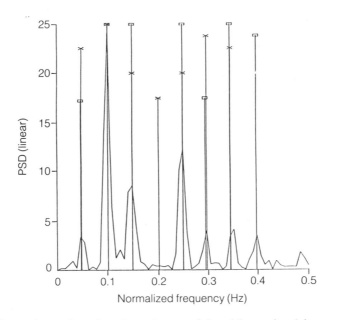

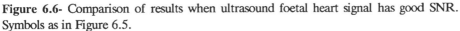

Figure 6.6- Comparison of results when ultrasound foetal heart signal has good SNR. Symbols as in Figure 6.5.

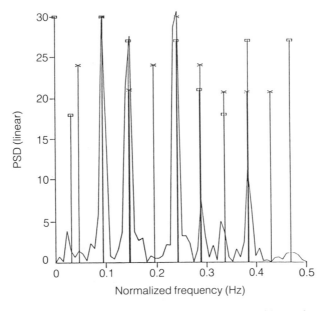

Figure 6.7- Comparison of results showing low frequency problem when ultrasound foetal heart signal has good SNR. Symbols as in Figure 6.5.

The fundamental heart rate is estimated using the AI algorithm of Section 5 and the results are shown in Figure 6.8 over 100 individual blocks of data. The solid line with crosses marking each point indicates the heart rate determined from the scalp data and the plain solid line indicates the ultrasound data. The ultrasound results follow the scalp results very closely except at a few points. These results compare very favourably with alternative transform techniques, [3], which collapse the power of the harmonics into the fundamental.

6.3 Other Example

One of the advantages of the AR algorithms is the good resolution in high SNR environments. An application that could make use of this is one that must detect closely spaced peaks. In the case of short data records the periodogram cannot perform this task.

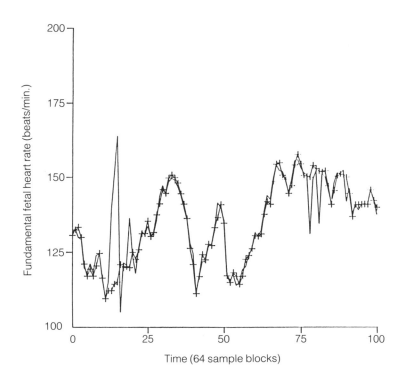

Figure 6.8- Fundamental heart rate estimation using AI algorithm over 100 blocks of data. Ultrasound data / plain solid line. Scalp data (reference) / solid line with crosses marking each point.

The example involves three sinusoids in additive white gaussian noise. The data record length is 32, with zero padding to 128 samples. These three sinusoids have the following properties:

Frequency	0.23575	0.265625	0.36
SNR(dB)	10	20	30

The results are shown in Figure 6.9. They show that the periodogram cannot pick out the low level peak but the AI algorithm can easily identify its presence.

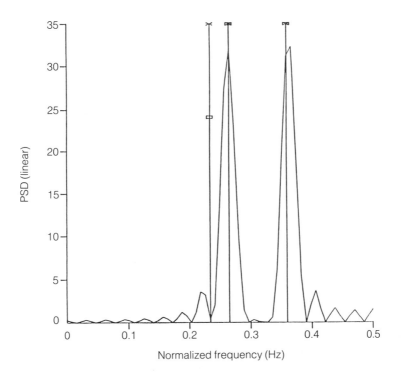

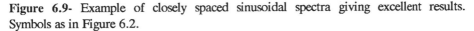

Figure 6.9- Example of closely spaced sinusoidal spectra giving excellent results. Symbols as in Figure 6.2.

6.4 Implementation Overhead

The processing requirement of this system is an important item to consider in real-time applications. The processing time can be divided into two areas, the time required for the signal processing algorithms and the time for the intelligent decision procedures. In the Prolog blackboard implementation of this system the signal processing time requirements are insignificant compared to the intelligent decision procedures. This, of course is due to the Prolog environment that was used to implement the decision procedures. In the C environment the decision procedures consist mainly of IF statements. Many of the C functions are recursive and thus the actual time overhead depends on the data being processed. The data processed to date indicate that the decision procedures consume approximately 20 percent of the processing time. Thus it appears that the increased overhead is not significant relative to the improved results using this technique.

7 Conclusions

The purpose of this study was to determine if AI techniques can be used to improve spectral analysis for short data record applications. The project concentrated on developing a rule-based system to determine the best model order for the AR algorithm. This AI technique used as input the PSD's generated from applying the AR and periodogram analysis of harmonic signals. The system was designed to find the best model order automatically and also to use other information from the AR and periodogram PSD's to eliminate spurious peaks and produce a confidence ranking for the chosen peaks. The confidence ranking is useful because it gives the user more information about the spectrum. The user can choose to accept or reject the less confident peaks. An AI algorithm was also developed and shown to be capable of further estimating the fundamental frequency of the harmonic spectrum.

It should be noted that there are analytical techniques for selecting the best AR model order. These criteria are known as the final prediction error, the Akaike information criteria and the criterion autoregressive transfer [2]. These criterion have not been investigated in this project since it has been found [13], that for short data records, none of them work very well. However, it may be worthwhile, in future work, to compare the AI results with these techniques. The AI spectral estimation algorithm was developed for harmonic signals. The results of the final section indicate that it may be worthwhile to apply these techniques to other signals such as those with closely spaced frequency components (and short data records). Another worthwhile extension is the addition of other signal processing algorithms for functions other than spectral analysis.

8 References

[1] S.L. Marple Jr, *Digital Spectral Analysis with Applications*, Prentice-Hall, 1987.

[2] P.M. Grant, C.F.N. Cowan, B. Mulgrew and J.H. Dripps, *Analogue and Digital Signal Processing and Coding*, Chartwell Bratt, UK, 1989.

[3] B.L.F. Daku, P.M. Grant, C.F.N. Cowan and J. Hallam, "Intelligent Techniques for Spectral Estimation", *IERE Journal*, **Vol-159**, pp 275-283, December 1988.

[4] E.S. Angel, H.E. Fox and E.L. Titlebaum, "Digital Filtering and Foetal Heart Rate Variability", *Computers and Biomedical Research*, **Vol-12**, pp 167-180, 1979.

[5] W. Jarisch and J.S. Detwiler, "Statistical Modeling of Foetal Heart Rate Variability", *IEEE Trans. BME*, **Vol-27**, No-10, pp 582-589, October 1980.

[6] S.J. Cahill and G. McClure, "A Microcomputer-Based Heart-Rate Variability Monitor", *IEEE Trans. BME*, **Vol-30**, No-2, pp 87-93, February 1983.

[7] AI Applications Institute, University of Edinburgh, *Edinburgh Prolog (The New Implementation) User's Manual*, **Version 1.4**, October 1986.

[8] L. Erman, F. Hayes-Roth, V.R. Lesser and D.R. Reddy, "The Hearsay-II: Speech Understanding System: Integrating Knowledge to Resolve Uncertainty", *Computing Surveys*, **Vol-12**, No-2, June 1980.

[9] M. Kaveh and G.A. Lippert, "An Optimum Tapered Burg Algorithm for Linear Prediction and Spectral Analysis", *IEEE Trans. ASSP*, **Vol-31**, No-2, pp 438-444, April 1983.

[10] S.M. Kay and S.L. Marple Jr., "Spectrum Analysis - A Modern Perspective", *Proc. IEEE*, **Vol-69**, No-11, pp 1380-1419, November 1981.

[11] KES Knowledge Base Author's Manual. Software Architecture and Engineering, Arlington, Virginia, 1987.

[12] H. Feigenbaum, *Echocardiography*, Lea and Febiger, Philadelphia, 1986.

[13] T.J. Ulrych and R.W. Clayton,"Time Series Modelling and Maximum Entropy", *Phys. Earth Planet. International* , **Vol-12**, pp 188-200, August 1976.

Appendix A : Blackboard Rules

The end result of this set of rules is the term [ar_ar, order_list(A1,A2,A3,done,Lr), true] which specifies the list of peaks, Lr, that is common to the selected orders A1, A2 and A3. These AR orders indicate the region of "stability" determined by the following rules.

Rules 1 and 2 determine the significant results for the case where the initial order is 2*N in Table 2. Rules 3, 4 and 5 search for the common peaks over the best six consecutive orders as described in Section 4.2. Rules 6, 7, 8, 9 and 10 perform the bandwidth tests as described in Section 4.2. Rule 11 presents the result described above.

The Prolog terms required for some rules (located at the "then" portion of the rule) have not been included in this appendix. In most cases the purpose of the Prolog term should be self-evident.

```
%       Rule 1
if      [ar_ar, best_bw(done), true]
and     [plan, run(plan_2,Op), true]
then    true
to      add [ar_ar,plan2_order_list(12,14,16), true]
est     5.


%       Rule 2
if      [ar_ar,plan2_order_list(O1,O2,O3), true]
and     [ar, freq_list(O1,L1), true]
and     [ar, freq_list(O2,L2), true]
and     [ar, freq_list(O3,L3), true]
and     [user_data, peak_tolerance(Tol), true]
then    pick_peaks_plan2(L1,L2,L3,Tol,Lr)
to      add [ar_ar, tot_peaks_list(Lr), true]
and     [ar_ar, psd_cont, true]
and     [ar_ar, order_list(O1,O2,O3,done,Lr), true]
est     6.
```

```
%      Rule 3
if     [ar_ar, best_bw(done), true]
and    not [plan, run(plan_2,Op), true]
and    [dom_ar, order(Ord), true]
and    [user_data, samples(Max_ord), true]
then   get_ini_order_list(Ord,O1,O2,O3,Max_ord)
to     add [ar_ar, s_order_list(O1,O2,O3,1,Ord,no,repeat,L), true]
est    6.


%      Rule 4
if     [ar_ar, s_order_list(O1,O2,O3,S,Ord,Skip,repeat,L), true]
and    [ar, freq_list(O1,L1), true]
and    [ar, freq_list(O2,L2), true]
and    [ar, freq_list(O3,L3), true]
and    [user_data, peak_tolerance(Tol), true]
and    [user_data, samples(Max_ord), true]
then   pick_peaks(L1,L2,L3,Tol,Lr,O2,A1,A2,A3,Ord,Max_ord,
                    S,S1,Skip,Sk,Stat)
to     add [ar_ar, temp_order_list(A1,A2,A3,S1,Ord,Sk,Stat,Lr),true]
est    6.


%      Rule 5
if     [ar_ar, temp_order_list(A1,A2,A3,S,Ord,Skip,Stat,L), true]
then   true
to     add [ar_ar, s_order_list(A1,A2,A3,S,Ord,Skip,Stat,L), true]
est    5.


%      Rule 6
if     [ar_ar, s_order_list(O1,O2,O3,S,Ord,Skip,done_peaks,Lr), true]
then   read_list(Lr,ar_ar,bw_freq, Items_to_add)
to     add Items_to_add
est    4.


%      Rule 7
if     notnow [bw, bw_tot, true]
then   assert(bw_tot(0))
to     add [bw, bw_tot, true]
est    1.


%      Rule 8
if     [ar_ar, s_order_list(O1,O2,O3,S,Ord,Skip,done_peaks,L), true]
and    [ar_ar, bw_freq(F), true]
and    [ar, ar_peak(order(O3),peak(freq(F),_,bw(B),_)), true]
```

```
and    [user_data, accept_bw(Best), true]
then   (Best >= B)
to     action one_more
est    5.

%      Rule 9
if     @[ar_ar, s_order_list(O1,O2,O3,S,Ord,Skip,done_peaks,L), true]
and    [user_data, samples(Max_ord), true]
then   chk_bw_size(L,O2,A1,A2,A3,Stat,Ord,Ordn,S,Skip,Max_ord)
to     amend [ar_ar, s_order_list(A1,A2,A3,S,Ordn,Skip,Stat,L), true]
est    6.

%      Rule 10
if     [ar_ar, s_order_list(A1,A2,A3,S,Ord,Skip,done_peaks,Lr), true]
and    @[bw, bw_tot, true]
then   + bw_tot(_)
to     delete
est    3.

%      Rule 11
if     [ar_ar, s_order_list(A1,A2,A3,S,Ord,Skip,done,Lr), true]
then   true
to     add [ar_ar, tot_peaks_list(Lr), true]
and    [ar_ar, psd_cont, true]
and    [ar_ar, order_list(A1,A2,A3,done,Lr), true]
est    5.
```

Chapter 7

Rule-Based Processing
of Foetal Phonocardiograms

E. McDonnell

1 Introduction

Signal processing may be defined as the operation or operations
whereby the useful information in a set of data is extracted from the
irrelevant. What constitutes useful, or conversely irrelevant,
information is very much dependent on those features which are being
sought from the signal.

Traditionally, signal processing has been concerned with the
application of numerical algorithms to improve the signal-to-noise ratio
or to transform the domain of the signal thereby accentuating certain of
its features. In both cases the characteristics of the signal and the noise
are known beforehand. These numerical techniques rely on a
mathematical model of the system and certain idealizing assumptions.
Such an analytical approach fails when the signal characteristics are not
well defined, or when there is insufficient understanding of the
underlying mechanism of signal production, or again, where the system
is too complex to be modelled mathematically. In these situations a
more pragmatic approach is required. Such an approach is provided by
the knowledge-based formalism as applied to signal processing [6]. The
rationale behind this formulation is essentially empiricism, insofar as the
knowledge which represents the associations within and between events
is induced from accumulated observations of specific instances.
Thereafter, this knowledge about the domain, which is usually
represented as condition-action pairs [6], will, in an individual case,
provide the inference to be made whenever its conditional antecedent is

satisfied. This 'domain knowledge' represents the captured experience of someone who has expertise in analysing that particular type of signal, e.g. ECG analysis. The power of this formalism lies in the specificity of the domain knowledge which is inherently close to reality. Obtaining this knowledge is one of the difficulties which arise in systems which use knowledge-based methodologies [3]. The use of such methods of signal processing does not preclude the deployment of numerical signal processing algorithms, as these may be accommodated within the system as yet another aspect of the expert's knowledge.

The goal of the processing in this domain is to identify automatically certain events in the cardiac cycle from the acoustic signal produced by the functioning of the foetal heart. This task is doubly complicated because, firstly, the clinician is more concerned with the extremes of variation and irregularities than the norms and, secondly, the signal generators and transmission medium are non-linear, non-stationary, non-deterministic, time-varying, noisy, and prone to transients. Due to such variability in the signal, the only recourse was to imitate the procedures used by the clinician while analysing foetal phonocardiograms. This was embodied within the framework of a rule-based procedural expert system. The flexibility offered by such a formalism allows the variability in the signal to be accommodated.

2 Foetal Monitoring

The aims of foetal monitoring are primarily to prevent foetal death and morbidity, and to deter unnecessary intervention. The foetal heart rate and its derivates are the most commonly measured among all the foetal parameters which can be accessed non-invasively. The significance of certain changes in heart rate patterns has long been known to be associated with foetal distress [4].

By the eighth week of gestation, the foetal heart is fully formed; from about the twenty-fourth week, it can be detected aurally. This acoustic signal represents the sounds produced by the functioning of the heart. Traditionally, the obstetrician would listen to these heart sounds with a stethoscope to determine the foetal heart rate. Although the ear is unequalled in detecting sounds over a particular frequency range, the spectrum occupied by the foetal heart tones is on the threshold of audibility. This aural processing has always posed problems relating to accuracy and inter-auditor agreement. For these reasons, it has been superseded by phonocardiography. The greater low-frequency sensitivity of the phonocardiographic transducer allows all the acoustic information to be registered. The visual processing of the phonocardiogram is the only reliable way of judging heart rate from the cardiac sounds. This visual processing is satisfactory when only short lengths of data are considered. However, when long term monitoring is used, the amount of data produced is considerable. There is, consequently, a pressing need for the automation of the process.

A record of the variation of this acoustic signal with time is known as the phonocardiogram (PhCG) (Figure 7.1), and is obtained with a phonocardiographic transducer [9] attached to the mother's abdomen. Identification of the two principal heart sounds in the cardiac cycle permits measurement of the instantaneous foetal heart rate, beat-to-beat differences, and duration of the systolic and diastolic phases. These measures are sensitive indicators of cardiac function, which in turn reflects foetal well-being.

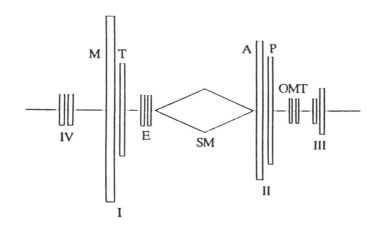

Figure 7.1- The normal phonocardiogram *(idealized)*

Legend:

I	First Heart Sound	II	Second Heart Sound
III	Third Heart Sound	IV	Fourth Heart Sound
E	Ejection Sound	SM	Systolic Murmur
OMT	Opening Sound of MT valves	M	Mitral Component
T	Tricuspid Component	A	Aortic Component
P	Pulmonary Component		

2.1 The Foetal Heart

The anatomy of the foetal heart is illustrated in Figure 7.2. The heart is divided into four chambers of which the upper and lower pairs are called the atria and ventricles, respectively. The atria are connected to the veins which convey blood to the heart, while the ventricles are connected to the arterial network which transports blood away from the heart. These four chambers are actually pumps of which the atria are the primer pumps for the ventricles, which are the power pumps.

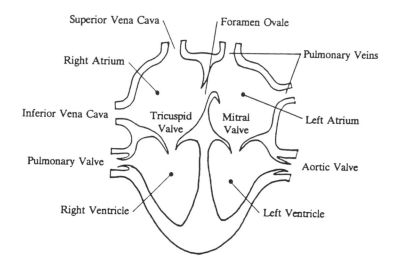

Figure 7.2- The foetal heart

The heart has four valves: the mitral, the tricuspid, the aortic, and the pulmonary. The mitral and tricuspid (MT) valves connect the atria to the ventricles, while the aortic and pulmonary (AP) valves connect the ventricles to the arteries. These valves are composed of tough but flexible leaflets of fibrous tissue, whose movements are essentially passive; that is, their openings and closings are effected by the direction of blood flow rather than any voluntary movement on their part. The valves by virtue of their structure, restraining tendons and orientation permit only a uni-directional flow of blood through, and away, from the heart.

One anatomical difference between the foetal and new-born/adult heart is the orifice which shunts the atria together. This so-called *foramen ovale* causes most of the oxygenated blood from the placenta which enters the right atrium, to pass directly through into the left atrium and thence, by cardiac action, into the arteries.

2.2 Production of Heart Sounds

The functioning of the heart produces two principal sounds (I,II), and two subsidiary sounds (III,IV) per cardiac cycle. The generally accepted hypothesis for the origin of the principal heart sounds is that they are caused by the sudden halting through closure of valve leaflets which had been moving at high speed [5]. The third and fourth sounds, which are not of valvular origin, are caused by vibrations of the cardiac walls and are usually inaudible.

Blood returning to the heart through the great veins, and oxygenated blood from the placenta continually flows into the atria. However, when ventricular pumping is in progress, the MT valves are shut which prevents this blood gaining access to the lower cardiac chambers, hence blood accumulates in the atria. Once ventricular contraction has ended, the pressure differential across the MT valves forces them to open, and the blood to flow rapidly into the flaccid ventricles. This valvular opening is usually silent as it evolves relatively slowly. At the onset of cardiac depolarization, the atria contract and thereby force the remaining blood in the atria into the ventricles. This atrial contraction is associated with barely audible vibrations arising from the flow of blood into the ventricles. These vibrations produce the fourth heart sound (IV). An increase in the pressure of the blood contained in the ventricles, brought about by the contraction of the ventricular walls, causes the MT valves to shut (first heart sound - I) preventing a reflux of blood into the atria. The MT valve leaflets are tightly sealed by this rising ventricular pressure. This valvular closure approximately marks the beginning of systole (cardiac action phase), or conversely the end of diastole (cardiac relaxation phase). The ventricular walls continue to contract, which increases the pressure in the enclosed blood until, unable to withstand the pressure, the AP valves open. Blood is rapidly ejected into the arteries. When, after contraction, the ventricular pressure drops, the high pressure blood in the arteries attempts to flow back into the ventricles. The cusps of the AP valves are caught by, and abruptly arrest, this reflux which gives rise to the second heart sound (II). This approximately marks the end of systole or conversely the beginning of diastole. The third heart sound (III) occurs early in the diastolic phase, and is thought to be the result of vibrations caused by the rapid filling of the left and right ventricles.

3 Domain Anomalies

In contrast to adult phonocardiography, where a strong sound generator is close to the transducer, foetal phonocardiography has to contend with a weak sound generator which is separated from the sensor by up to ten heart diameters.

Whenever the closing of the cardiac valves creates a sound, this energy packet must travel through a complex and dynamic system up to the maternal abdominal surface. At the outset the intensity of a principal sound depends on factors such as pressure differential across the valve, size of the valve leaflets, the initial extent of separation of the leaflets, and the volume of blood which is modulated by foetal breathing [1]. All of these factors, except leaflet size, would be expected to change from beat to beat. The inherent variability of the foetal heart rate (60-220 bpm), the irregularity of which is an indication of normality, originates in the variability of the durations of the systolic and diastolic phases. This again is reflected in the relative instants of closure of the valves.

The sound transmission path is made up of the fluid-filled amniotic cavity, the muscular wall of the uterus, layers of fat, tissue, and possibly bony and cartilaginous material. Each of these substances will attenuate the forward-going sound energy both in the bulk of the material, and by reflection arising from the impedance mismatch which occurs at the boundary of each of these layers [9]. This natural screen surrounding the foetus has the effect of diminishing the energy of the principal heart sounds reaching the phonographic transducer. In addition to this, there will be extraneous sounds produced by the umbilical cord, foetal movements, and environmental noise which will superimpose themselves onto the acoustic signal from the heart. Finally, at the maternal abdominal surface, the position of the transducer will also considerably alter the shape of the sound waveform.

This complex system would be expected to modify every characteristic of the original signal. Not only will this system be varying on a short-term basis, but also in the longer term as the gestation progresses and the foetus grows in size.

Overall these factors combine to produce "heart sounds" which often change markedly from one beat to the next in frequency, amplitude, duration, morphology, and in instant of occurrence relative to the previous beat, and even to the complete attenuation of a sound. Along with this are the other sounds/noises produced by the mechanical

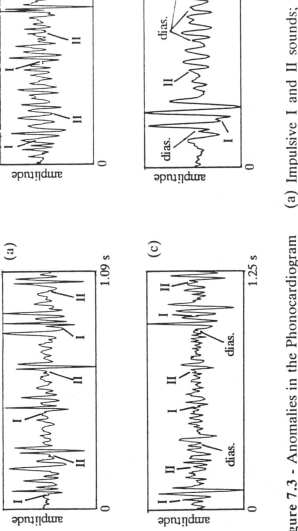

Figure 7.3 - Anomalies in the Phonocardiogram

(a) Impulsive I and II sounds; large systolic and diastolic sounds; similarity of I and II sounds.

(b) Continuum of events; I and II sounds barely distinguishable from background.

(c) Weak I and II sounds; large diastolic sound.

(d) Oscillatory pattern of all sounds; poorly defined end points; weak II sound; diastolic murmurs.

functioning of the heart: blood circulation sounds, ejection sounds, entry sounds and eddies; these all contribute to further complicate the already difficult task of identifying the principal cardiac sounds.

This variability in the characteristics of the principal heart sounds precludes compiling a syllabus of types for each sound either for a particular gravida or on a per data block basis.

Figure 7.3 illustrates occurrences of certain of these anomalies in the phonocardiogram. They were all recorded within 60s from the same gravida.

4 Knowledge-Based Pre-Processors

The low-level processes of the system, i.e. those closest to the primary data in the processing hierarchy, are arranged into detection, and segmentation modules which are themselves KAs (knowledge areas) [2] (Figure 7.4) within the overall signal analysis expert system. These KAs consist of an *invocation part* and a *body*. The invocation, which is similar to the antecedent of traditional production rules, is used to trigger a KA. The body of the KA, which performs a function similar to the consequent of a production, consists of a large amount of domain-specific procedural knowledge. The function of these pre-processing stages is to remove noise, and to enhance the principal sounds in the PhCG prior to classification.

4.1 Detection

Detection is the process whereby certain events in the PhCG are discriminated from the background. In conventional signal processing algorithms detection is achieved using numerical computation. Such techniques are of limited use in this context because of the non-deterministic and variable nature of the data. The knowledge required to perform the task of detection is the least expert of all the knowledge embodied in the system. However, it performs a function on which depend all the other KAs and ultimately, the quality of the subsequent PhCG analysis. A layman on examining Figure 7.7 could easily spot *significant* events in the data record. Although a simple task for the human eye, it is a difficult one to emulate by computer.

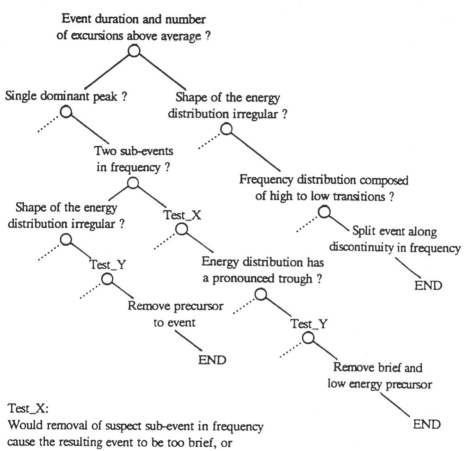

Event duration and number
of excursions above average ?

Single dominant peak ?

Shape of the energy
distribution irregular ?

Two sub-events
in frequency ?

Frequency distribution composed
of high to low transitions ?

Shape of the energy
distribution irregular ?

Test_X

Split event along
discontinuity in frequency

Test_Y

Energy distribution has
a pronounced trough ?

END

Remove precursor
to event

Test_Y

END

Remove brief and
low energy precursor

END

Test_X:
Would removal of suspect sub-event in frequency
cause the resulting event to be too brief, or
have too few cycles, or to have too low an energy ?

Test_Y:
Would removal of suspect sub-event in time
cause the resulting event to be too brief, or
have too few cycles, or to have too low an energy ?

Figure 7.4- Part of the segmentation knowledge area

What makes certain events visually significant is primarily their local amplitude contrast and, secondly, their frequency and structure. The structure refers to the smooth continuity of the PhCG from the beginning to the end of an event. Contrasted with this is the ill-structuredness of the background. The background is here taken to mean not only noise in the conventional sense, but also certain sounds of non-valvular origin.

The detection process cannot be discriminating between principal sounds and non-valvular sounds as one may masquerade as the other. Furthermore, no morphological similarities have been observed experimentally within a class, or consistently during the block processing interval.

The detection process acts on a per excursion basis. An excursion is defined to be that part of the phonocardiogram bounded between two immediately adjacent transitions across the horizontal. If the excursion meets the criteria for being classed as significant, *viz:* the combination of local amplitude contrast, frequency and continuity, it is assigned a weighting in proportion to these three factors. This metric has been designed to absorb and erase both the local and global variations in signal morphology.

4.2 Removal of Insignificant Excursions

It has been found that whenever the clinician inspects the PhCG, he subconsciously takes account of the global scenario first. Then working at the local level he accepts or rejects events in the context of the overall scenario while progressing causally, i.e. left to right, across the phonocardiogram.

This procedure has also been adopted here for the automated removal of insignificant excursions. Although the detection process extracts the significant excursions, within this class there will be varying degrees of significance. Once the excursion processing has been completed, which furnishes global information and corresponds to the expert's initial broad overview, the local level is revisited in the light of this extracted global knowledge. An adaptive thresholding technique has been employed to remove the insignificant excursions. This threshold takes account of how the excursion energy levels are varying with time in the context of both the local and global energy fluctuations. As sometimes happens a weak valvular sound may be discarded at this stage. Although undesirable, this situation can be recovered later by the higher level processes which rely on information from the model and expectations drawn from the context.

4.3 Grouping of Excursions

The outcome of this global/local processing is termed the *significant* excursions of the PhCG. The term significant excursion implies a locally pronounced and bounded part of the PhCG which exhibits the characteristics of a component of a valvular sound. This, however, does not imply that it necessarily is one.

Contiguous excursions are grouped together to form the so-called significant events. The terminal points of these groupings are established when an *insignificant* excursion is encountered. These groupings inherit the attributes of their constituent excursions so that the whole event assumes the quality of being heart-sound like.

4.4 Feature Extraction

Once the significant events have been located, the feature extraction process transforms these events into a set of features. These features are: start time, end time, duration, total energy content, number and location of the *dominant* energy peaks, number of excursions, information about the rate of change of excursion duration, and energy distribution. Each event is represented as a vector of these features. These vectors, which are data structures, are then assembled into a linear array which constitutes the first level of data abstraction.

The variability in all aspects of an actual valvular sound has the effect that the discriminating criteria which delimit a significant event cannot be stringent, with the consequence that many more events are taken to be significant than are valvular sounds in the PhCG trace. This overestimate will depend on the quality of the data, for example, in the case of a moderately noisy PhCG there will typically be twice as many spurious valvular sounds as actual ones. The advantage of a weak discriminant is that the chance of rejecting a valvular sound as *insignificant* is small. Consequently the higher level processing stages do not have to contend with biased information. This deferral of discrimination until more knowledge can be brought to bear prevents premature decisions. Its disadvantage is that the higher levels are more taxed to ascertain which of all the events are the valvular sounds.

4.5 Segmentation

Whenever the grouping module proposes the concatenation of certain excursions as an event, it does not consider the possibility that the resulting "event" may not be homogeneous. That is, the event may be composed of more than one sound. This conglomeration arises mainly from the juxtaposition of the sounds within the "event" (Figure 7.3), and a smooth continuum of the previously outlined metrics (Section 4.1) across the sounds. Segmentation is the process which attempts to decompose these coalesced sounds. The localizing of a sound depends on the determination of its endpoints, particularly the starting point, which in turn effectively marks the endpoint of the preceding event.

Segmentation is performed in two passes: initially excursions are clustered (Section 4.3), then each cluster is tested for homogeneity. When segmentation is first attempted, i.e. at data base initialization therefore without contextual information, it is still possible to decompose some of the combined sounds, e.g. when the constituent sounds exhibit an obvious dissimilarity. Although the amplitude distribution in the primary data may give no clue to a coalescence, both the energy and the excursion duration distributions may reveal its presence. One of the commonly occurring coalescences is that of a diastolic sound and a I heart sound (Figure 7.3). Although it cannot be said what are the particular features of a valvular sound, there are certain characteristics which disclose a non-valvular sound, e.g. an instantaneous frequency spectrum across the event which increases with time. In these circumstances the non-valvular event is removed. However, non-valvular events are not always identified at this stage, so segmentation of coalescences must be delayed until reprocessing under the guidance of contextual information.

Once segmentation has been completed, the feature extraction module (Section 4.4) is recalled to process the resulting events. This refined version of the significant events is posted in the data base as the second level of data abstraction.

Although the segmentation KA has been included under the section dealing with pre-processors, it may be, if required, later recalled under interpretation control [10] to reperform its function on certain stretches of the PhCG. As such, segmentation is also a guided data re-processor.

4.6 Abstracted Data

By this stage in the processing chain the abstracted data is still noisy. This acoustic "noise" generally arises from events within the heart rather than noise originating in the non-cardiac events which will have been removed.

There now exists two levels of data abstraction which are maintained in the data base along with the primary data. The lower level of the abstraction consists of the significant events and the higher level these same events — segmented or partially reconfigured where applicable (Figure 7.5).

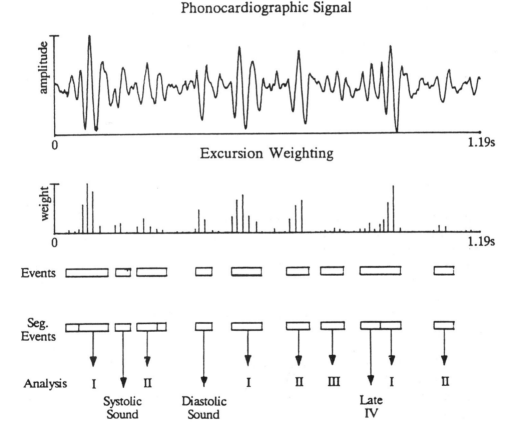

Figure 7.5- The levels of data abstraction

Although the primary data is not reprocessed, it is retained for records of problem areas and sounds. Problems that do occur are mostly attributable to high noise levels in the data, and the non-registration in the PhCG of an expected event through either a "soft" valve closure or some anomaly in the sound transmission path. In these cases the nature of the problem and a record of the primary data surrounding it are catalogued to await later investigation by the expert.

5 Classification

The process of classification assigns labels (I, II, or noise) to the significant events. To achieve this necessitates removing all sounds whose origin is non-valvular (noise), while this in turn demands that the prior identification of the principal sounds has been either totally or partially achieved; but the principal sounds are only identified when the noise has been removed. To break this impasse certain areas of the PhCG which from machine inspection can easily be resolved into valvular/non-valvular sounds are exploited to provide a bridgehead into the more ambiguous regions.

6 System Control

The preceding detection, and segmentation KAs operate under the direction of a central classification-directed control system. The control component is executed by control KAs. These differ from the other KAs in that their expertise derives from their ability to direct the application of knowledge. For this reason these control oriented KAs are referred to as meta-KAs. The control knowledge has access to both the low-level and high-level KAs, the primary data and its abstractions, and the unfolding analysis of the data. Under its direction certain KAs will be selected and possibly activated, depending on their suitability for the required task.

The control is organized hierarchically on two levels: strategy or policy level, and task level. The strategy KA and the task KA are on the higher and lower levels respectively (Figure 7.6).

Architecture of the control system

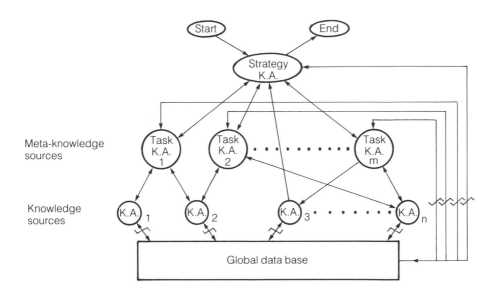

Figure 7.6- The Architecture of the Control System
Lines marked thus :⌐ƒ are data lines; all others are control lines.

6.1 Strategy Knowledge Area

In the context of the control structure, the strategy level KA is a control meta KA, and is the originator of the top-down control process. Its knowledge is embedded as rules within the KA. The brief of the strategy KA is to: set up the data base, determine whether prima facie it is worthwhile attempting a analysis, establish solution islands q.v., control solution island expansion, focus attention on a particular area, revisit the lower levels of data abstraction in the light of contextual information, know when to abandon the analysis, and know when a total, or the best partial analysis has been achieved. When control originates or is passed up to the strategy level, it will examine the data base on the basis of the outcome of the last task it tried to accomplish, and then decide what to do next. As the number of entries in the data base is small — approximately 40 for 4s — its re-examination on each strategy control cycle is permissible within the time constraints.

6.2 Task Knowledge Area

Once the **strategy KA** has determined what to do it will invoke one or more of the **task KAs**. The task KAs autonomously guide the application of the data-level KAs using knowledge embedded as rules. Each task has a certain area of expertise, e.g. finding a solution island, which it will use in the region defined by the strategy KA. The task KA will run until completion, or relinquish its aim due to failure.

6.3 Data-Level Knowledge Areas

A data-level KA is under the control of one or more of the task KAs. It is these KAs which are, of all the KAs, the only ones which may generate, modify, or delete entries in the database. Each KA at this level may be viewed as a local expert in some aspect of the data analysis. The body of a KA consists of domain knowledge in rule format. The knowledge may be in the form of facts and/or heuristics relevant to the particular area of expertise. Although data-level KAs are independent, i.e. one KA cannot fire another, they may influence one another through the entries they generate in the database.

Each data-level KA is interfaced within the system in the same format as the control KAs, i.e. its precondition is held at the controlling level above it. When a data-level KA is tested for applicability, its condition part will respond with either "true" or "false". *True* signifies that the state of the database is such that the KA appears to be able to advance the analysis — which immediately entails KA firing — whereas *false* implies that that particular KA was unsuitable in the prevailing circumstances. Upon firing, the data-level KA will again report back with "true" or "false": *true*, if it has successfully achieved its aim, or *false*, if it failed to do so. Like the control KAs, the data-level KAs have access both to the data abstractions and the unfolding analysis of the PhCG.

6.4 Control Execution Cycle

Control originates at the strategy level and proceeds down the hierarchy. The strategy level elects one or more of the task level KAs to execute some policy. The power of control now resides in the selected task KA and the strategy KA is suspended. This task KA will autonomously attempt to realize its function until it either succeeds or fails whereupon, in either case, control resumes to the strategy KA. When the task KA causes an applicable data-level KA to fire, control will pass down to this — the lowest level. When the data-level KA reports back to the task level, it also transfers control. This brings the task KA out of suspension. This passing of control between the two lowest levels will continue until the task has been accomplished or it terminates its execution. Control will then return to the strategy KA which will reanimate.

6.5 Knowledge Application

The method used to decompose the problem is that which the expert himself employs. This involves examining the PhCG to ascertain areas where, with confidence, he is able to identify certain of the significant events as being of valvular origin. This is accomplished using an initial data-driven approach, which switches to a model-driven approach relying on generate-and-test, where verification is provided by domain constraints. Once these solution islands [8] have been identified, the goal is to expand outwards into regions where the analysis is not so immediately obvious. Ultimately this expansion will, depending on the quality of the data and its abstractions, result in all solution islands being fused together to provide a complete analysis of the PhCG.

Although it is not always possible to achieve a complete analysis, a partial solution, i.e. resolution of certain areas of the PhCG, will still provide the required cardiac parameters. If a region should prove to be difficult to analyse because of very high levels of noise or many missing expected events — it is abandoned. For the sake of confidence in the analysis it is better to spend time in the more easily resolved regions where solution integrity is high than where there is an increased possibility of an incorrect assessment.

Expansion of solution islands is effected using the model of Figure 7.1 combined with the physical/temporal constraints of the underlying physiological process. Projections are made in either advancing or receding time, with respect to the time instant of an identified event, as to the type of the next expected event and the region within which it is to occur. Several events will fit these criteria but hopefully all but the sought event will be eliminated using factual, contextual and heuristic knowledge within the generate-and-test paradigm.

7 Explanation Facility

The analysis of the PhCG presents a "dynamic" problem, i.e. one which is constantly changing with time, which needs to be continuously monitored. As the duration of the monitoring is of the order of hours, to be clinically useful the system must be able to run unsupervised. This unsupervised mode of operation can only be a realistic proposition when there is sufficient confidence in the accuracy of the analysis produced — as is the case. This confidence arises primarily from the quality of the captured expertise and from the characteristics of this domain. In other applications where the domain is polydimensional, less constrained, more convoluted and the knowledge widely disparate, e.g. HASP/SIAP [7] there is a need to have an extensive explanation facility.

The ability of this system to justify its actions is restricted to its reasons for abandoning a particular PhCG region or record†, i.e. problem cataloguing (q.v.). A fuller explanation is possible, however, which was relied upon during debugging and testing. This was a list of solution islands along with a terse summary of progress at each step which comprised the task, the region under scrutiny, KA firings, and a justification for any changes to entries in the database.

8 Implementation

The system as a whole was realized in the *C* language under *UNIX* mainly because *C* produces very fast and efficient executable code. In this application the amount of processing required for long term monitoring is considerable, and the nature of the task, i.e. warning of foetal distress, needs speed of response. The disadvantage of using a non-AI language is the lack of the built-in facilities which these possess, consequently the *C* code tends to be rather long and complex.

The database is realized as arrays of data structures. Each structure is divided into elements which each represent some attribute of the significant event which it represents.

The meta-KAs and KAs are composed of *C* functions. Each function is tested for applicability as previously described and if selected returns a value of either *true* or *false* corresponding to the success or otherwise of its objective.

---

† This is for the benefit of the knowledge engineer rather than the clinician.

9 Example‡

Although the signal is continuous in time, it would be unrealistic to expect events to be interpreted on arrival, as the analysis of the PhCG is so dependent on supporting evidence derived from the context. To provide this context, data is captured in frames of 4s duration which gives sufficient "context" for even the lowest foetal heart rates.

After suitable sampling and filtering, the PhCG of Figure 7.7 is presented to the system for analysis. The main difficulties posed by this particular PhCG are: the similarity of events, the plethora of non-valvular events, and the presence of systolic sounds of large amplitude (a,b,c). The latter has the effect of obscuring the end of the I sounds and the beginning of the II sounds. Uncharacteristically, the I sound has consistently the same shape across the trace and likewise the II sound in the latter half. At the beginning and the end of the record ((d,e),(f,g)), the I sound and adjoining II sound are almost identical, and throughout the trace they have similar parameters and shape except for a phase reversal. The principal sounds have approximately the same duration which is uncommon — normally the I sounds will be the longer by up to three times the duration of the II sounds. Certain other phenomena present in the trace are: diastolic sounds (h,i,j), a fast transient from an unknown source (k), amplitude variability, and IV sounds coalescing with I sounds (l,m).

After detection and removal of insignificant detail Figure 7.7b results, illustrating those events in the PhCG which are regarded as significant. This is a rather contrived illustration as by this stage each event has been converted into a string of attributes. The segmentation KA was fired in the three instances (n,o,p) where the sub-event dissimilarities were obvious, however, sound complex "Q" went unnoticed as a conjunction of a systolic sound and a II sound. Event complex "R" presented itself for consideration as a solution island because of its relatively noiseless local context. Upon closer examination it met the criteria to allow it to be established as an identified I,II couple. These criteria, which are embedded within a verification KA, are: the inter-sound gap (systolic time) must be within the allowed range, if it were not a I,II couple would the resulting eventless time gap between valvular sounds suggest an impossibly low foetal heart rate, establish that it is not the coupling of a systolic and diastolic sound and that it is not a II sound pairing with a systolic sound or a I sound pairing with a diastolic sound, and that all possible I,II couplings on

---

‡ Letters in parentheses in the following text refer to Figure 7.7.

either side do not link to this couple? Once a solution island has been established it will allow the elimination of many of the surrounding events which purport to be valvular sounds. An expansion from the solution island will then be effected in either advancing or receding time depending on the most promising direction. A direction is taken to be promising if there are fewer events to be resolved and hence fewer decisions. In this case both the forward and backward directions are equally promising so backward is chosen quite arbitrarily. Of the two possible candidates (s,t) for the expected II sound only "s" fulfills all the conditions necessary, which eliminates "t" and thereby suggests "u" as the valvular couple of the II sound. This process of expansion continues until the PhCG is resolved as completely as possible. As this particular PhCG was deliberatly chosen for its relative straightforwardness a complete analysis was achieved. This is not always so. There may be cases where the data is so noisy that no solution islands are found or where the noisiness inhibits expansion from already identified solution islands.

In the case of event complex "Q" the preceding I sound was identified but the corresponding II sound could not be located. This suggested that the long and high energy systolic event "c" might have coalesced with the II sound to form an apparently homogeneous cluster. The frequency spectrum of the event was re-examined now that more information was available on the likely region of occurrence and the nature of the sought event. This permitted the re-segmentation process to be more specific and the II sound "v" was isolated from the total event.

The most convenient measure of how well the system is performing is provided by a visual comparison of the analysis achieved by the system with that of the expert. This also enables those shortcomings to be identified, e.g. underestimating the extent of a sound, which in the main are invisible to the embedded problem cataloguing facility.

No system can ever surpass the expert from whom it derives its knowledge. No matter how sophisticated the processing is, if the signal quality is poor this will be reflected in the analysis. Of course, this system, like the expert, will make mistakes, especially in such a volatile domain. However, the system performs sufficiently well, and automatically provides the parameters of cardiac function over extended periods to make it a valuable aid for the clinician.

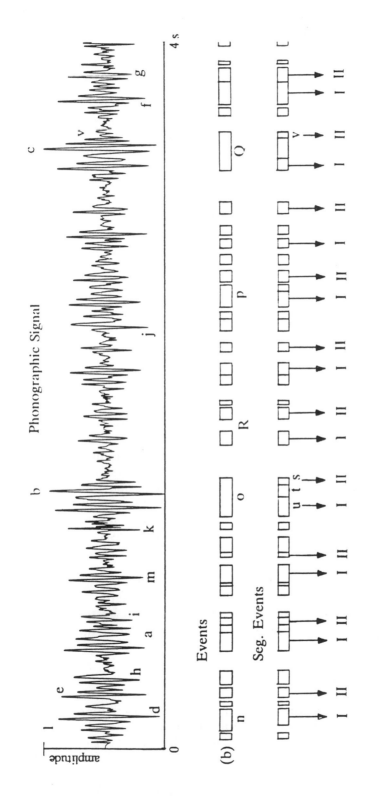

Figure 7.7

10 Conclusion

This chapter has presented the implementation of a knowledge-based expert system for the continuous identification of the principal heart sounds in the foetal phonocardiogram. The power of such methods of signal processing derives from expert knowledge of the domain captured in the system. For the most part this knowledge is domain-specific and empirical. Although lacking the rigour of analytic methods, this technique has the advantage that it remains close to reality, and benefits from the very specificity of its knowledge and meta-knowledge.

10.1 Summary

The essential feature of this expert system is its organization as a hierarchical procedural expert system. This formulation allows an efficient search for applicable rules in an application where speed of response is important. The fundamental problems with the domain are the noisiness of the signal, and the variability of every parameter in the sought-after events.

The analysis of the PhCG begins with the detection and segmentation of events. These events are then searched for solution islands, i.e. areas of data where the identification of the principal sounds is obvious. From these islands the system attempts to expand the analysis into the more ambiguous regions. A complete analysis of a data block is reached when all the principal heart sounds have been identified. In cases where the expansion is irretrievably terminated by high levels of noise these solution islands, which are complete partial analyses rather than intermediate steps in an analysis, can still provide the required heart rate information albeit over a shorter time interval.

Incorporated within the expert system is a feedback mechanism from the higher to the lower levels of data abstraction. This allows the weight of contextual information on the higher level to be brought to bear on areas where initially local processing was not sufficient to resolve ambiguities.

10.2 Future Work

Another transducer which is commonly used in monitoring the foetal heart besides the phonocardiograph is the ultrasound foetal cardiograph (uFCG). This transducer relies on the Doppler principle for its operation. A beam of ultrasound energy is directed towards the foetal heart and is frequency-shifted in proportion to the velocity of the moving structures it encounters in its path. As the cardiac valves move much more quickly than any of the other components of the foetal heart or the blood flow, this permits the separation of the valvular movements from the extraneous signal generators. In theory the uFCG can register not only the closings of the valves but also their openings.

The ultrasound transducer used in conjunction with the phonocardiograph provides a different perspective on certain cardiac events which are registered in common. The more different sensory information that can be integrated into the system the more confidence there will be in the ultimate analysis. Using two different types of transducer also minimizes the amount of information required from each independently. The resulting information redundancy can be exploited to: prompt the analysis of the other transducer signal, act as an independent source of verification for the already identified events in the other signal, and to combat noise which will be uncorrelated in both signals.

The complete system which will incorporate both transducer signals is shown in Figure 7.8. The *information synthesizer* will perform the function of exploiting the redundancy between the transducer signals to facilitate complete analysis of each signal. Ultimately, the information synthesizer should output the instants of closure of the MT and AP valve pairs and the AP opening. From these can be derived all the temporal parameters of cardiac function.

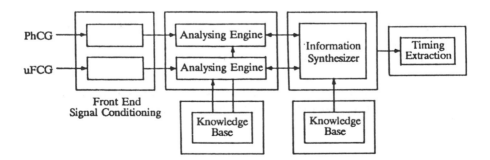

Figure 7.8- Proposed system for fusion of transducer information

References

[1]   N. Colley, et al., "The Foetal Phonogram: A Measure of Foetal Activity", *The Lancet*, pp 931-934, April 26, 1986.

[2]   M.P. Georgeff, "A Framework for Control in Production Systems", *IJCAI*, pp 328-334, 1979.

[3]   F. Hayes-Roth, et al., *Building Expert Systems*, Addison-Wesley, 1983.

[4]   E.H. Hon, et al., "Electronic Evaluation of the Foetal Heart Rate Part VIII Patterns Preceding Foetal Death", *Am. J. Obstet. Gynecol.*, **87**, pp 814, 1974.

[5]   A. Leatham, *Auscultation of the Heart and Phonocardiography*, Churchill, 1970.

[6]   H.P. Nii, et al., "Rule-Based Understanding of Signals", *Pattern-Directed Inference Systems*, D.A Waterman & F. Hayes-Roth (eds.), Academic Press, 1978.

[7]   H.P. Nii, et al., "Signal-to-Symbol Transformation: HASP/SIAP Case Study", *The AI Magazine*, pp 23-35, Spring 1982.

[8]   H.P. Nii, "Blackboard Systems", *The AI Magazine*, pp 38-53, Summer 1986.

[9]   D.G. Talbert, et al., "Wide Bandwidth Foetal Phonography Using a Sensor Matched to the Compliance of the Mother's Adbominal Wall", *IEEE Trans Biomed Eng*, **BME-33**, pp 175-180.

[10] J.M. Tenebaum, et al., "Experiments in Interpretation Guided Segmentation", *Artificial Intelligence*, **8(2)**, pp 241-274, 1977.

Chapter 8

BOFFIN: A Blackboard System for Sonar Interpretation

D.M. Lane

1 Introduction

The first published implementation of the blackboard architecture was the Hearsay-I speech-understanding system [1]. Since then, a number of variants on the theme have been reported [2-4], each using a different implementation for different applications, but with the same underlying spirit.

Figure 8.1 shows a simple diagram outlining the component parts of the blackboard approach. (For more detailed description of the blackboard architectures and systems see Chapter 2 of this volume.) At the heart of the system is a global memory area, the blackboard, employed as a hierarchical store of goals, data and information concerning the information processing task. Confidence or belief attributes are usually associated with each of these, and hence the blackboard is a store of hypotheses (uncertain facts) about the problem domain. Its role is therefore passive.

Activity on the blackboard is created by independent processing modules called knowledge sources or KS for short. Each knowledge source contains expertise appropriate to one very small part of the problem domain. The number of knowledge sources in a knowledge base will depend on the extent of the problem domain, and the granularity of the knowledge employed.

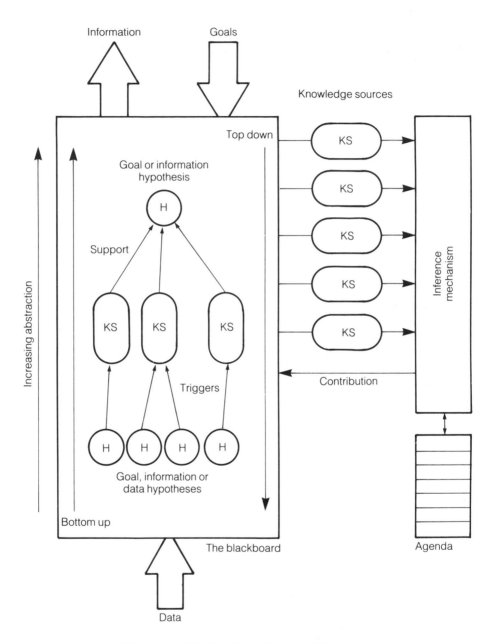

Figure 8.1- The blackboard system philosophy.

The KS all play the role of independent experts looking at the information, data and goals stored on the blackboard. Execution is initiated by the blackboard inference mechanism. At each inference cycle, all KS examine the blackboard to see if they are able to contribute new hypotheses/facts, or provide additional confirmation or denial for those already in existence. In a single processor implementation, those KS which have something to contribute (i.e write on the blackboard) are labelled as triggered and stored according to some priority mechanism in a list called the agenda. To execute the next KS, the inference mechanism merely activates the KS currently at the top of the agenda. Once running, a KS must complete execution without interruption, and is therefore indivisible in operation.

The result of a KS execution will be the assertion of information or goals on the blackboard, which may form the trigger field for other KS. Such an assertion is termed a blackboard event. Each event may provide support for a hypothesis which is in agreement with other support (co-operative), or in disagreement (competitive). Execution continues in this way until there are no more KS waiting. The blackboard is then said to be idle. In the absence of any further goals, data or knowledge, the competing hypotheses expressing the most confidence are taken as the best guess at the problem solution. If the knowledge base or the furnished data are inadequate, then only a subset of the system goals may have been satisfied, leaving a partial solution.

Support for a hypothesis is maintained using links on the blackboard, showing which KS were responsible for its existence, and the confidence they have that the hypothesis is correct. Goals, data and information, therefore, can be thought of as a connected network of hypothesis nodes, each connection representing support provided by a KS. As KS execution proceeds, so "islands" of hypotheses evolve, until eventually these independent fragments expand and merge to form the overall solution. In this respect the blackboard architecture employs an incremental approach to information processing, where any or all of the hypotheses and facts can be completely revised at any stage. It functions as both a means of communicating between KS, and a store of the current state of the processing task.

In implementing any blackboard system, a number of design issues must be addressed. In summary these are [5]:

(a)   What knowledge representation formalisms should be used?

(b)   Should hypotheses on the blackboard be static (i.e. exist for all time once created) or dynamic (exist for only a period of time)?

(c)   What structure should a knowledge source have?

(d)   Should knowledge sources be polled at each cycle to test their trigger fields, or should each KS declare its interest in a hypothesis to the inference mechanism?

(e)   What mechanism should be used to order the execution of triggered knowledge sources (so called focus of control)?

(f)   What formalism should be used to represent and propagate uncertainty measures associated with each hypothesis on the blackboard, and with each KS?

(g)   In the event that KS are allowed to re-trigger and alter their contribution, what mechanism should be used to propagate the change to other dependent hypotheses and thus keep entries on the blackboard consistent?

(h)   How will closed loops of unnecessary KS re-triggering and hypothesis updating (also known as illusions) be detected and broken?

(i)   What form will the user interface take for knowledge-base development, inspection and execution?

This chapter shows how some of these issues can been addressed by describing the approach used in the BOFFIN system. Although designed initially for sonar interpretation, it has subsequently been used in other vision domains, and has potential for other applications.

2 BOFFIN Implementation

The BOFFIN system is a blackboard system implemented in C to run on DEC and SUN workstations which forms the first realization of a generic concept for a network of distributed and interacting blackboard processing nodes termed rational cells. It has been used since 1986 as a tool for researching processing techniques for performing automatic interpretation of sonar images [5,6], machine vision using fourier descriptors and colour recognition [7] and for research into distributed problem solving [8].

2.1 Hypothesis Representation

The nature of the problem domain for BOFFIN dictated that a hierarchy of hypothesis abstractions, comprising symbols, propositions, numerical parameters and images be implemented on the blackboard. To this end, a framelike structure was chosen, following the general format of Figure 8.2. Every instance of a hypothesis employs a structure of this form.

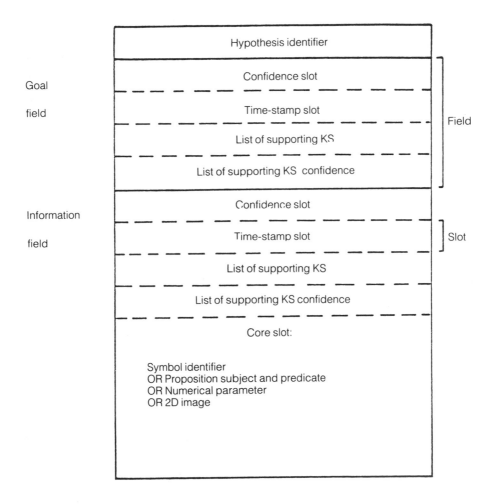

Figure 8.2- Structure of a hypothesis frame.

Hypotheses within BOFFIN are interpretable as both goal and information. The hypothesis frame therefore contains separate fields for both of these, each containing further units called slots.

Slots within the information field are accessed by KS triggering or triggered in a data-driven mode of inference. The confidence slot is used to maintain the overall belief associated with the hypothesis information. For KS triggering purposes, the time-stamp slot stores a value indicating the last inference cycle in which a KS updated the information field. The two support slots are used to maintain the identities of triggering KS, and the degree of belief they contribute.

Support from a KS for a hypothesis will be either competitive or co-operative depending on its agreement with the conclusions of other KS. The information support slots store the identity and confidence assertions of these supporting KS, so that the most favoured version of the hypothesis can be derived at any time.

Entries into the core slot provide the hypothesis information content, such as a symbol, the value of single or grouped parameters, the subject and predicate of a proposition or the 2D array of numbers constituting a digitized image. Because KS may disagree with this information, competing versions are maintained to correspond with entries into the support slots.

Slots within the goal field are accessed by KS triggering or triggered in a goal-driven mode of inference. As with the information field, goal slots maintain confidence in the hypothesis as a worthwhile goal, and time-stamp information identifying when the goal field was last updated. Support fields are used to maintain the identity and belief associated with KS supporting the goal. KS may only support goals in a constructive way, indicating to what extent they agree with its pursuit. In order to express criticism or disagreement, they must affirm support for an alternative goal. Hence all support for a goal is considered co-operative.

An additional field containing a single slot resides at the head of the hypothesis frame, indicating its location on the blackboard.

2.2 Hypothesis Creation

In general, hypothesis creation may use a static or dynamic approach. The static approach has implementation advantage, in that the total number of hypotheses can be identified from KS trigger and contribution fields. However, the dynamic approach has advantage for vision work, where an unknown number of objects may be detected in an image and separate hypotheses are required for each. BOFFIN employs both hypothesis creation mechanisms, at the expense of some clumsy programming required to specify the trigger fields of KS which react to dynamically created blackboard contributions.

The system further implements a mechanism for storing the state of the blackboard, and for re-initializing static hypotheses to a don't know condition (Figure 8.3). Such an action can be synchronized with any desired blackboard event, so that KS can have access to the time history of a hypothesis. Thus for a vision application, image sequences can be employed, with critical temporal information maintained at all levels of abstraction on the blackboard.

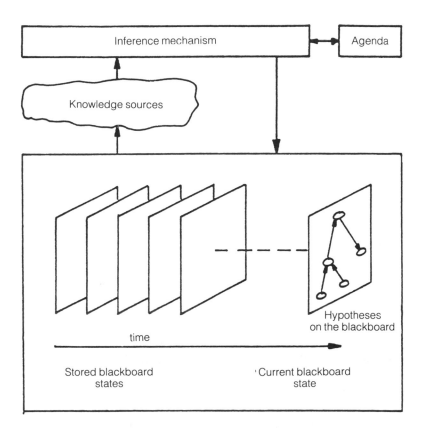

Figure 8.3- Storage of blackboard states.

2.3 The Inference Mechanism

Ideally, the inference mechanism must support data-driven, goal-driven or hybrid application of knowledge sources. For the defined hypothesis frames, tests associated with calculating KS triggers are simple and straightforward, and do not justify being sorted into the agenda as is done with some systems. For BOFFIN a KS polling scheme was therefore adopted, where all KS triggers are tested at each cycle.

For modularity and flexibility, meta-KS are used to implement the mechanism itself. Meta-KS are knowledge sources which reason about the execution of KS with expertise in the problem domain. They are therefore concerned with scheduling, and with creating and executing the problem domain agenda, and are driven by a simple cyclic scheduling mechanism.

Currently only four meta-KS are employed to perform:

(a) Polling of KS triggers for data and/or goal-driven inference.

(b) Focus of attention, using some performance metric or reasoning strategy to sort triggered KS into an agenda. Agendas may be maintained separately or combined for hybrid data and goal-driven inference. Knowledge of real-time constraints outwith the cell may be part of the strategy.

(c) Activation of the KS currently at the top of the agenda(s).

(d) Detection and action when no more KS are triggered.

(e) Storage and initialization of the blackboard state when a specified event occurs (e.g. (d)).

In addition, however, other meta-KS could be used for:

(f) Initialization of KS, the KS noticeboard and static hypotheses.

(g) Checking and correcting closed loop updating of hypotheses.

(h) Monitoring of efficiency according to some metric or reasoning strategy.

(i) Inter-cell communication in a distributed network, propagating goals, data and knowledge to and from other nodes [9].

The focus of control is achieved using a simple mechanism which combines fixed KS priorities (specified when the knowledge base is created) with the levels of abstraction at which KS contribute. KS contributing at the highest level (processing symbols and propositions) are given priority over KS at lower levels (processing images) to allow strategic processing to be carried out in advance of more computationally costly numerical processing. KS contributing at similar levels are sorted into the agenda using their fixed priorities.

The inference mechanism must also implement a strategy for combining competitive and co-operative KS support, and for propagating confidence through the application of KS. A number of quantitative techniques have been published with varying applications and success [10]. Thus, for BOFFIN an *ad hoc* approach has been employed based on common sense. The confidence values employed within hypothesis frames are used as a quantitative measure of certainty. Each measure is an integer value in the range 0% to 100% representing the "don't know" condition and full confidence respectively. No representation of falsehood is maintained, so that a system of constructive criticism is used. In order to disagree with a hypothesis, a KS must assert some form of alternative, with appropriate belief. The "don't know" confidence value therefore constitutes a condition of no information, rather than falsehood.

Computing the overall confidence associated with a hypothesis requires combination of the co-operative and competitive support values. The i competing confidence value is first calculated from the m supporting KS confidences according to:

$$C_i = Max \ \{C_1, C_2, ..., C_m\}$$

The overall confidence for the hypothesis is then derived from the n competing versions according to:

$$C_o = Max \ \{C_1, C_2, ..., C_i, ..., C_n\}$$

In propagating confidence to a KS contribution hypothesis, the conservative assumption is made that a chain is only as strong as its weakest link. The propagated confidence from the l triggering hypotheses is therefore:

$$C_o = Min \ \{C_1, C_2, \ . \ . \ . \ , C_k, \ . \ . \ . \ , C_l\}$$

Currently, the mechanism assumes there is no uncertainty associated with the KS knowledge, although this could easily be included.

2.4 Knowledge Sources

Knowledge sources are diverse in nature, triggering and contributing in a data or goal-driven mode of inference. For the example of Figure 8.4 hypotheses H1, H2 and H3 are interpreted as information/data during data-driven inference, and trigger the KS to support a further information hypothesis, H4. During goal-driven inference, the hypothesis H4 is interpreted as a goal, and triggers the KS to support hypotheses H1, H2 and H3 as sub-goals.

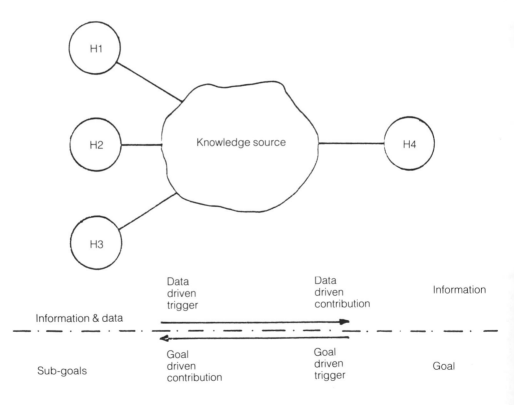

Figure 8.4- Goal and data-driven KS application.

To structure the knowledge base, and to identify data-driven context, KS are constrained to contribute only one hypothesis during data-driven inference. To enable the inference mechanism successfully to implement these trigger and contribution actions, all KS maintain information about themselves on the blackboard, and use a set format in their implementation.

Knowledge Source Noticeboard

Information about individual KS is maintained within BOFFIN on a section of the blackboard called the knowledge source noticeboard. Entries for each KS on the noticeboard use the frame structure of Figure 8.5. As with hypotheses, fields containing slots are used for data and goal-driven inference. The goal field maintains slots to indicate the context (i.e. blackboard level) at which sub-goals are contributed, the KS trigger status (not triggered, triggered, already contributed), the priority value associated with making sub-goal contributions, and a time-stamp, indicating the last inference cycle during which the KS made a goal-driven contribution. Two further fields maintain the hypothesis identifiers (Figure 8.2) for the most recent trigger and contribution goals. The information field, used during data-driven inference, maintains a similar set of slots for the same purpose.

KS within the cell may contain knowledge associated with the problem domain or with inference. An additional meta field is therefore used to identify which of these the KS contains. Furthermore, in future implementations it is hoped that KS may be created as a result of the processing actions of other KS. A support field is therefore maintained to indicate the KS which have contributed this KS, and the belief they have asserted. The belief indicates the validity of the knowledge.

Knowledge Source Structure

All KS have their processing ability structured within the fields of Figure 8.6, independent of the form of their knowledge. Processing sections are identified according to the different ways in which the inference mechanism may execute part of the KS. The initialization section is executed when the cell is first activated, to allow KS to assert their presence onto the knowledge source noticeboard. The cost section provides the focus of attention meta-KS with some means of evaluating the cost (according to the defined metric) of executing the KS. Thus its priority rating and position in the agenda are influenced.

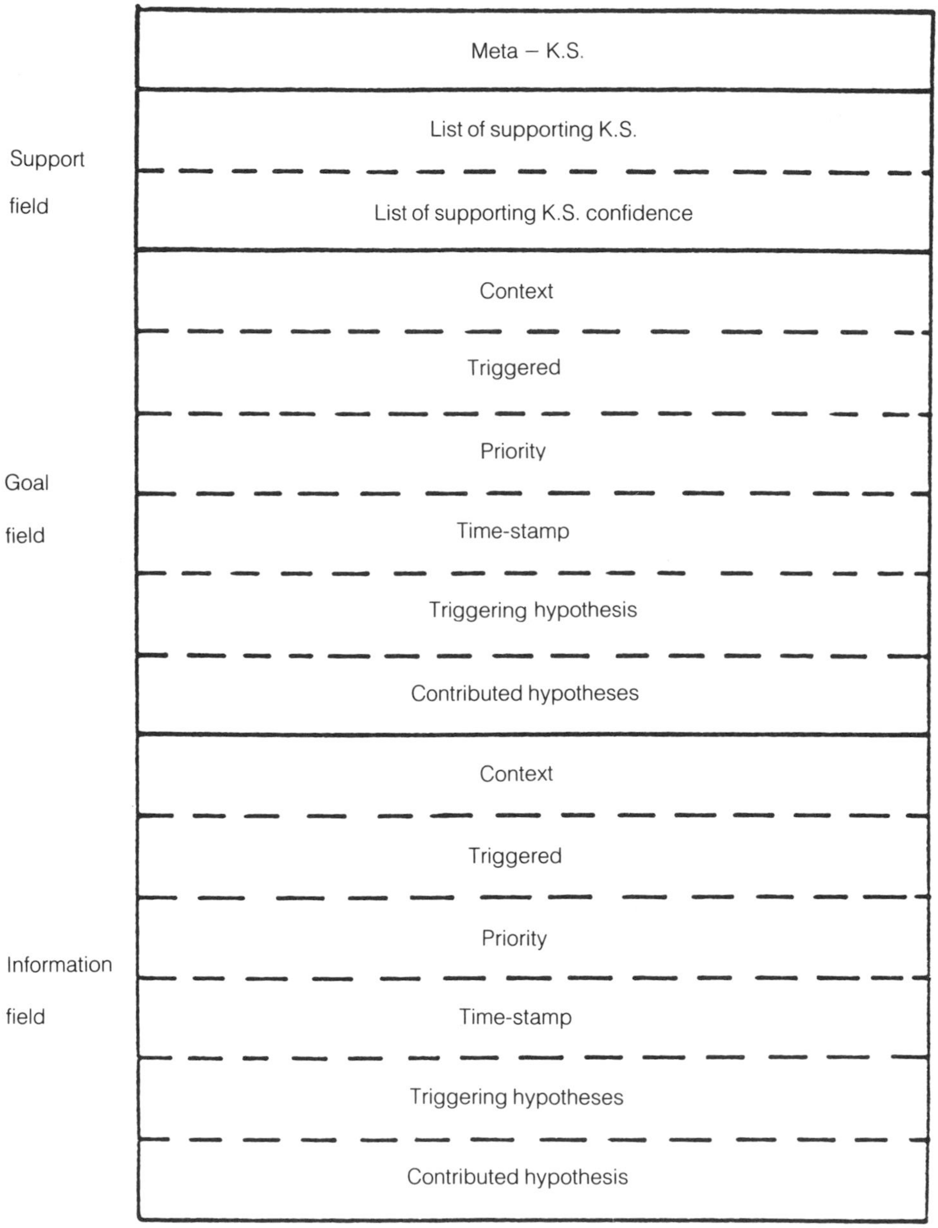

Figure 8.5- Structure of a KS noticeboard frame.

The heart of the knowledge source is contained within the data-driven and goal-driven trigger and contribution fields. The trigger fields are executed by a meta-KS to establish if the KS is triggered. If it is, the appropriate entry is made onto the KS noticeboard and the KS sorted into the agenda. The contribution fields contain the active knowledge which the KS brings to the problem domain. They are executed if the KS is at the top of the agenda after sorting is complete.

Knowledge Source Trigger and Contribution Mechanism

KS triggering is achieved by ensuring there is confidence in all the triggering hypotheses, and by comparing the time-stamps on the KS noticeboard with the goal or information time-stamp on the hypothesis. The KS will only trigger if at least one of its triggering hypotheses has been updated since it last executed.

To resolve the issues of blackboard consistency and hypothesis update a mechanism is required for KS to alter their support for a contribution when their triggering hypotheses are altered. Performing this operation rapidly will reduce the duration of any blackboard inconsistency. To this end, KS are constructed so that they can remove support for a contribution from within their trigger fields, without re-applying their knowledge. Thus, updating any hypothesis on the blackboard may cause a number of KS to withdraw their support for other hypotheses during the next inference cycle.

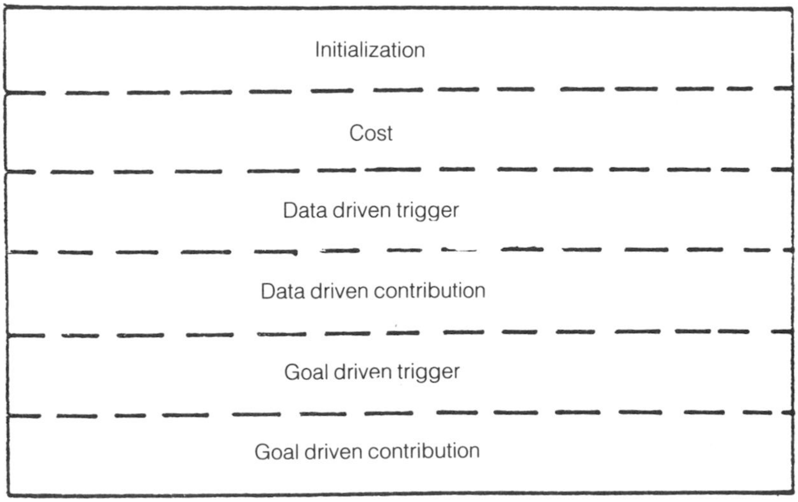

Initialization

Cost

Data driven trigger

Data driven contribution

Goal driven trigger

Goal driven contribution

Figure 8.6- Structure of a KS.

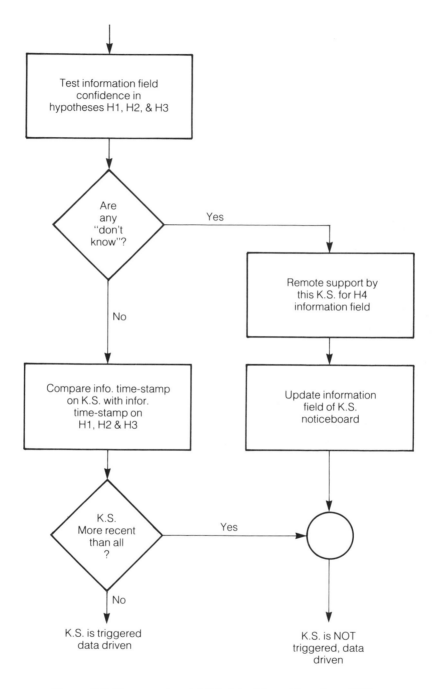

Figure 8.7- Sequence to establish data-driven triggering of KS.

Subsequently, however, they may re-trigger to assert their new conclusions. Inconsistencies between linked hypothesis frames only exist, therefore, for the duration of a single inference cycle. Typically it takes two or three inference cycles for these ripples of support removal to propagate across the blackboard.

Figure 8.7 shows a flow chart for the evaluation of a KS data-driven trigger section. By way of example, it employs the three hypotheses H1, H2 and H3 (Figure 8.4) as triggers for the information contribution H4. The information confidence slots in H1-H3 are initially tested. If any have no confidence, the KS removes any of its existing support for H4 as information, and labels the KS as not-triggered in the information field on the KS noticeboard. If H1, H2 and H3 are all supported, the information field time-stamp in each hypothesis is compared with the information field time-stamp on the KS noticeboard. If any of the hypotheses have been updated since the last time the KS contributed or removed support for H4, the KS is labelled triggered in the information field on the KS noticeboard. The inference mechanism then sorts it into the agenda. Figure 8.8 shows a similar diagram for goal-driven inference, where the triggering hypothesis is H4, interpreted as a goal. All updates to the goal or information fields in hypotheses and on the KS noticeboard cause the associated time-stamp to be updated.

To contribute in a data-driven mode, the problem domain knowledge is applied using the information in H1, H2 and H3, generating the supported version of H4. This is then incorporated into the H4 information field in a competitive or co-operative fashion, and the H4 information time-stamp is updated. Any support for H4 as a goal is removed, and the information field on the KS noticeboard is updated and time-stamped.

Contributing in a goal-driven mode (Figure 8.9) employs the same steps, with some additional stages. Confidence in the information fields of H1, H2 and H3 are first tested. If there is confidence in all of them, then the goal H4 has been satisfied to some degree. KS support for it is generated using the above data driven application of KS knowledge. If not, the KS updates the goal support and time-stamp slots for those of H1, H2 and H3 which contain no information, and for the goal field of the KS noticeboard.

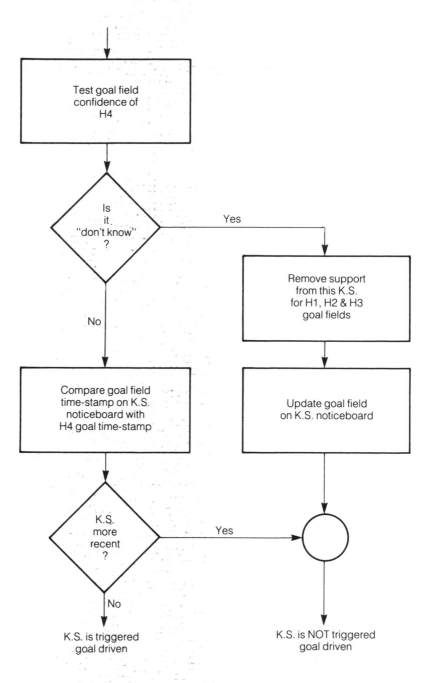

Figure 8.8- Sequence to establish goal-driven triggering of KS.

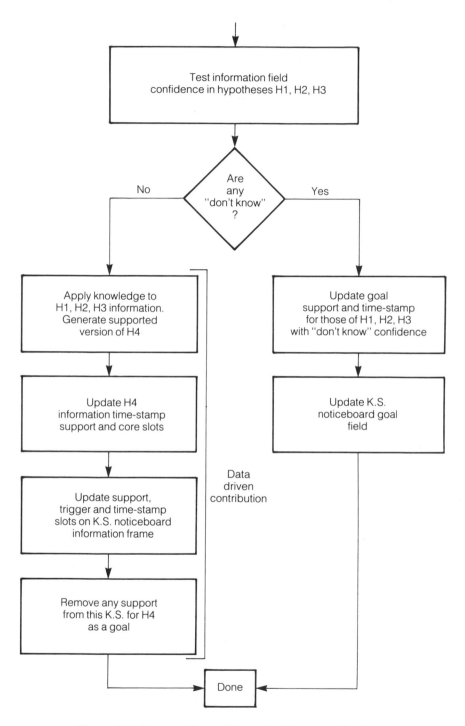

Figure 8.9- Sequence for making goal-driven contribution.

3 Application to Sonar Interpretation

To conclude this chapter, some consideration is given to the problem domain for which BOFFIN was originally employed to illustrate the basic structure of a typical blackboard system knowledge base.

3.1 Sonar Interpretation

Sonar interpretation is the task of automatically analysing sonar data in order to extract information concerning the marine environment surrounding the sensing device. For many practical applications, this will typically involve detecting and describing objects such as pipelines, wellheads, underwater vehicles and also divers. For geophysical work it may equally involve analysing image textures to describe different geological layers such as sand, rock, shingle or oil. The task is non trivial because the sonar data are typically corrupted by both the anomalous behaviour of the acoustic transmission medium (e.g. unwanted boundary and volume reverberation, varying propagation speeds throughout the medium) and by the nature of the sonar device itself (e.g. secondary sidelobe scanning, multipath and multipulse reflections). This creates various kinds of uncertainty in the data being processed, such as noise spread throughout the image, seabed clutter, ghost objects which do not correspond to real objects (so called anomalies) and inaccurate estimation of a boundary's range.

Once formatted as an image, a human expert working with such data seems to use two levels of processing to carry out an interpretation. At a subconscious level, image segmentation is carried out automatically, to effortlessly identify characteristic features such as regions, boundaries or texture. At a conscious level, more rule-based reasoning employing a priori knowledge of the characteristics of the sonar device and the surrounding marine environment is used to accept or reject candidate features as resulting from a bona-fide object, and to classify objects of known types.

To automate this task it appears reasonable to employ a knowledge-based approach to integrate image processing and symbolic reasoning activities (corresponding to the subconscious and conscious levels of human processing) within a vision pyramid. Thus, the decision-making associated with rejecting or selecting candidate features, and with selecting image processing tools and parameters can be carried out explicitly. It further provides a framework within which subsequent classification and identification operations can be carried out to label these candidate objects uniquely, and allows for the integration of data (sensory or available a priori) from elsewhere.

3.2 Sonar Interpretation Knowledge Base

With these techniques in mind, some consideration can be given to the information and process requirements for a blackboard implementation of a sonar perception and interpretation knowledge base. As with human expertise, a hierarchical approach is appropriate, using a classification such as that of Figure 8.10.

At the lowest level, raw sonar image data is placed on the blackboard, and operated upon by image processing knowledge sources forming the first part of the perception operation. These KS contain expertise in pre-processing of the sonar scan, and segmentation to identify candidate object and shadow regions. The second stage of the perception operation involves describing these regions in some more abstract quantitative way, providing the basis for subsequent interpretation operations. These feature-calculating KS take the segmented image information, and produce a series of sightings which contain numerical measures of position, shape and pixel statistics for the hypothesized region. The role of the KS implementing each of these tasks in combination is therefore analogous to the subconscious, low-level vision processing of the human operator.

The first stage of the interpretation process involves the classification of each candidate object and shadow sighting into object/shadow, anomaly and noise components typically observed in such images. These KS therefore take the position, shape and statistical values for each candidate, and use rule-based and algorithmic knowledge to perform the classification according to known phenomena concerning the device and the medium. The second stage of the interpretation process takes those sightings classified as object or shadow, and attempts to identify them at the symbol level. These KS therefore use rule-based and algorithmic knowledge to perform scan-to-scan correlation of object and shadow sightings and to implement simple reasoning functions based on the 3D world model, its expected appearance viewed through the sonar, and the candidates that have been identified. Such processing would make use of appropriate pattern recognition distance metrics as a means of comparing individual feature descriptions.

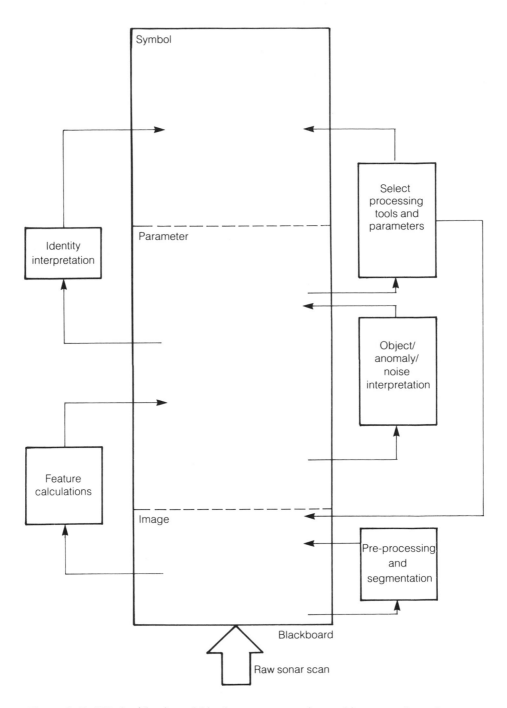

Figure 8.10- KS classification within the sonar perception and interpretation sub-system.

In tandem with these activities, a model-driven mode of processing uses information concerning the sonar position, orientation and status, and the topography of the local marine environment, to select the most appropriate image processing tools and to calculate the parameter values required. Low level signal processing is therefore guided according to more abstract forms of information and knowledge.

3.3 Knowledge Base Execution

To completely describe a KS execution sequence within BOFFIN is complex, and beyond that which can be described here. By way of illustration, however, the blackboard events which lead up to the application of a moving average filter designed to remove sea bed clutter are described, taken from [6].

The system is initially presented with hypotheses postulating the sonar position and orientation, the frequency, scan sector, gain and range of the sonar device, the material (rock, silt, etc.) which constitutes the sea bed, and a raw sonar scan. To identify the local blackboard level of each hypothesis and KS, the abbreviations S (symbol), F (float parameter) and I (image) are used. Percentages refer to the confidence values for each hypothesis. It is assumed that the sonar is mounted on an unmanned remotely operated underwater vehicle, termed an ROV.

The following KS trigger and contribution fields were invoked:

KS   Trigger and contribution hypotheses

1.(F) Sonar frequency (F 100%) & Saltwater (S 100%) ->
       acoustic attenuation coefficient (F 100%).
2.(F) Vertical sonar beam angle (F 100%) & ROV pitch (F 80%)
       & ROV height (F 85%) -> Sonar beam sea bed intersection
       range (F 80%).
3.(S) Sonar range setting (F 100%) & Sonar beam sea bed
       intersection range (F 80%) -> Sea bed intersects sonar
       scan (S 80%).
4.(F) Sonar gain setting (F 100%) & Sonar beam sea bed
       intersection range (F 80%) -> Time varying gain at
       intersection range (F 80%).
5.(F) Sonar frequency (F 100%) & Sea bed material (S 60%) ->
       Sea bed backscatter coefficient (F 60%).
6.(S) Sea bed backscatter coefficient (F 60%) & Time varying
       gain at intersection range (F 80%) & acoustic attenua-

tion coefficient (F 100%) & Sonar beam sea bed intersection range (F 80%) -> Sonar gain high enough for clutter (S 60%).

7.(S) Sonar gain high enough for clutter (S 60%) & Sea bed intersects sonar scan (S 80%) -> Sea bed clutter present (S 60%).

8.(F) Raw sonar image (I 100%) -> Mean of raw sonar image (F 100%).

9.(S) Mean of raw sonar image (F 100%) -> Sea bed clutter present (S 60% & 100%).

10.(F) Sea bed material (60%) & Sea bed clutter present (S 100%) -> Moving average filter time-constant (F 60%).

11.(I) Seabed clutter present (S 100%) & Raw sonar scan (I 100%) & Moving average filter time constant (F 60%) -> Sonar scan with sea bed clutter removed (I 60%).

Thus, the symbolic hypothesis asserting the presence of sea bed clutter in the image is supported by two co-operative KS with confidence 100% (KS 9) and 60% (KS 7). KS 11 therefore triggers to implement the moving average filter. Had KS 9 not supported the presence of sea bed clutter (i.e. the mean level in the raw sonar image was too low), then the sea bed clutter symbol would have remained with a confidence of 60%. The various levels of hypothesis and knowledge representation within the system thus co-operate in forward chaining, data and model-driven modes to identify the need to use a particular image processing algorithm on the raw sonar data, and to select one of the parameters that are required.

By way of illustration, Figure 8.11 presents a series of images showing the results of image processing stages leading up to the final segmentation of typical sonar scan into candidate object and shadow regions (c.f. the sonar operator's subconscious level of expertise). Figure 8.11a shows the original scan digitized from a UDI AS360 sector scanning sonar. The sonar is a mechanically scanned device typical of those used during offshore energy exploration and production activities. The image is a 360 degree scan on the 40*m* range setting and shows a diver (bottom left) a diving bell (top left) and a sea bed scar and ridge (centre right). The large symmetrical bright region occupying the centre of the scan is due to reflection from the adjacent sea bed and is regarder as clutter for the purpose of this work.

Figure 8.11b shows the image hypothesis which constitutes an estimate of the sea bed clutter derived from an image processing KS triggered during the above chain of inference. Figure 8.11c shows the image hypothesis produced by subtracting Figure 8.11b from Figure 8.11a to estimate the scanned environment with sea bed clutter removed. Figure 8.11d shows the final segmentation which results where bright areas correspond to candidate regions in the original image and mid-grey is a don't know condition. Regions containing acoustic shadows are of equal importance in carrying out interpretation and so the dark regions in Figure 8.11d correspond to candidate shadow regions in Figure 8.11a. Figure 8.11e and 8.11f present the original scan image overlayed by boxes showing the boundaries of the object and shadow regions respectively.

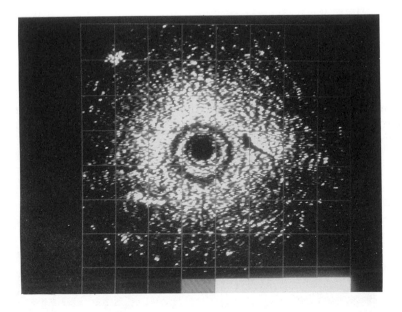

Figure 8.11a- Original sonar data.

(b)

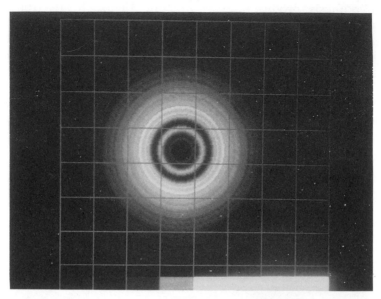

(c)

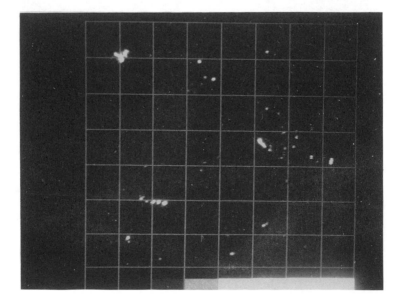

Figure 8.11- Sonar data.

(d)

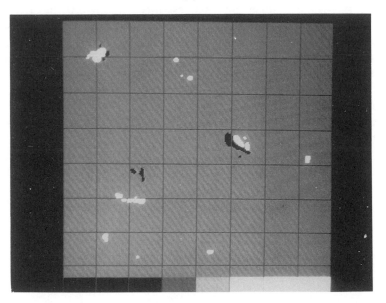

(e)

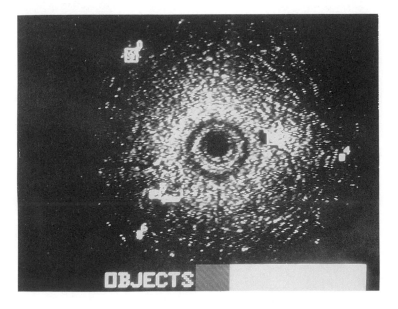

Figure 8.11- Sonar data.

The knowledge base has successfully identified the diving bell (object 0) in the scan, but has separated both the diver and sea bed ridge into separate objects (1 & 5 and 2 & 3 respectively). Two further candidates have also been detected which may or may not represent actual objects. The knowledge base has had less success in detecting shadow as a result of the lower signal-to-noise (S/N) ratio in the shadow pixel information. Furthermore, it has failed to identify a long, narrow horizontal shadow adjacent to shadow number 2 and also the shadow to the rear of the diver.

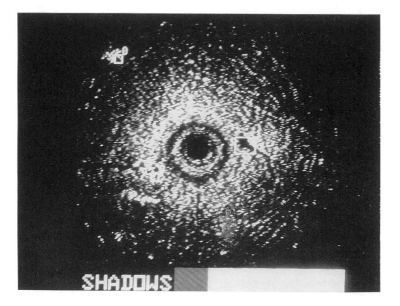

Figure 8.11f- Sonar data.

The results have demostrated the value of using a KB architecture such as the BOFFIN blackboard to structure the application of rule-based and algorithmic processing to carrying out segmentations of the raw sonar data. The knowledge base developed here has performed adequately, but does not demonstrate robust performance in the presence of poor signal information at the pixel level. This could be improved by developing the quality of image processing tools available. An alternative and more interesting approach would be to include extra KS operating in a model-driven mode, using a priori information about the known environment to reject candidate regions with low certainty values derived from portions of the image with a low S/N ratio.

4 Conclusion

This chapter has briefly described a blackboard system BOFFIN which has been used as a research tool for helping structure processing modules for sonar interpretation. Some detail concerning the architecture of BOFFIN was followed by a consideration of the problem domain for which it was originally developed, and an example of a sequence of KS trigger and execution actions.

Although successful as a prototyping tool for experimenting with processing modules and their interactions, the BOFFIN system as it stands is not suitable for inclusion in a stand-alone real-time environment. This is primarily because the blackboard acts as a bottleneck in a single processor implementation, and because basic real-time mechanisms such as pre-emptive scheduling are not present. The system cannot easily be synchronized to events in the outside world therefore.

Our current research effort is thus concentrating on using a distributed network of blackboard processing nodes (rational cells), to carry out the same interpretation task [8]. The aim is to speed up the processing time for interpretation, to synchronize the system with external events, and to investigate some fundamental issues in distributed problem solving.

References

[1]   D.R. Reddy, L.D. Erman, R.D. Fennell and R.B. Neely, "The HEARSAY Speech Understanding System: An Example of the Recognition Process", *Proc. 3rd Int. Joint Conf. on AI*, Stanford, Calif., pp 185-193, August 1973.

[2]   L. Erman, F. Hayes-Roth, V.R. Lesser, and D.R. Reddy, "The HEARSAY II Speech Understanding System: Integrating Knowledge to Resolve Uncertainty", *Computing Surveys*, **Vol-12**, No-2, June 1980.

[3]   H.P. Nii, E.A. Fiegenbaum, J.J. Anton and A.J. Rockmore, "Signal To Symbol Transformation: HASP/SIAP Case Study", *The AI Magazine*, Spring 1982.

[4]   H.P. Nii, "Blackboard Systems: The Blackboard Model of Problem Solving and the Evolution of the Blackboard Architecture", *The AI Magazine*, pp 38-53, Summer 1986.

[5]   D.M. Lane, "The Investigation of a Knowledge Based System Architecture in the Context of a Subsea Robotic Application", *Ph.D. thesis*, Dept. of Electrical & Electronic Engineering, Heriot-Watt University, Edinburgh, 1986.

[6]   G.T. Russell and D.M. Lane, "A Knowledge Based System Framework for Environmental Perception in a subsea Robotic Context", *IEEE Journal of Oceanic Engineering*, July 1986.

[7]   D.T. Berry, "A Knowledge Based System For Machine Vision", *Ph.D. Thesis*, Dept. of Electrical and Electronic Engineering, Heriot-Watt University, Edinburgh. 1987.

[8]   D.M. Lane, M.J. Chantler, A.G. McFadzean and E.W. Robertson, "A Distributed Problem Solving Architecture for Sonar Image Interpretation", *Underwater Technology J. of the Society For Underwater Technology*, **Vol-14**, No-3, Autumn 88.

[9]   E.W. Robertson, "An Investigation of a Distributed Problem Solving Architecture For A Knowledge Based Vision Task", *M.Sc. thesis*, Dept. of Electrical and Electronic Engineering, Heriot-Watt University, Edinburgh 1989.

[10] R. Martin-Clouairc and H. Prade, "On The Problems of Representation and Propagation of Uncertainty In Expert Systems", *International J. of Man Machine Studies*, *Vol-22*, pp 251-264, 1985.

Chapter 9

Automatic Speech Recognition

J.S. Bridle

1 Introduction

One of the most difficult areas of artificial intelligence is concerned with reproducing the ability of animals to turn sensory data into useful interpretations. Artificial perception (AP) can be defined as the goal of building artificial systems that could exhibit a degree of robustness and flexibilty, in responding to real-world data, that we normally associate with animals (including humans). Automatic speech recognition (ASR) is a problem in artificial perception: the input is a continuous, undifferentiated, flowing pattern of sound (no symbols!) but the desired output is symbolic (words-label, meanings, or text). We briefly review two of the established styles of approach to ASR, which can be called the strong knowledge (conventional symbolic AI) approach and the strong algorithms (stochastic models) approach. We then present our experience and insights into the merits of feed-forward non-linear adaptive networks (or "multi-layer perceptrons") compared with more conventional approaches to speech and pattern recognition. We conclude with an opinion on the important relationships between the methods, both theoretically and from the practical point of view of developing improved automatic speech recognition technology.

Speech is essentially a function of time, and any serious attempt at ASR has to deal with time in a principled way. Normal, natural speech recognition is performed (apparently effortlessly) by our brains, without the need for conscious thought. Speech can be described at many levels, ranging from the shape of waveforms to the meaning of whole sentences. Speech science is largely concerned with identifying useful levels of description and relating descriptions at different levels. Speech technology typically deals with methods for moving between levels automatically.

The input to most automatic speech recognition systems is a single pressure waveform picked up by a microphone near the speaker's mouth although we know that multiple microphones, and even images of the speaker, could help. Figure 9.1 shows such a sound pressure waveform, for an utterance of the word "zero".

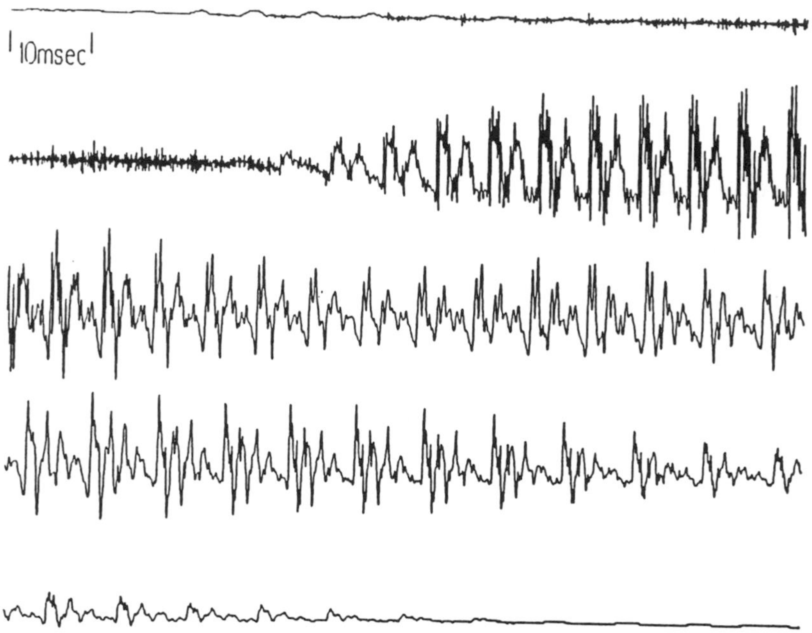

Figure 9.1- Waveform of an utterance of word "zero".

It is usual to convert the waveform to a pattern of energy as a function of time and frequency (see Figure 9.2), with high frequencies at the top, low frequencies at the bottom, and brightest areas corresponding to greatest energy density. There are several methods of producing such representations, but ours uses a bank of frequency-selective (band-pass) filters and short-term energy detectors. The process deliberately smoothes out the fine structure caused by e.g. the pitch of the voice, while retaining (we hope) the changing spectrum shape caused by the changing shape of the speaker's mouth.

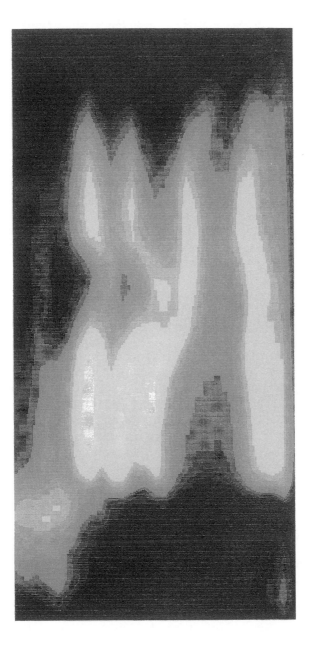

Figure 9.2.- Time-frequency pattern of an utterance of word 'zero'.

Repetitions of the same word produce different, but similar, patterns. Different words produce very different patterns (usually). Figure 9.3 shows a selection of utterances of digits from several persons. Each one is the same format as Figure 9.2.

The automatic speech recognition systems available today compare such patterns with reference patterns ("models"), one or more for each word, stored in the system's memory, and a decision is made about the most likely word or sequence of words.

We review three styles of approach to ASR which have each been in fashion (at least once) in the past 20 years. The strong knowledge approach starts with the assumption that what speech experts (phoneticians) know about speech is relevant and applicable to ASR. In the stochastic model and connectionist approaches, most of the speech knowledge comes from automatic analysis of speech in terms of the models and networks to be used in recognition ("the speech speaks for itself").

2 Strong Knowledge Approaches

The strong knowledge approach starts with the assumption that what speech experts (mainly phoneticians) know about speech is relevant and applicable to ASR. It is clear that a much better performance should be possible, if only we could build into ASR machines more of the rich and useful-looking knowledge about the structure of speech that seems to exist in the domains of phonetics, psychology, physiology and linguistics. The technology is normally that of mainstream applied artificial intelligence (i.e. somewhere between the simulation of conscious reasoning and the use of high-level symbolic programming techniques). However, some SK approaches to ASR have also incorporated techniques from statistical pattern recognition and combinatorial search algorithms.

The relationship between acoustic pattern and meaning is very complicated. We suspect that it would be useful to describe the relationship via several intermediate concepts such as words. Speech science provides several other useful-looking intermediate concepts, such as formant and phoneme. Unfortunately, when we come to apply such ideas we typically find them lacking in the kind of precise definition that we need in order to translate directly into computationally useful form.

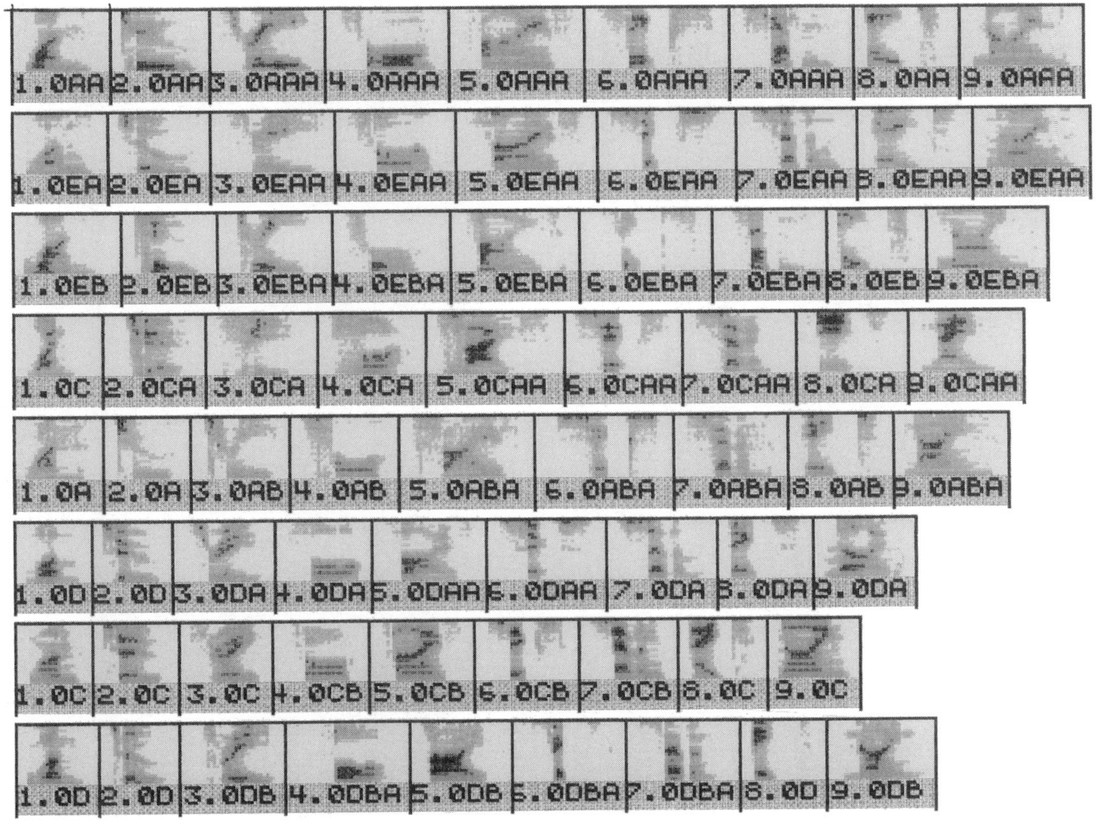

Figure 9.3- Examples of the multi-speaker isolated digit data.

Since most knowledge from speech science is in symbolic form, it is natural that most attempts to apply such knowledge to ASR have tried to convert speech signals to some symbolic form early on... usually far too early! The most visible products of AI research are based on a symbolic mode, appropriate, perhaps, to emulating conscious thought processes. (The main exceptions are in the field of computer vision, where numerical methods are dominant for the early stages.)

Smolensky dramatizes our ignorance of the representations, processes and mechanisms which mediate between sensory data and conscious thought as a "conceptual abyss", and suggests [1] that the symbolic level of description of our minds is best seen as an approximation to the much richer *sub-symbolic* level at which the computation actually takes place.

By the above definition, artificial perception is a branch of engineering, and its products can be judged by results independently of any relationship to theories of the operation of biological systems. However, the argument that "Nature's way is best" has a great deal of force in speech processing, because it is reasonable to assume that the speech code has evolved to make maximum use of the available (and co-evolving) processes of perception.

The issues for such an approach to ASR are of two kinds: the suitability and adequacy of the speech knowledge, and the suitability of the "knowledge engineering" techniques.

There have been many attempts to use strong speech knowledge and AI techniques for ASR. One of the biggest was the ARPA speech understanding systems project, in the early 1970s [2]. The emphasis was on the use of "higher level" knowledge (syntactic, semantic and pragmatic) to make up for the ambiguities of the acoustic signal. One of the most interesting system architectures was that of Hearsay. The basic idea was that the recognition process was divided up into separate but interacting "knowledge sources", for example acoustic, phonetic, syntactic and semantic. The knowledge sources communicated using a "blackboard". Although the Hearsay blackboard architecture is now standard in expert systems, (see Chapter 2 of this volume) the original speech recognition system did not perform particularly well. It can be argued that the blackboard architecture idea has served as stimulus to connectionist approaches to speech and language processing [3].

The only ARPA SUS system that met all the original specifications was called Harpy. It worked in a quite different way, with two quite separate phases. In the first phase (model building) all the grammatical, lexical and phonological knowledge was "compiled" into a single huge network-type structure, which was a compact way of specifying all possible valid utterances in the task domain. In the second phase (recognition) the utterance to be recognized was compared with the whole network to find the path for which the acoustic expectations were closest to the input. Because of the restricted form of the network it was possible to use a powerful and near-optimal search technique, which is the same as that used in the stochastic model paradigm described below. Indeed, Harpy was the result of combining speech knowledge techniques from Hearsay with the stochastic model representation and search methods developed for the Dragon [4] speech recognition system.

The current big US government attempt to push back the frontiers of automatic speech recognition was also founded on an assumption that better speech knowledge needed to be used, and that techniques were available to exploit it. This DARPA speech programme has also seen a swing to stochastic-model based techniques and a (relatively) crude interpretation of current phonetic knowledge, (although significant advances have been made in techniques for incorporating speech knowledge and training in the details [5]. In the U.K. the Alvey Programme's big ASR demonstrator project has similarly swung towards stochastic model-based methods, both at the acoustic-phonetic level and the grammatical level.

It is not clear whether the relative failure of the knowledge intensive methods has been because the knowledge or the techniques were not up to the job, or because the approach was not pursued far enough. For the "higher levels" of spoken language processing we might expect methods using explicit symbols and rules to be more appropriate, particularly if the style of the language used is rather formal, such as in some military, technical or legal areas. There is no doubt that some form of reasoning is needed in systems which are to maintain a useful dialogue in a human-like way.

3 Stochastic Models

In strong algorithms approaches to ASR the emphasis is on the ability to solve well-defined mathematical problems which, it is hoped, are relevant to speech processing. Powerful mathematical techniques are typically used for finding optimal "decodings" of speech patterns, in the sense of minimizing an error or "energy", or maximizing a likelihood.

One particularly powerful set of algorithms derives from treating the speech data as if it were the output of a *stochastic* system. A stochastic system is one that evolves in time or space according to probabilistic laws [6]. In a *stochastic model* (SM) approach the patterns are treated as if they are outputs of a stochastic system. Information about the classes of patterns is encoded as the structure of such "laws" and the probabilities that govern their operation. The word *model* is used for this representation of a hypothetical generator of data. It should not be confused with a "connectionist model", which is likely to be a computational embodiment of a theory of perception. In an SM approach the "perception" is done by an algorithm designed to suit the form of the model. It is necessary to choose the form of the models as a careful compromise between availability of good algorithms and faithfulness to the nature of speech patterns. The Stochastic Model approach makes no claims to be relevant to human speech recognition, but does have principled ways of dealing with uncertainty and temporal structure.

Figure 9.4 shows the general idea. The models are the result of statistical analysis of labelled examples of patterns for the various classes. The comparison process computes the likelihood with which each model would produce the unknown pattern, and the decision is made based on these likelihoods, together with prior probabilities of the classes, and costs of the various kinds of error.

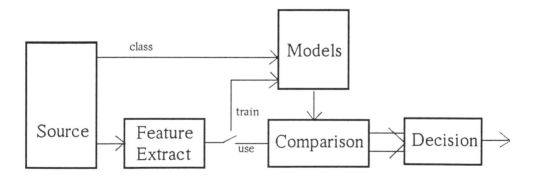

Figure 9.4- Block diagram of a stochastic model-based classifier.

A stochastic word model contains enough information to produce, with appropriate probabilities, many different "pronunciations" of a single word. (The variations in the spectrum and timescales would be realistic if the model were a very good one, but current stochastic models do not make good synthesizers.) Alternatively, the same information can be used to compute the probability with which the model would generate any particular pattern. Speech recognition decisions are made by choosing the stochastic word model which is "most likely" to produce the unknown speech pattern.

The best established type of stochastic word model has a mathematical form known variously as a "probabilistic finite state automaton", a "hidden Markov model" (HMM) or a "stochastic regular grammar". In a simple type of hidden Markov model the hypothetical pattern generating machine has an internal state which is not directly observed. A word model might have between 4 and 20 states. The machine proceeds through a sequence of these states, changing state every hundredth of a second (perhaps to repeat a state). The state sequence is a first-order Markov Chain, which means that the influence of past states on the current state can be expressed in terms of the dependence on the immediately past state alone. (The *state transition matrix*.) The observable acoustic data at each time depends directly on only the state at that time. (The *output distributions*.) The output distributions may be discrete, or continuous with parameters (e.g. multi-variate Gaussian) depending on the amount and type of pre-processing of the data. Variability of timescale and of structure is expressed in the state transition matrix, and variability of the spectrum shape is expressed in the output distributions [7,8,9].

Recognition of an unknown word pattern can be done by computing the probability with which each model would generate the given pattern. The most likely word is then chosen, or the word probabilities are passed on to higher levels of analysis. This recognition computation involves a probability-weighted sum over all state sequences (alternatively the probability of the best state sequence is computed). Because of the simple (Markovian) structure of dependencies between states, it is possible to compute such sums (and maxima) without a combinatorial explosion.

This approach can be extended to deal with sequences of words [10]. It is possible to take the integration of levels of representation of speech even further, and include models of language and phonetics. This amounts to probabilities for transitions between complete word models, and for transitions between "phonetic segment" units within a word. Using this approach, some success has been reported for the "decoding" of sentences dictated from real documents [11], and recently speaker-independent connected-word sentence recognition [5].

An HMM recognition algorithm is designed to find the best explanation of the input in terms of the model. It tracks scores for all plausible current states of the generator and throws away explanations which lead to a current state for which there is a better explaination (Bellman's Dynamic Programming [12]). It may also throw away explaintions which lead to a current state much worse than the best current state (score pruning, producing a beam search method [13]). (It is important to keep many hypotheses in hand, particularly when the current input is ambiguous.)

Model building is of crucial importance. Essentially it is a matter of estimating the conditional probabilities and the parameters of the output distributions. Elegant methods are available for "tuning" an initial word model using many examples of each word [7,14]. Figure 9.5 shows some aspects of a HMM word model for "zero". The lower picture is the same as Figure 9.2. The top line shows the structure of the model, a sequence of six states, each of which may be repeated or skipped. There are transition probabilities associated with all the transitions. The states of the model have been mapped onto the timescale of the particular utterance of "zero", as shown by the rays projecting down from the states. The synthetic word pattern shows the sequence of expected spectrum shapes for the states, aligned to the natural utterance. We can consider this picture as a best explanation of the utterance in terms of the model.

To build a set of word models for a speaker-independent isolated digit recognizer, we would need examples of the words from many speakers (say 100) recorded under conditions relevant to our intended application. Using any one of several acoustic analysis techniques the waveforms would be converted to one vector of say 10 numbers 100 times per second. We might further reduce this representation (using "vector quantization") to one integer 100 times per second. We would choose the number of states (about 10 for short words) and other aspects of the models, perhaps by experiment using part of the data. Initial settings of the parameters of the models might be set by dividing the timescale of each word pattern equally between a sequence of states. The re-estimation method needs time proportional to number of states per word times total amount of training data, and space proportional to number of states per word times total length of training data for a word.

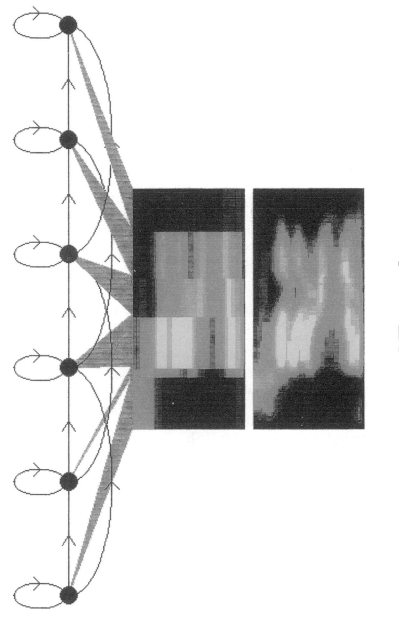

'Zero'

Figure 9.5- Alignment of a hidden Markov model to an utterance.

The art of applying the stochastic model approach is to choose a class of models which is realistic enough to be likely to be able to capture the distinctions (between speech sounds or words for instance) and yet have a structure which makes it amenable to algorithms for building the detail of the models based on examples, and for interpreting particular unknown patterns. Future systems will need to exploit the regularities described by phonetics, to allow the construction of high-performance systems with large vocabularies, and their adaptation to the characteristics of each new user.

4 Neural Network Approaches

Whereas the strong knowledge approach starts with the prior information which should be used, and the stochastic model approach starts by assuming a form for the generator of the data, Connectionist (or PDP or "neural network") approaches (Chapter 4) start with an idea of the *types of process* to be used to transform the data into answers. Connectionist or NN approaches can claim some legitimacy by reference to new (or renewed) theories of cognitive processing. The actual mechanisms used are simpler than those of the SM method, but the mathematical theory (of what can be learnt or computed for instance) is more difficult, particularly for structures which have been proposed for dealing with temporal processing. Some will be interested in the potential for connectionist methods to be relevant as models of perception, or for their potential compatibility with future methods of fabrication, be that electronic or something more exotic. For a comprehensive review of attempts at applying neural network approaches to speech recognition, see [15].

Figure 9.6 shows the general idea of a trainable classifier for static, fixed-size input patterns. There are no explicit models — just a discrimination process with many parameters ("knobs") which need to be adjusted to make it perform well for the given task. There is one output from the discriminator for each possible class. The adaptation (or training, or learning, or knob twiddling) is done by observing the outputs for labelled examples, and adjusting the parameters to make those outputs closer to the desired outputs (high for the correct class and low for the incorrect class).

A typical adaptive network based discriminator, of the "multi-layer perceptron" type, would take several linear combinations (weighted sums) of the input values, pass these sums through sigmoid non-linearities (in "hidden units") and repeat this process to produce output values. The parameters are the weights. In the analogy with neurobiological pattern processing, the weights corespond to synaptic strengths, and the non-linearities correspond to transfer functions of neurons.

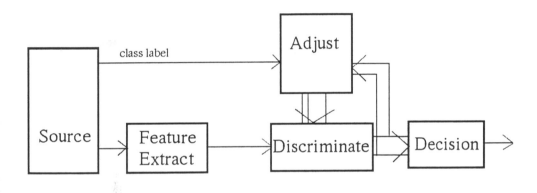

Figure 9.6- Block diagram of a "trainable" classifier.

One of the conceptually simplest approaches to speech recognition is to treat a whole time-frequency-amplitude array (resulting from initial acoustic analysis) as the input to a network, and require a (word) label as output. In the next section we describe one such method, which produced results not much worse than the best HMM methods available, on the same data. The problem of invariance to temporal position was dealt with simply by training the network with the patterns at random positions in a fixed time-window. This approach does not seem to be applicable to connected word recognition.

One of the dreams for connectionist approaches to speech is a network whose inputs accept the speech data as it arrives. It would have an internal state which contains all necessary information about the past input, and the output would be as accurate and early as possible. The training of networks with their own dynamics is particularly difficult, especially when we are unable to specify what the internal state should be. The trace model was constructed to have an appropriate kind of dynamics. Almeida [16] and Rohwer [17,18] are developing methods for training the fixed points of continuous-valued recurrent non-linear synchronous networks. There is work (e.g. [19,20]) on the theory of the dynamics of systems composed of large numbers of binary "neurons" with time delays and assymetrical connections. Watrous [21] limits his recurrent connections to self-loops on hidden and output units, but even so the general theory of such recursive non-linear filters is formidable.

Waibel [22] use an arrangement which can be thought of either as the replication of smaller networks across the time-window (a time-spread network [23]) or as a single small network with internal delay lines (a time-delay neural network, TDNN). There are no recurrent links (except for simple ones at the output), so training (using Backpropagation) is no great problem. We may think of the hidden layers of a TDNN as a finite-impulse-response non-linear filter, as distinct from a recursive filter in the case of recurrent networks. Reported results on consonant discrimination are encouraging, and better than those of a HMM system on the same data.

Kohonen has constructed and demonstrated large vocabulary isolated word [24] and unrestricted vocabulary continuous speech transciption [25] systems which are inspired by neural network ideas, but implemented as algorithms more suitable for current programmed digital signal processor and CPU chips. (Omohundro [26] has pointed out that most of the desirable properties of neural network type systems can often be achieved much more efficiently using appropriate algorithms.) Kohonen's *phonotopic map* technique can be thought of as an unsupervised adaptive quantizer constrained to put its reference points in a non-linear low-dimensional sub-space. His *learning vector quantiser* technique used for initial labelling combines the advantages of the classic nearest-neighbour method and discriminant training. The *redundant hash addressing* process used for subsequent lexical access in the isolated-word system is related to hash coding and also to some learning networks such as WISARD [27]. (See also Chapter 1 of this volume.)

Among other types of network which have been applied to speech we must mention an interesting class based not on correlations with weight vectors (dot-product) but on distances from reference points. *Radial basis function* theory [28] was developed for multi-dimensional interpolation, and was shown by Broomhead and Lowe [29] to be suitable for many of the jobs that feed-forward networks are used for. The advantage is that it is not difficult to find useful positions for the reference points which define the first, non-linear, transformation. If this is followed by a linear output transformation then the weights can be found by methods which are fast and straightforward. (The reference points can be adapted using methods based on back-propagation if required.)

5 Experiences with MLPs for Speech

Mathematical techniques for solving problems in automatic speech recognition have been the subject of research at the RSRE speech research unit for many years. An awareness of some of the limitations of the most successful approaches (which are based on stochastic models) led to an interest in adaptive discriminative ("neural") networks. We have concentrated on finding out the strengths and weaknesses of variations on the error back-propagation technique for multi-layer perceptrons (MLPs), compared with more conventional approaches to speech and pattern recognition.

Our experiences of a NETtalk-like system for learning letter-to-sound rules for English were interesting [30], but the performance was definitely worse than our (inadequate) hand-crafted rule system [31]. In speaker-independent vowel labelling from spectrum shape a simple MLP performed rather better than a variety of standard pattern recognition techniques [32]. Preliminary experience with MLPs for visual discrimination between vowels was encouraging [33]. Perhaps the most obvious way of using an MLP for word recognition is to present a whole-word pattern to a network and let the output indicate the word. Our experiments with such networks have demonstrated performance which is not quite as good as that of our best hidden Markov models for single and multiple speaker digit recognition (see below). For onset-aligned English alphabet letters ("b,c,d,e,g,p,t,v") best results were obtained using radial basis function networks. Theoretical analysis and experiments with carefully constructed artificial data have produced some insights relevant to speech recognition using networks [34].

We shall now consider more specifically some experiments which compare performance of MLPs and HMMs on a multi-speaker isolated digit recognition task. For full details see [35,36].

Each of the 40 speakers was seated in an acoustically treated room. They were prompted by the words "zero, one, ..., nine" appearing in psuedo-random order [37] on a computer-driven display [38]. Initial acoustic analysis used a 19-channel filter bank analyser designed for a communications vocoder [39]. Start and end points for each utterance were established using an automatic system with manual checking. The lengths ranged between 17 and 60-frames. A representative selection of digit patterns from some of the speakers is shown in Figure 9.3. Each line shows the digits 1 to 9 from one talker. In each small digit picture the time (frame) axis is horizontal and the frequency (channel) axis vertical.

All the MLPs were static, with a fixed input field large enough to accept the longest utterance: 60 frames by 19 channels, giving 1140 input units. To reduce the dependence on endpoint detection, and to introduce relevant variability into the training data, each utterance was positioned randomly within this 60 frame window each time it was presented to the network for training or testing. The extra frames at the ends were filled with a standard silence pattern corresponding to the lowest level of the vocoder for all channels. Five network structures were investigated. Each had 1140 input units and 10 output units (one for each class). The simplest network had no hidden units (1140-10). the others had one or two hidden layers of 8 or 50 units, giving structures we shall write as 1140-8-10, 1140-8-8-10, 1140-50-10 and 1140-50-50-10. Each layer was fully connected to the next, using semi-linear logistic units [40]. Figure 9.7 shows the general arrangement, with a 2D array of inputs, a set of hidden units and 10 output units.

In a multi-speaker experiment data from all the speakers are used for training and testing. A separate set of 10 utterances of each digit by each talker was used for testing. The optimization criterion for the training was sum-squared error between the 10 outputs of the network and the targets (all 0 except for a 1 at the position of the correct class). Backpropagation of partial derivatives was used to obtain estimates of the gradient of the criterion with respect to each of the weights. An online gradient descent method with momentum was used to modify the weights, updating after every set of 10 patterns of different classes. Testing simply picked the largest output and compared with the correct class.

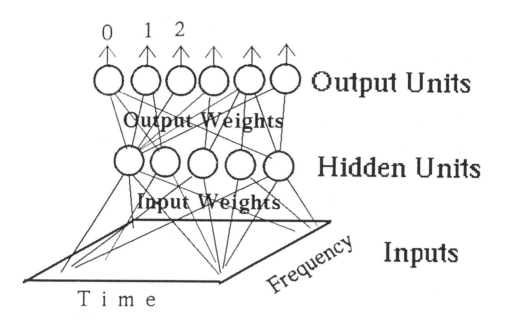

Figure 9.7- Arrangement of input, hidden and output units.

Structure	η=0.15 α=0.75		η=0.07 α=0.50		η=0.25 α=0.50	
	Train	Test	Train	Test	Train	Test
1140-10	18	23	7	12	20	22
1140-8-10	5	12	2	10	6	14
1140-8-8-10	9	11	7	14	9	16
1140-50-10	0	4	0	3	0	3
1140-50-50-10	1	5	1	4	0	4

Table 9.1- Percentage errors from a 400-digit training set (one per speaker) and 4000-digit test set (10 per speaker). An entry of 0 means 0 or 1 errors.

There are several practical matters that needed to be dealt with, such as: range of initial conditions (weight starts), values of the adaptation parameters (stepsize term η and momentum term α), stopping rule, and choice of network for test. A series of pilot experiments established a useful small set of adaptation parameters (η, α) which were used subsequently. Up to five random weight starts were used for each condition, and the one with minimum classification error on the training set was used. (This was cut short if zero error was obtained.) Each run was stopped when the average squared error per pattern (averaged over 200 patterns) was less than 0.001.

Results using one example of each digit from each speaker are shown in Table 9.1. Note that the training errors are out of 400 digits and the testing errors out of 4000 digits. Best generalization (ability to predict performance on test data from performance on training data) was by the simplest networks. The best performance on the test data (3% to 5%) was for networks with 50 first-layer hidden units. These systems were producing almost no errors on the training data.

This performance should be compared with between 1% and 2% error rates on the same test data by a range of hidden Markov model based methods [41,42]. (The padding to 60 frames was not used for the HMMs, but generally we expect HMMs not to have much difficulty with such a perturbation.)

Further experiments on MLPs using two or three utterances of each digit from each speaker gave a reduction of error rates to around 2% for the 1140-50-10 network.

A visual inspection of the weight patterns developed by the learning algorithm reveals some interesting structures. In Figure 9.8 each large rectangle shows the pattern of weights from the input array to a single hidden unit. The narrow row at the top of each rectangle shows the weights from the first-layer hidden unit to the 50 hidden units in the next layer. Some of the hidden units will respond to the average spectrum shape over the whole input array, some are more local, and a few seem to have a periodic structure, thus responding to a given feature if it appears in any one of several positions. There is also a suggestion of sets of hidden units with similar patterns at different horizontal offsets.

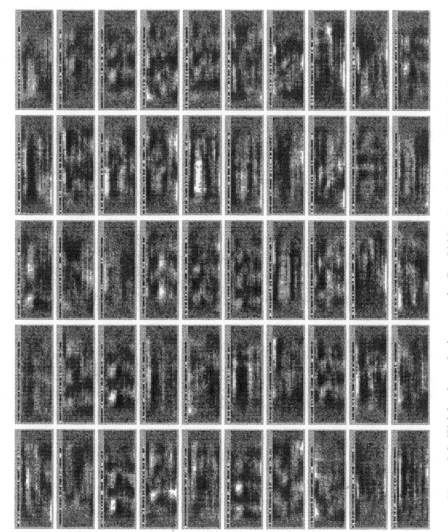

Figure 9.8- Weights from the input to the first hidden layer in the net 1140-50-50-10.

My conclusions from this experience are as follows. Considering how crude and inappropriate the MLP configuration seems, performance was surprisingly good (the superior HMM systems are the product of many years research.) It is quite difficult to design an experiment to make a fair comparison between methods with such different requirements. It is likely that improvements could be made by imposing more structure on the MLP [43,22].

6 Comparisons and Prospects

There is no doubt that the Stochastic model-based methods work best at present, but current systems are generally far inferior to humans even in situations where the usefulness of higher-level processing is minimal, so there is a long way to go. Stochastic model-based methods offer principled ways of dealing with uncertainty and with temporal structure, plus powerful algorithms for decoding (recognition) and for model building (learning). There is no clear limit to development of SM methods for speech, and the recognition algorithms are not difficult to map on to parallel hardware. However, there seems to be a culture gap between the type of mathematics underlying SMs and most speech scientists: the number of individuals who appreciate both fields is quite small.

The connectionist (neural network) approach offers a different viewpoint, and a language for thought and communication. It is a way of making contact with many ideas which may not have been applied to speech before. The training methods for neural network classifiers are based on improving discrimination between classes, whereas SM methods usually model each class separately [44]. (But see [45]) It seems that speech scientists find it easier to see how to use neural networks than stochastic models, so we can expect to see NN approaches with a good basis in appreciation of the subtleties of speech. For examples of NN methods applied in a knowledge-intensive way, see [46,47].

I feel that much more should be possible by mimicking in neural networks the type of computations which take place in a SM based speech recognition system, where the state of the recognizer is a vector of scores for alternative states of the (hypothetical) generator at the current time, plus information needed to recover the best interpretation (traceback pointers). Although there is great theoretical and long-term interest in the possibility of adaptive networks which process continuous speech using their own internal dynamics, at present there is most promise in using MLPs as adaptive nonlinear feature extractors, preceding phoneme- or word-recognition systems of conventional type.

I predict that the next generation of ASR systems will be based on a combination of connectionist and SM theory and techniques, with mainstream speech knowledge probably used in a rather soft way to decide the structure. This can be done in a small way already, if NNs are treated as a way of parameterizing a set of more or less high-order correlations, which can be used as an alternative to the usual discrete or continuous output distributions [48]. It should be possible to integrate the training of an MLP feature transformation and the HMM-based sequential processing by exploiting underlying relationships.

Alternatively, it should be possible to use backpropagation-based adaptation to design non-linear transformations of the acoustic pattern data such that simple Euclidean distances are appropriate when comparing speech sounds, and irrelevant perturbations (caused e.g. by background noise or speaker differences) are ignored. A good starting point is the *linear* transformation which optimizes a measure of the ratio of the within-class to between-class variance [49].

A related area is the design of parameterized transformations which 'take out' systematic acoustic differences between the voices of different people [50]. Adapting the speaker parameters on-line should provide the ability to tune-in to new accents.

We can look forward to a successful marriage of domain knowledge, stochastic model-based methods and connectionist methods which will be part of a revolution in artificial intelligence, both in the importance given to perceptual pattern processing and in the types of processing paradigms.

References

[1] P. Smolensky, "Connectionist AI, Symbolic AI and the Brain", *Artificial Intelligence Review*, 1, pp 95-109, 1987.

[2] D.H. Klatt, "Review of the ARPA Speech Understanding Project", *J.Acoust.Soc.Amer.*, 62, pp 1345-1366, 1977.

[3] M.A. Arbib, *Brains, Machines, and Mathematics* (second edition), Springer-Verlag, 1987.

[4] J.K. Baker, "The Dragon system: An Overview", *IEEE Trans. ASSP-23*, (1), pp 24-29, February 1975.

[5] K.F. Lee, "On Large-vocabulary Speaker-independent Continuous Speech Recognition", *Speech Communication*, 7, pp 375-379, 1988.

[6] D.R. Cox and H.D. Millar, *The Theory of Stochastic Processes*, Methuen, 1965.

[7] S.E. Levinson, L.R. Rabiner, and M.M. Sohndi, "An Introduction to the Application of the Theory of Probabilistic Functions of a Markov Process to Automatic Speech Recognition", *Bell Syst. Tech. J.*, 62(4), pp 1035-1074, April 1983.

[8] S.E. Levinson, "A Unified Theory of Composite Pattern Analysis for Automatic Speech Recognition", F.Fallside and W.Woods, editors, *Computer Speech Processing*, Prentice Hall, 1984.

[9] M.R. Russell and R.K. Moore, "Explicit Modelling of State Occupancy in Hidden Markov Models for Automatic Speech Recognition", *IEEE ICASSP*, 1985.

[10] J.S. Bridle, M.D. Brown, and R.M. Chamberlain, "Continuous Connected Speech Recognition Using Whole-word Templates", *The Radio and Electronic Engineer*, 53(4), pp 167-175, 1983.

[11] L. Bahl, *et. al.*, "Recognition of Isolated-word Sentences from a 5000-word Vocabulary Office Correspondence Task", *Proc. IEEE Int.Conf. on Acoustics Speech and Signal Processing*, 1983.

[12] R. Bellman and S. Dreyfus, *Applied Dynamic Programming*, Princeton University Press, 1962.

[13] B.T. Lowerre, *The HARPY Speech Recognition System*, PhD thesis, Carnegie-Mellon University Comp.Sci., April 1976.

[14] L.E. Baum, "An Inequality and Associated Maximisation Technique in Statistical Estimation for Probabilistic Functions of a Markov Process", *Inequalities*, 3, pp 1-8, 1972.

[15] R.P. Lippmann, "Review of Neural Networks for Speech Recognition", *Neural Network Computation*, 1, 1989.

[16] Almeida, "A Learning Rule for Asynchronous Perceptrons with Feedback in a Combinatorial Environment", *Proc. First IEEE Intl. Conf. on Neural Networks*, June 1987.

[17] R. Rohwer and B. Forrest, "Training Time-dependencies in Neural Networks", *Proc. First IEEE Intl. Conf. on Neural Networks*, June 1987.

[18] R. Rohwer and S. Renals, "Training Recurrent Networks", *Proc. N'Euro-88*, June 1988.

[19] A.C. Coolen and T.W. Ruijgrok, *Phys. Rev. A*, 38, 1988.

[20] H. Sompolinsky and I. Kanter, "Temporal Association in Assymetrical Neural Networks", *Physical Review Letters*, 57, pp 2861-2864, 1986.

[21] R.L. Watrous, "Connectionist Speech Recognition Using the Temporal Flow Model", *Proc. IEEE Workshop on Speech Recognition*, June 1988.

[22] A. Waibel, T. Hanazawa, G. Hinton, K. Shikano, and K. Lang, "Phoneme Recognition Using Time-delay Neural Networks", *IEEE Trans. ASSP*, March 1988.

[23] J.S. Bridle and R.K. Moore, "Boltzmann Machines for Speech Pattern Processing", *Proc. Inst. Acoust.*, pp 1-8, November 1984.

[24] T. Kohonen *et. al.*, "On-line Recognition of Spoken Words from a Large Vocabulary", *Information Sciences*, 33, pp 3-30, 1984.

[25] T. Kohonen, "The 'Neural' Phonetic Typewriter", *IEEE Computer*, March 1988.

[26] S.M. Omohundro, "Efficient Algorithms with Neural Network Behaviour", *Complex Systems*, 1, pp 273-347, 1987.

[27] W.V. Thomas, I. Aleksander and P.A Bowden, "Wisard - a Radical Step Forward in Image Recognition", *Sensor Review*, pp 120-124, July 1984.

[28] M.J. Powell, "Radial Basis Functions for Multi-variate Interpolation: A Review", *Proc. IMA Conf. on algorithms for the approximation of functions and data*, 1985.

[29] D. Broomhead and D. Lowe, *Multi-variable Interpolation and Adaptive Networks*, Technical Report 4148, Royal Signals and Radar Est., 1988.

[30] N. McCulloch, M.D. Bedworth, and J.S. Bridle, "NETspeak - A Re-implementation of NETtalk", *Computer Speech and Language*, 2, pp 289-301, 1987.

[31] J.A. Edward, *Pronunciation Rules for English Text*, JSRU Research report 1014, RSRE Malvern, 1982.

[32] N. McCulloch and W. Ainsworth, "Speaker Independent Vowel Recognition Using a Multi-layer Perceptron", *Proc. 7th FASE Symposium*, pp 851-858, August 1988.

[33] S.M. Peeling, R.K. Moore, and M.J. Tomlinson, "The Multi-layer Perceptron as a Tool for Speech Pattern Processing Research", *Proc. IoA Autumn Conf. on Speech and Hearing*, 8(7), pp 307-314, 1986.

[34] M.D. Bedworth and J.S. Bridle, *Experiments with the Back Propagation Algorithm: a Systematic Look at a Small Problem*, Memo 4049, RSRE, 1987.

[35] S.M. Peeling and R.K. Moore, *Experiments in Isolated Digit Recognition Using the Multi-layer Perceptron*. Memo 4073, RSRE, 1987.

[36] S.M. Peeling and R.K. Moore, "Isolated Digit Recognition Experiments Using the Multi-layer Perceptron", *EURASIP Journal Speech Communication*, 7, pp 403-409, 1988.

[37] R.S. Vonusa *et. al.*, "Nato ac/243 (Panel iii rsg10) Language Database", *Proc. NBS Speech I/O Stand. Workshop*, 1982.

[38] J.C.A. Deacon *et. al.*, *RSRE Speech Database Recordings (1983) Part 1: Specification of Vocabulary and Recording Procedure*, Report 83010, RSRE, 1983.

[39] J.N. Holmes, "The JSRU Channel Vocoder", *Proc. IEE*, 127 Pt.F(1), pp 53-60, 1980.

[40] D.E. Rumelhart, G.E. Hinton, and R.J. Williams, "Learning Internal Representations by Error Propagation", D.E Rumelhart and J.L McClelland, editors, *Parallel Distributed Processing: Explorations in the Microstructure of Cognition*, Vol-1, MIT Press, 1986.

[41] M.J. Russell and A.E. Cook, "Experiments in Speaker-Dependent Isolated Digit Recognition using Hidden Markov Models", *Proc. IoA Autumn Conf. on Speech and Hearing*, 8(7), pp 291-298, 1986.

[42] M.J. Russell and A.E. Cook, "Experimental Evaluation of Duration Modelling Techniques for Automatic Speech Recognition", *Proc. IEEE International Conf. on Acoustics, Speech and Signal Processing*, , pp 2376-2379, 1987.

[43] J.S. Bridle and R.K. Moore, "Boltzmann Machines for Speech Pattern Processing", *Proc. Institute of Acoustics Autumn Conf.*, 6(4), pp 315-322, 1984.

[44] L. Niles, H. Silverman, G. Tajchman, and M. Bush, "How Limited Training Data Can Allow a Neural Network to Outperform an 'Optimal' Classifier", *Proc.ICASSP89*, 1989.

[45] L.R. Bahl, P.F. Brown, P.V. DeSouza, and R.L. Mercer, "A New Algorithm for the Estimation of HMM Parameters", *Proc. IEEE ICASSP88*, pp 493-496, 1988.

[46] I.S. Howard and M.A. Huckvale, "Acoustic-phonetic Attribute Determination Using Multi-layer Perceptrons", *IEE Colloquium Digest 1988/11, 1988*.

[47] Y. Bengio, R. Cardin, R. DeMori, and E. Merlo, "Programmable Execution of Multi-layered Networks for Automatic Speech Recognition", *Comm. ACM*, 32(2), pp 195-199, February 1989.

[48] H. Bourlard and C.J. Wellekens, "Links Between Markov Models and Multilayer Perceptrons", *Computer, Speech and Language*, 1989.

[49] M.J. Hunt and C. Lefebre, "A Comparison of Several Acoustic Representations for Speech Recognition with Degraded and Undegraded Speech", *Proc. IEEE Int. Conf. Acoustics Speech and Signal Processing*, 1989.

[50] S.J. Cox and J.S. Bridle, "Unsupervised Speaker Adaptation by Probabilistic Spectrum Fitting", *Proc. IEEE Int. Conf. ASSP*, 1989.

Chapter 10

Fault Diagnosis of Microwave Digital Radios

K.E. Brown, C.F.N. Cowan and T.M. Crawford

1 Introduction

This chapter considers fault detection and diagnosis in 16-quadrature-amplitude-modulated (QAM) digital microwave radio relay equipment. 16-QAM digital radio relays are widely used to transmit telephony and other data signals over microwave line of sight (LOS) networks. The data rates over these LOS networks are high (140Mbits/s) over a relatively low bandwidth (40 MHz) and to achieve this transmission efficiency, while still maintaining low error rates, requires complex transmitting and receiving equipment.

Initial adjustment of the equipment, to ensure that it meets its performance specifications, and readjustment to remove the effects of equipment malfunctions during operation is a complicated task requiring operators with considerable expertise. The removal of the impairments, by correcting the settings of the different sub-systems of the radio, is performed by a skilled operator after visually interpreting the information from the radio's 16-QAM signal constellation. The information contained within the signal constellation is also used by the diagnostic systems to perform their fault diagnosis.

The basic structure of a typical digital radio and 16-QAM modulation/demodulation are explained to introduce the systems under consideration. Some of the possible sources of impairments and their effects on a 16-QAM radio are discussed, indicating some typical equipment malfunctions. The signal constellation which is used to provide the information for the fault diagnosis is characterized by a set of geometric features. These features, which form the inputs to the knowledge-based systems, are listed and their attributes cited.

Two methods of performing the detection and diagnosis of impairments in the radio equipment are considered. In the first approach, a production rule system is employed which uses a set of geometric features (that characterize the signal constellation) as its input. The generation of the rules and the stucture of the system are explained. In the second technique, a machine learning system is utilized to map the geometric features of the signal constellation to adjustment commands which will improve the performance of the faulty/maladjusted equipment. The merits of both systems' performance are highlighted and the drawbacks are also detailed. This comparison leads to the proposal of a hybrid method, using a combination of both systems. Using the hybrid system, the fault diagnosis of 16-QAM radio equipment is evaluated, underlining the benefits and problems of employing the joint system. Finally, the feasibility, based upon the results presented in this chapter, of using this type of system to perform the required impairment removal for 16-QAM radios is discussed.

2 Digital Radio

Digital modulation techniques are increasingly being used for radio transmission. These methods are used in satellite/earth stations and in terrestrial line of sight radios. Using signal regeneration techniques and error detecting and correcting codes [1], digital transmission allows the carrier-to-noise ratio (CNR) to be reduced without increasing the error rates.

The introduction of spectrally efficient modulation techniques [2,3] has led to digital transmission becoming more widely applied. These techniques, such as quadrature amplitude modulation (QAM), offer the advantages of digital transmission including: signal regeneration; error detecting and correcting coding; and signal encryption.

2.1 Typical Radio

The block structure of a typical digital radio is shown in Figure 10.1. The radio modulates, demodulates and performs the required filtering, amplification and up/down frequency conversions on the signal to provide satisfactory transmission and reception of the data.

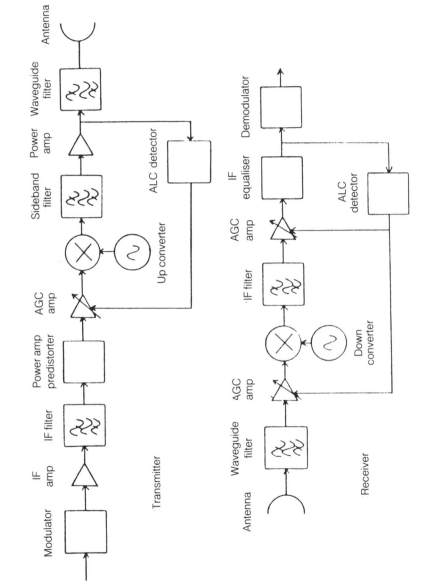

Figure 10.1- Block structure of a typical digital radio.

Some radios may not include all of these elements, or may contain additional components, e.g. additional filtering stages. However, Figure 10.1 shows the outline of a radio which provides the functions of an operational system.

2.2 16-QAM Modulation

There are many types of digital modulation techniques currently in use. All of these alternatives have tradeoffs with regard to bandwidth efficiency, noise immunity and technical realisability. Feher [4] details the currently available spectrally efficient digital modem techniques.

Figure 10.2 shows the two-dimensional amplitude phase diagram of the 16 different signal states of a 16-QAM signal constellation [5]. This diagram illustrates how the 16 different signal states are separated by amplitude and phase. There are three distinct amplitudes ($\sqrt{2}$, $\sqrt{10}$, $3\sqrt{2}$) and 12 distinct signal phase values (18°, 45°, 72°, 108°, 135°, 162°, 198°, 225°, 252°, 288°, 315°, 342°) in a 16-QAM signal constellation.

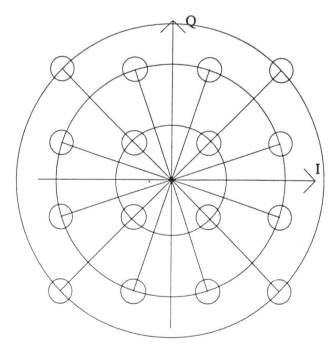

Figure 10.2- 16-QAM constellation showing 3 distinct amplitudes and 12 distinct phases present.

2.3 Fault Sources in Digital Radio

There are many possible sources of faults in digital microwave radio relay equipment. Faults can occur in the channel which include: interference in the form of noise or a specific tone, multipath effects or blockage of the direct path by a solid object such as a building. These channel faults are of considerable importance to the operation of a radio system; they can vary between those which are catastrophic in nature and so prevent any data transmission, or are relatively minor and increase the bit error rate (BER). However, since they are not part of the actual radio equipment, and so are not faults in the transmitter or receiver, these channel impairments will not be discussed further here. This chapter concentrates on the detection and analysis of equipment malfunctions.

In the transmitter and receiver of a digital radio, Figure 10.1, faults can occur in the filtering sections, amplification stages and the quadrature phase splitting during modulation and demodulation. Any of the amplifiers, in either the transmitter or the receiver, can be driven at an incorrect level causing their output signal to be at an unsuitable level which can cause the radio to fail completely or the BER to increase. However, the RF power amplifier in the transmitter, usually a travelling wave tube (TWT) amplifier, will have highly non-linear characteristics and so a small maladjustment of this section will create a large signal distortion. This maladjustment is termed either an amplifier overdrive or underdrive from the preferred level, depending upon the precise input signal levels.

The quadrature splitters, both in the transmitter and the receiver, do not always split the signal by exactly $90°$, and so the two signals may not be truly orthogonal. If the deviation from $90°$ is sufficiently great then a non-orthogonal carrier fault will result.

In the transmitter modulator if either the I or the Q channel 2 to 4 level coder is incorrectly adjusted, one or more of the signal amplitudes (or spacings) will be incorrect. This can occur in either or both channels (I and Q) and will cause the signal at the demodulator output to possess incorrect amplitude and phase information. This fault is termed a gap spacing level error.

Figure 10.3a shows a normal 16-QAM signal constellation. A radio with a 3-dB TWT amplifier overdrive generates a signal constellation as illustrated in Figure 10.3b. This shows how the outermost states of the constellation are rotated clockwise and compressed in amplitude, while the innermost states are contra-rotated and expanded in comparison to the normal signal constellation. Figure 10.3c shows a signal constellation of a radio with a non-orthogonality of the I and Q carriers of 5 degrees. The signal constellation must now be described by a set of parameters which provides a basis for describing the effect of each introduced impairment. The set of constellation features detailed in the next section have been developed to describe the 16-QAM constellation.

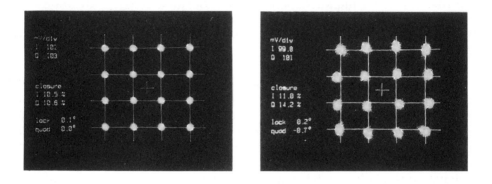

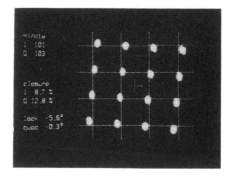

Figure 10.3- (a) Typical 16-QAM signal constellation; (b) with 3-dB TWT overdrive; (c) with 5° carrier non-orthogonality.

2.4 16-QAM Signal Constellation Features

The signal constellation of a 16-QAM digital radio is viewed by a constellation analyser [6] connected to the receiver demodulator. The signal constellation is an amplitude-phase diagram of the position of the signal states and the spread of each of these states. In signal constellations the inphase component lies along the x axis direction and the quadrature component along the y axis direction. The distance from the centre of the constellation (the origin) to each signal state provides a measure of the amplitude of that signal state. The angle formed between the x axis and a line through the origin and the centre of the state is the phase of the signal. The 16-QAM signal has three distinct signal amplitudes and 12 discrete signal phase values to describe the 16 signal states as shown in Figure 10.2.

Human experts who perform fault diagnosis on digital microwave radio use the signal constellation as their information source for the diagnoses. To allow a knowledge-based system to exploit the information in the signal constellation, for digital radio fault diagnosis, a method is required that represents the information in the signal constellation. A geometric feature set was developed to describe the signal constellation using a set of geometric parameters calculated from a set of 16000 signal sample values. The use of approximately 1000 samples per signal state, provides a suitably averaged description of the signal constellation. The geometric features calculated comprise:

(1)   % Expansion of outer states
(2)   % Expansion of inner states
(3)   %I + %Q gap spacing error
(4)   %I - %Q gap spacing error
(5)   Constellation rotation (degrees)
(6)   Differential rotation of inner to outer states (degrees)
(7)   Non-orthogonality of constellation (degrees)
(8)   Ratio of number of inner points to outer points in sample set
(9)   I pool deviation (sum of I squared)
(10)   Q pool deviation (sum of Q squared)
(11)   I Q pool variance (sum of $I \times Q$)
(12)   Correlation coefficient

This geometric feature set primarily describes the location (in amplitude and phase) of the signal states. Faults other than those considered here (e.g. phase jitter) can affect the shape of the signal state. If these faults were to be diagnosed, further geometrical features would be required. The feature set is calculated by first forming two reference squares from those of the eight signal states which are neither among the four innermost or four outermost signal states. The position of each signal state is taken to be the mean position of the cluster of points forming that state. Figure 10.4 shows these two reference squares. These squares are used to help determine the expected amplitudes and phases of the inner and the outer signal states of an undistorted constellation. The calculation of these features is described in detail by Brown [7].

These simply calculated geometric features define the positions of each of the constellation states. They can be used as the information input to a knowledge-based diagnostic system for 16-QAM radio equipment analysis.

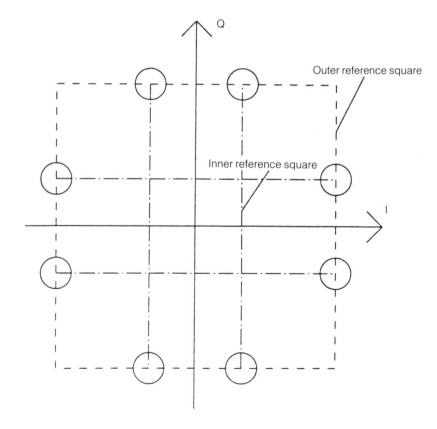

Figure 10.4- Construction of inner and outer reference squares.

3 Rule-Based System

A rule-based system was selected for the task of fault diagnosis in a digital radio. This method was chosen because it is currently the most commonly used technique for implementing diagnostic expert systems, and intuitively rules with a set of conditions for a given conclusion are the most direct solution to this type of problem. Rule-based systems can require a great deal of "expert" knowledge about the problem and can take a long time to produce, but they do provide an understandable solution to the problem. This comprehensibility arises from the ability to examine the actual rules being used to find out how the diagnosis is actually being performed.

3.1 Rule Generation

Certain features formed a distinct relationship to specific fault conditions. Other features, however, demonstrated a less pronounced association with the fault conditions. The TWT power amplifier overdrive and underdrive faults were most closely related to: the outer compression and the inner expansion of the constellation states, and to the differential rotation of the inner and outer constellation states. The geometric features bearing the clearest association to the introduced gap spacing error in the modulator were the I gap and the Q gap spacing errors. The parameter which demonstrated a clear correlation with the introduced non-orthogonality of the I and Q carriers was the non-orthogonality of the signal constellation.

These six geometric features formed the basis for the "generation" of the rules to perform the fault detection and to determine the levels of the faults which are present. Some of the geometric parameters showed such a weak coupling to all of the faults under examination, that it was impossible to extract from them the information about which of the distortions were present. These geometric features were not used to generate any of the rules, but they would be employed to determine other unexamined fault types which affected these parameters in a quantifiable manner. The constellation features which were unused were: the I pool deviation, the Q pool deviation, the IQ pool variance and the correlation coefficient.

The remaining constellation features were used, in conjunction with the features which exhibited a clear relationship to specific faults, to determine whether the radio was well adjusted. A rule was generated which determines if the radio is "normal" (or well adjusted). This is the first test to be carried out on the constellation and it checks that the expected level of each feature within the constellation is, in fact, found. If the radio is established as being correctly adjusted the system will indicate this to the user and terminate its analysis.

To identify the possible fault conditions, it is necessary that rules be written to attribute the variation of specific features to specific fault conditions. This is not a trivial task since the geometric features which vary in a certain manner due to one of the introduced faults can be altered by the presence of another fault. The non-orthogonality of the I and Q carriers and the constellation spacing faults only affect their own determining features. However, when the TWT amplifier overdrive is 6 dB or greater all of the geometric features start to vary. The variation of all of the parameters is caused by incorrect decisions being made about which signal state specific symbols belong to. The changes can aid the correct determination of the level of TWT overdrive, but adversely affect the diagnoses of the other fault types.

There are also rules which provide an explanation of the fault diagnosis that has been performed. The explanatory rules examine which faults are present, and indicate to the user the values of the features which were used to determine the faults.

3.2 Rule-Based System Structure

A structure for the system had to be decided upon. The method an "expert" would use to go about performing the fault diagnosis was first examined. One possible approach an expert might use is a blackborad type structure, where the expert initially forms a hypothesis as to what faults are present and stores this as if on a "blackboard". A set of rules then uses this hypothesis to form a further set of hypotheses on the magnitude of each of the fault conditions which are present. This information is then examined to determine if it agrees with the data available from the signal constellation feature set. If there is any disagreement the process is repeated to alter the non-conforming hypotheses. When the constellation data and the hypotheses agree, the faults, their levels and an explanation of the reasoning behind the diagnosis is given.

The rule-based system written in C has a similar structure to the expert's approach, but without the option to rerun the process to alter incorrect hypotheses. The rule-based system does not have the option to alter hypotheses because all of the information available to the knowledge base is embedded in the rules for generating the diagnoses. The expert probably has additional information which he does not initially use for his diagnosis and this helps him to decide whether the final diagnosis is correct or not. This may be information previously learned (from another expert, literature of experience), or it may be something that was not originally noticed. The rule-based system has to use all the knowledge available in one pass to perform the fault diagnosis, and it has no facility to "learn"; any extension to the operation has to be achieved by physically modifying the rule base. The lack of a built-in "learning" capability is the main operational difference between the C rule-based system and the human "expert".

The system performs its fault diagnosis by initially accessing the signal constellation features which provide the information about the constellation states' geometry, forming the input for the rules. The possible radio conditions are combinations of:

(1) Radio is normal
(2) TWT amplifier overdrive or underdrive
(3) Error in the signal constellation levels
(4) Non-orthogonal I and Q carriers
(5) Unknown fault.

When the features all correspond to the expected values for a normal working radio, the system indicates no fault and ceases processing.

The initial hypothesis about which distortions are present is used as the input for the rules which establish the magnitude of the faults. If there is a TWT amplifier overdrive fault present, its magnitude is estimated from the inner to outer expansion and the inner to outer rotation values. These two features are also used to determine the value of the TWT amplifier underdrive if it is present. TWT amplifier overdrive and underdrive are mutually exclusive fault conditions. The level of spacing error, if present, is estimated using the sum of the I and Q spacing errors when there is no TWT amplifier overdrive. If there is TWT amplifier overdrive and constellation spacing errors, the difference between the I and Q spacing is used to establish the value of the spacing error. To determine the level of the non-orthogonality of carriers the value of the measured non-orthogonality of the signal constellation is used. These should give an estimate of the levels of the faults which have been detected. However, if a fault's presence is indicated, the geometric features may not exactly match the PREMISE of any of the rules detailed above. If this is the case then the next set of rules is triggered.

This set of rules will estimate the level of the faults using a subset of the information available from the signal constellation features. The confidence in the conclusions of these rules is not as great as the confidence in the previous set of rules since some information has been ignored. These rules use the geometric feature which has the strongest dependence on the introduced distortion.

When all of the distortions which are present and their levels have been established, the rules which provide an explanation of the fault diagnosis are implemented. These rules detail the determining features of each detected distortion. When the indicated faults have been identified, their levels and explanations of the diagnosis are output to the user to aid decisions about what remedial action should be taken. The explanations are included to permit the user to make a separate evaluation of the diagnosis. If he disagrees with any aspect of the system's conclusions, then different action from the recommended can be taken.

This structure for the system was chosen as it seemed a "natural" way to perform the diagnosis, while still remaining relatively easy to implement in C. By partitioning the rule base into sets of rules, which put forward hypotheses about the faults and their levels, the ordering of the rules was simplified. The various sets of rules also ensured that the addition and modification of rules would be less complicated than if one large rule set had been used. This follows because the rules in each rule set take the problem only one step further without involving complicated interactions between rules. The transfer of information between rule sets is performed by the intermediate hypotheses, with the outputs from one set forming the inputs to another rule set.

This modular approach provided a workable technique for producing a rule-based expert system for performing the fault diagnosis. The constellation data and the required quantization levels form the input to the program. The rules are of the form:

If PREMISE then CONCLUSION

Where the PREMISE can be any combination of conjunctions and disjunctions of propositions, and the CONCLUSION is a combination of conjunctions of conclusions.

3.3 Performance of the Rule-Based System

The main elements of a 16-QAM radio were modelled using two HP 4948A analysers [8], one as the transmitter and one as the receiver. This model is described in detail by Brown [7]. The simulation of the radio was used to assess the performance of the diagnostic knowledge-based systems. Impairments were deliberately introduced into the model and the diagnoses from the knowledge-based systems was compared to the introduced faults.

The rule-based system was tested with a variety of introduced fault conditions. Initially the testing examined the performance when diagnosing faults on the radio model with only one distortion type present at any given time. The faults investigated were: TWT amplifier overdrive and underdrive, non-orthogonality of the I and Q carriers and errors in the constellation spacing levels. Table 10.1 summarizes the results obtained from single fault condition tests. The system was seen to correctly identify all of these fault conditions.

The system was then tested with combinations of two faults introduced at one time. These results are detailed in Table 10.2. Finally, the performance of the rule-based system was examined with three simultaneously occurring faults. Table 10.3 details the results obtained from the system for three faults present at one time.

The single fault conditions were all correctly detected by the rule-based system for all the ranges tested. The TWT amplifier overdrive and underdrive faults were detected in 2-dB steps over the full range. With an 8-dB or 6-dB TWT amplifier overdrive a spacing error was also indicated but with a value of 0%. The non-orthogonal I and Q carrier faults were correctly identified over the range 0 degrees to 5 degrees in 1-degree steps. However, for a 5-degree non-orthogonality a spacing error of 0% was again indicated. The spacing errors were correctly detected from -10% to +10% in 1% steps, while a non-orthogonal carrier fault of 0 degrees was specified. Thus the rule-based approach correctly detected all the individually present faults. In certain cases additional faults were indicated as occurring, but with zero level.

The detection of the multiple fault conditions, including both double and triple fault conditions, was not as accurate as that of the single fault conditions. For the cases where there was no TWT amplifier overdrive of 6 dB or greater, the diagnoses of the radio condition were as accurate as for singly occurring faults. However, for multiple faults with TWT amplifier overdrive of 6 dB or more there were some errors. The system always specified the correct level of TWT amplifier overdrive, but the other faults were erroneously diagnosed. The presence of the other faults was detected, but their levels were incorrectly identified. This problem arises from the fact that the high levels of TWT amplifier overdrive affect the features which were used to determine the other fault conditions. The features that establish the TWT amplifier overdrive were not sensitive to the levels of the other faults present.

Faults	Abbreviation and units
Non-orthogonal carriers	NOC degrees
Gap spacing	GS %
TWT overdive	OD dB
TWT underdrive	UD dB

Faults Introduced	Faults Detected
NOC 1	NOC 1
NOC 3	NOC 3
NOC 5	NOC 5, GS 0
GS -9	GS -9, NOC 0
GS -6	GS -6, NOC 0
GS -3	GS -3, NOC 0
GS 3	GS 3, NOC 0
GS 6	GS 6, NOC 0
GS 9	GS 9, NOC 0
OD 8	OD 8, GS 0
OD 6	OD 6, GS 0
OD 4	OD 4
OD 2	OD 2
UD 2	UD 2
UD 4	UD 4
UD 6	UD 6
UD 8	UD 8

Table 10.1- The output of the rule-based system for diagnosing single fault conditions. Abbreviations: NOC non-orthogonal carriers (degree), GS gap spacing (%), OD TWT overdrive and UD TWT underdrive (dB).

Faults Introduced	Faults Detected
GS 3, NOC 3	GS 3, NOC 3
UD 4, NOC 3	UD 4, NOC 3
OD 8, NOC 3	OD 8, NOC 0, GS 1
OD 2, NOC 3	OD 2, NOC 3, GS 0
OD 6, NOC 3	OD 6, NOC 2, GS -4
UD 4, NOC 1	UD 4, NOC 1
OD 8, NOC 1	OD 8, NOC 0, GS 0
UD 4, GS 6	UD 4, GS 6, NOC 0
OD 2, GS 6	OD 2, GS 6, NOC 0
OD 6, GS 6	OD 6, GS 5, NOC 0
OD 8, GS 6	OD 8, GS 1, NOC 0
UD 4, GS 3	UD 4, GS 3, NOC 0
OD 2, GS 3	OD 2, GS 3, NOC 0
OD 6, GS 3	OD 6, GS 2, NOC 0
OD 8, GS 3	OD 8, GS 1, NOC 0

Table 10.2- The output of the rule-based system for diagnosing double fault conditions. Abbreviations: as in Table 10.1.

Faults Introduced	Faults Detected
OD 2, GS 9, NOC 1	OD 2, GS 9, NOC 1
OD 6, GS 3, NOC 3	OD 6, GS 0, NOC 2
OD 6, GS 6, NOC 1	OD 6, GS 6, NOC 1
OD 8, GS 3, NOC 3	OD 8, GS 2, NOC 0
OD 2, GS 3, NOC 3	OD 2, GS 1, NOC 3

Table 10.3- The output of the rule-based system for diagnosing triple fault conditions. Abbreviations: as in Table 10.1.

4 Machine Learning System (MLS)

Knowledge-based systems in general require a considerable amount of work from a knowledge engineer to imbed in the system the information that is required to perform the specified task. The great effort needed will not necessarily prove prohibitive to the system construction if there are many identical units required, or the benefits accrued from one or a few units are considerable. However, certain applications require many similar systems (units with the same structure but different contents of their knowledge-bases) to cover all of the different uses of the system. This is the case for fault diagnosis of 16-QAM digital radios. There are many different types of 16-QAM radio, each of which could use the same structure of system to perform the fault diagnoses, but would require slightly different knowledge bases.

One method of overcoming the problem of the quantity of work required from a knowledge engineer is to produce a system of a suitable structure which can generate its own knowledge base. This is termed a machine learning system and the "learning", or creation of the knowledge base, is performed by training the system on specific examples of fault conditions. A machine learning system requires work by a knowledge engineer to produce a satisfactory structure for the system, and operation initially in a training mode to encode the information into the system.

The machine learning system uses techniques from two separate areas: distance classifiers from geometry and pattern analysis [6], and a recursive least squares (RLS) algorithm from adaptive filtering [10]. The structure of the machine learning system, and the ways in which the distance classifier and adaptive filtering techniques are implemented within the structure, are detailed in Chapter 5.

4.1 Performance of the (MLS) on a Real Radio

The machine learning system was tested on a real radio in the laboratory. The digital radio used was an 11-GHz (16-QAM) digital radio looped back at RF. The constellation data was collected using a constellation analyser (HP3709) directly connected to the I and Q monitor points of the radio receiver demodulator. A data signal was provided by the radio's 17-stage pseudo-random binary sequence (PRBS) scrambler. The machine learning system was trained on a set of four deliberately introduced quantified faults. The training was performed by altering the settings on the pre-set potentiometers by a specific number of turns, or by adding external filters to the receiver IF section to introduce known amounts of passband asymmetry into a correctly set up radio. Four types of fault were introduced: output amplifier overdrive; phase-lock potentiometer out of adjustment; quadrature capacitor maladjustment; and an asymmetry in the receiver's IF filters. The output amplifier overdrive was measured using an external power meter; the turns of the phase-lock potentiometer and the quadrature capacitor were assessed by eye; and the bandpass filter was adjusted off-line using a separate system with different instrumentation.

After training on these faults, the system was connected to the radio with an arbitrary set of introduced faults. This was done for several sets of faults and when the adjustments recommended by the system were completed the radio was again correctly set up. The output from the machine learning system was a graphical bar display of the faults which indicated the distance of the radio under test from a correctly aligned radio. Figure 10.5 shows the output from the machine learning system (which has been trained on four fault types) connected to a maladjusted radio. The adjustments recommended by the machine learning system correspond exactly to the deliberately introduced impairments. The output of the machine learning system when connected to the radio with the appropriate adjustments completed indicated no impairments present.

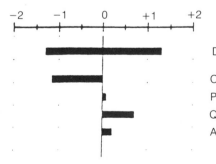

Radio well conditioned

Distance from radios which passed BER test

Output overdriven (1 unit = 2dB overdrive)
Phase-lock pot adjustment (1 unit = ½ turn)
Quadrature capacitor adjustment (1 unit = ¼ turn)
Asymmetry in bandpass filter

Figure 10.5- The output of the MLS connected to a maladjusted radio.

These results demonstrate that the machine learning system can deal with several simultaneously occurring faults and accurately determine their levels. These faults all formed tolerably linear relationships with their input feature sets, making them suitable candidates for use with the linear combiners. Fault conditions which exhibit a highly non-linear relationship with the input features would not have been so accurately detected.

4.2 Tests of the MLS on the Digital Radio Model

The machine learning system's performance was tested with the same data used to test the rule-based system in Section 10.3. The same ranges of each impairment were investigated. First, the system was tested with only one fault present at one time; these results are shown in Table 10.4. Then combinations of two simultaneous impairments were tested; these results are summarized in Table 10.5. Finally the performance of the machine learning system was tested with three faults occurring at once; these findings are detailed in Table 10.6.

Faults Introduced	Faults Detected
NOC 1	NOC 0.5
NOC 3	NOC 2.5
NOC 5	NOC 5.4
GS -9	GS -9
GS -6	GS -6
GS -3	GS -2.5, UD 0.7
GS 3	GS 3, UD 0.5
GS 6	GS 6
GS 9	GS 9
OD 8	OD 8.1
OD 6	OD 6.6
OD 4	OD 4.2
OD 2	OD 2.1, GS 0.4
UD 2	UD 1.4
UD 4	UD 3.4
UD 6	UD 5.4
UD 8	UD 7.5

Table 10.4- The output of the MLS for diagnosing single fault conditions. Abbreviations: as in Table 10.1.

Faults Introduced	Faults Detected
GS 3, NOC 3	GS 3.3, NOC 3
UD 4, NOC 3	UD 3.4, NOC 2.4
OD 8, NOC 3	OD 16, NOC -10
OD 2, NOC 3	OD 2, NOC 1.9
OD 6, NOC 3	OD 2, GS 10.1
UD 4, NOC 1	UD 3.3, NOC 0.5
OD 8, NOC 1	OD 3.6, GS 4
UD 4, GS 6	UD 3.2, GS 6
OD 2, GS 6	OD 2.6, GS 4.8
OD 6, GS 6	OD 1.8, GS 16, NOC 2
OD 8, GS 6	OD 10.5, GS 7.5, NOC 0.8
UD 4, GS 3	UD 3.5, GS 1.5
OD 2, GS 3	OD 1.3, GS 1.3
OD 6, GS 3	OD -1.3, GS 9.8
OD 8, GS 3	OD 3.5, GS 10, NOC 1.1

Table 10.5- The output of the MLS for diagnosing double fault conditions. Abbreviations: as in Table 10.1.

Faults Introduced	Faults Detected
OD 2, GS 9, NOC 1	OD 3, GS 7.5, NOC 0
OD 6, GS 3, NOC 3	OD 1, GS 8, NOC 0.6
OD 6, GS 6, NOC 1	OD 10, GS 1.5, NOC 0.3
OD 8, GS 3, NOC 3	OD 3.7, GS -1, NOC 0.2
OD 2, GS 3, NOC 3	OD 1, GS 2.5, NOC 2

Table 10.6- The output of the MLS for diagnosing triple fault conditions. Abbreviations: as in Table 10.1.

The machine learning system indicated the correct level of the single TWT amplifier faults to within 1 dB for an overdrive of 8 dB through to an underdrive of 8 dB. The levels of the non-orthogonality of the I and Q carriers for single faults were detected to within 1I of the actual level. The levels estimated for single spacing errors were within 0.5% of the introduced error. The differences between the output of the system and the introduced fault levels arose from errors caused by the approximations used in the selected filter tap weight algorithm.

With multiple introduced fault conditions the machine learning system's performance degraded significantly. Fault estimates of multiple impairments which included high levels of TWT overdrive proved very unreliable. Estimates were up to: 8 dB in error for the TWT overdrive level; 10% in error for the signal constellation spacing fault; and up to 3I in error for the level of the non-orthogonality of the I and Q carriers. The fault detection for the cases with TWT underdrive or only low levels of TWT amplifier overdrive, 2 dB to 4 dB, were much better except that the system always failed to detect low levels of spacing error because the training sequence included high levels of TWT overdrive. These errors in the multiple fault cases were caused by the non-linear changes in the feature set versus fault relationships for certain fault levels. The nature of the adaptive combiners, which are linear classifiers, does not permit them accurately to model these non-linear relationships.

5 Hybrid System

The machine learning and the rule-based systems both provide solutions to the problem of fault diagnosis for digital microwave radio equipment, using the signal constellation geometric features as the information source. The geometric parameters accurately represent the positions of the signal states of a 16-QAM signal constellation, and from these features the faults present can be diagnosed. Faults which do not affect the signal constellation (faults in the slicer and decoder circuitry) are undetectable using these systems and extra information would be required to correctly diagnose them.

The rule-based system requires much work by a knowledge engineer, examining the relationships between the faults in the radio equipment and the changes in the geometric features. Once these relationships have been established the knowledge engineer has to write a set of rules (in an appropriate form for the system) which express these relationships. The number of rules required increases as the required accuracy of the diagnoses is increased. The work by the knowledge engineer is appreciable; moreover, it must be repeated for each different type of 16-QAM digital radio that the system is used with. The rules written for one specific type of 16-QAM radio would not necessarily work when applied to a different type of 16-QAM radio.

The machine learning system also requires to be trained separately on each type of radio with which is it used. However, this training needs only a few examples of each fault condition, and this can be performed in a few minutes. The training of the machine learning system will not produce a working system if it is trained on highly non-linear fault/feature relationships. This limitation of the machine learning system restricts the variety of fault conditions that the system can correctly diagnose.

The rule-based and the machine learning systems complement each other, with the areas of weakness of one system being the areas of strength of the other system.

Without developing any new techniques, or using any other methods than those already detailed, an improved system is possible. This would take advantage of the robustness of the rule-based system to non-linear fault/feature relationships, and the accuracy, fine tuning capabilities and ease of training of the machine learning system. A hybrid of the two systems was formulated which consisted of a combination of the conventional rule-based approach and of the machine learning system. The overall structure of the system remained the same as that of the machine learning system, described in Chapter 5. However, the adaptive algorithm section of the system also contains some rules as well as the adaptive combiners. The structure of this new section, which replaces the adaptive combiner section of the machine learning system, is detailed in Figure 10.6.

The rules are used to determine the level of the fault conditions which exhibit a non-linear fault/feature relationship. If these rules establish that there is a fault corresponding to a non-linear relationship, then the level of the fault is output and no more analysis is performed by the system. However, if only faults corresponding to linear fault/feature relationships are present, the system continues on to the adaptive algorithm and proceeds with the processing as in the unmodified machine learning system.

The combination of the two systems in this form provides several advantages. The size of the rule base and therefore the amount of work required to be done by the knowledge engineer is less. Rules are only required to cover the faults corresponding to non-linear relationships which are a small subset of all of the faults under examination. These rules prevent the adaptive processing section of the system having to make diagnoses from non-linear fault/feature relationships. The adaptive algorithms provide an accurate fault diagnosis of faults with linear fault/feature relationships and the rules limit the adaptive section to these cases. If there are no non-linear conditions among the faults being examined, then the rule base is left empty and the system reverts to the machine learning system. If rules are required the knowledge engineer will be required to write them, and then train the machine learning system in the conventional manner. On the one hand, the work required by the knowledge engineer is greater than if no rules were used and it was left simply as the machine learning system; on the other hand, considerably less effort is needed than that required to produce a complete rule-based system.

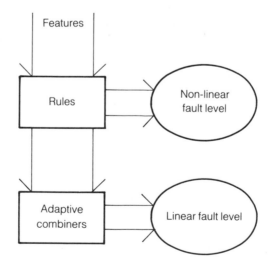

Figure 10.6- The structure of the hybrid system.

The benefits of this system are that first, it does not have to be limited to purely linear relationships as the machine learning system does and secondly, it can provide more accurate results than the rule-based system (without a very large number of rules and a great amount of work by the knowledge engineer). This approach does mean that for those cases where there is a non-linear fault the system will have to use two passes to diagnose all of the faults fully. On the first pass the non-linear condition will be diagnosed, and then corrected; the second pass will diagnose the remaining faults. However, this penalty is small compared to the greater range of conditions that can be treated by such a system.

5.1 Performance of the Hybrid System

The performance of the hybrid system was examined by testing it on a variety of induced fault conditions on the radio model. The results of these tests are summarized in Table 10.7. This system correctly diagnoses all of the TWT overdrive faults of 6 dB or greater without attempting to establish the levels of any of the other faults present. This method, which circumvents the problem of determining the other faults present when there is a high level of TWT overdrive, allows the number of rules needed for the system to be kept to a minimum. However, it does mean that a two-step process is required for the radio to be correctly adjusted. If initially there was only a TWT overdrive fault present, then the second examination of the radio by the system will show the radio as functioning correctly.

The performance of the system for detecting the remaining fault conditions (TWT overdrive up to 6 dB, TWT underdrive, spacing errors and non-orthogonality of carriers) proved excellent. The errors in the diagnoses remained constant for detecting single or multiple occurring faults. The results indicate that a radio could quickly and reliably be returned to correct adjustment provided the only faults present were those upon which the system had been previously trained.

6 Conclusions

Two separate approaches to implementing a diagnostic expert system (rule-based and machine learning methods) were examined and then combined to generate a third technique.

Faults Introduced	Faults Detected
NOC 1	NOC 0.5
NOC 3	NOC 3.5
NOC 5	NOC 4.8
GS -9	GS -9.5
GS -6	GS -5.9
GS -3	GS -3
GS 3	GS 3.1
GS 6	GS 5.8
GS 9	GS 9.8
OD 8	OD 8
OD 6	OD 6
OD 4	OD 3
OD 2	OD 1.7
UD 2	UD 1.9
UD 4	UD 3.1
UD 6	UD 5
UD 8	UD 9
OD 2, NOC 1, GS 9	OD 0.9, NOC 1.4, GS 9
OD 2, GS 3	OD 1.5, GS 2
OD 2, GS 6	OD 1.5, GS 6
UD 4, NOC 1	UD 3, NOC 0.5
UD 4, NOC 3	UD 3.4, NOC 3.2
UD 4, GS 3	UD 2.9, GS 2.8
UD 4, GS 6	UD 2.8, GS 5.8
OD 8, NOC 1	OD 8
OD 8, NOC 3, GS 3	OD 8
OD 8, GS 3	OD 8
OD 8, GS 6	OD 8
OD 6, NOC 1, GS 6	OD 6
OD 6, NOC 3	OD 6
OD 6, GS -3, NOC 3	OD 6
OD 6, GS 3	OD 6
OD 6, GS 6	OD 6
GS -3, NOC 3	GS -3, NOC 3

Table 10.7- Summary of the performance of the hybrid system.

Producing the ordered rules was a very slow process but, when completed, the system correctly diagnosed the faults present in the radio model under test. However, the accuracy of the diagnoses by the system was dependent upon the number of rules used. To increase the accuracy of the diagnosis of the faults in the radio, therefore, the stepsize between the estimates of the distortion levels made by the rules would have to be decreased. Almost any specified precision could be achieved, but at the expense of additional work by the knowledge engineer producing more rules. A rudimentary explanatory facility, consisting of a set of rules, was provided by the rule-based system.

It would be possible to diagnose other faults in a digital radio, apart from those examined, using the rule-based system. However, these faults would have to exhibit a clear unambiguous relationship between their magnitudes and the constellation features to permit rules to be written which estimate the fault levels from the feature set.

The second approach, using the machine learning system, was based on two separate techniques: a distance classifier and an adaptive filtering algorithm. The machine learning system was trained with data from the digital radio model. Its performance proved very poor when used to diagnose faults which included TWT overdrives of 6 dB or greater. This poor performance was caused by the non-linear relationship between high levels of TWT overdrive and the feature set. When limited to fault levels which did not form such non-linear associations within the feature set (TWT overdrives < 6 dB), the accuracy of the diagnoses made by the machine learning system was excellent and the training of the system was proved to be quick and simple.

The machine learning system was tested to evaluate its performance when used to diagnose faults in an actual radio. It correctly diagnosed the faults which had been deliberately introduced into the radio. None of the ranges of faults examined formed highly non-linear relationships with the feature sets. This limited the machine learning system to its efficient area of operation, thus producing accurate diagnoses of the fault conditions.

As with the rule-based system, the machine learning system could diagnose faults other than those already examined provided that they formed an unambiguous relationship within the feature set. If such a relationship did not exist, then additional features would have to be found. Additional constraints set by the machine learning system were that only faults exhibiting linear fault/feature relationships could be accurately diagnosed, and no explanatory facility to give the user information about the rationale behind each individual diagnosis was provided, although it should be noted that this has subsequently been developed, see Chapter 5.

Whilst the rule-based and machine learning systems both provided solutions to the problem of fault diagnosis of digital microwave radio equipment, each had its own limitations.

The strengths of these two techniques clearly complement each other, and this led to the choice of a hybrid system which combined both approaches. This hybrid system uses a small set of rules that diagnose those faults which exhibit strong non-linear relationships with the feature set. The machine learning system is thus partitioned from certain fault conditions to ensure its performance remains high. The work required to produce this hybrid for one particular radio type is greater than for the machine learning system, but is considerably less than for the rule-based system. The performance of the hybrid system proved to be excellent in diagnosing the faults in the radio model.

This work has demonstrated that it is possible to produce a knowledge-based diagnostic system for 16-QAM digital radio relay equipment. If the faults considered are limited to those which do not form highly non-linear relationships within the feature set, then the machine learning system is the most effective solution. However, if this constraint is not possible, then the hybrid system provides an excellent alternative.

The knowledge-based techniques provided valuable tools for performing the fault diagnosis of 16-QAM digital radio relay equipment. However, there is much further work required to develop and refine these methods before they could be used with actual radio equipment to perform all of their required tasks.

Before these knowledge-based techniques could be applied to an actual radio it would be necessary to ensure that the data (or information source) detailing the faults under examination adequately described all of the faults. The data used is the feature set and it must be expanded to form a more complete set which could be used to provide the required information for diagnosing a comprehensive set of fault conditions.

References

[1]   K. Feher, *Digital Communications Satellite/Earth Station Engineering* , Prentice Hall, New Jersey, 1983.

[2]   C.P Tou & D.A. Roy, "On Efficient Spectrum Utilization From the Standpoint of Communication Theory", *Proc. IEEE* , **Vol-68**, No. 12, pp 1460-1465, December 1980.

[3]   F. Amoroso, "The Bandwidth of Digital Data Signals", *IEEE Communications Magazine* , **No. 18-19**, pp 13-24, November 1980.

[4]   K. Feher, *Advanced Digital Communications* , Prentice Hall, New Jersey, 1987.

[5]   J.G. Proakis, *Digital Communications* , McGraw-Hill, New York, 1983.

[6]   D.J. Haworth, J.R. Pottinger & M.J. McKissock, "Dedicated Display Monitors Digital Radio Patterns", *Hewlett Packard Journal* , **Vol-38**, No-7, pp 4-13, July 1987.

[7]   K.E. Brown, "The Application of Knowledge-Based Techniques to Fault Diagnosis of 16-QAM Digital Microwave radio Equipment", Ph.D. Thesis, Dept. of Electrical Engineering, University of Edinburgh, 1988.

[8]   N. Carder, W.I. Dunn, J.H. Elliot, D.W. Grieve & G.W. Rhind, "In-service Transmission Impairment Testing of Voice Frequency Data Circuits", *Hewlett Packard Journal* , pp 4-15, October 1987.

[9]   B.S. Tze, *Pattern Recognition* , Marcel Dekker, 1984.

[10] C.F.N. Cowan & P.M. Grant, *Adaptive Filters* , Prentice-Hall, 1985.

Chapter 11

Waveguide Filter Alignment

A.R. Mirzai

1 Introduction

In many areas of manufacturing, there is a need to automate the procedures of fault diagnosis, adjustments and calibration. Historically, fault diagnosis and calibration have been carried out manually by skilled operators. This approach is very time consuming and expensive.

In recent years, intelligent systems have been successfully employed to carry out these tests and release skilled operators for other jobs. Chapter 10 illustrated the application of an expert system (ES) and a machine learning system (MLS) for the fault diagnosis of microwave digital radios. This chapter looks at the application of the MLS for the tuning of waveguide filters (WGFs). These filters are used in a wide range of communication systems for tailoring signals both during and after transmission.

The rest of the chapter is divided into four main sections. In Section 2 we consider the design, construction and manual tuning of WGFs. The adaptation of the MLS for the tuning of WGFs is described in Section 3 where we also discuss the feature extraction technique used. Section 4 presents some results and finally Section 5 discusses the limitation of this approach and ways for improving its performance.

2 Waveguide Filters (WGFs)

Waveguide filters (WGFs) are tuned once the filters have been assembled. The traditional approach to the tuning of these filters is to check the response of the filter at a number of critical frequencies and adjust a set of tuning screws in order to bring the filter response within some pre-defined specification. This procedure is carried out manually and can be thought of as a humanly performed real-time optimization. This tuning method is very time consuming, expensive and a skilled operator is required. Therefore automatic tuning of these filters would be a more desirable and cost effective alternative. In spite of the wide range of applications for waveguide filters, there have not been many contributions to the studies of computer aided alignment of WGFs. In the previous publications, people have described standard procedures for manual tuning of these filters [1-3], but these methods are not suitable for constructing a computer-based tuning system. Work on computer aided filter alignment has been very limited [4] and these methods are predominantly based on theoretical treatment and modelling of the filters.

Figure 11.1 shows the plan view and the cross section of a six cavity WGF. There are two types of screws. One type are the six tuning screws, bigger in size, and the other type are the seven coupling screws. The tuning screws are used to move the resonant frequencies of the corresponding cavities. The coupling screws between the two cavities are used to couple the adjacent cavities and the two end coupling screws are used to couple the filter to the outside word.

The effect of the tuning screws is much higher than the coupling screws and in some WGFs the coupling screws are not included. In general the coupling screws are used to compensate for any structural errors due to the manufacturing of the filters.

The design of a WGF involves the calculation of the WGF dimensions, i.e. a, b, c and d in Figure 11.1b. There are many different techniques for calculating these values [5-7]. Having got the WGF dimensions the next stage is to construct the physical filter. This is done by feeding the WGF dimensions into a numerically controlled machining process. In fact the design and the construction of the WGF are fully automated and require no expertise. After the filters are constructed, the next stage is to tune the filter for a certain set of specifications. The usual set of specifications are:

(1) centre frequency (Hz)
(2) bandwidth (Hz)
(3) insertion loss (dBs).

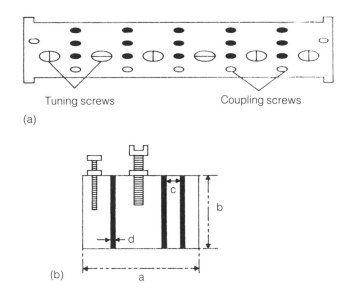

Figure 11.1- 6 cavity waveguide filter, (a) top view and (b) cross section.

A typical response of a WGF is given in Figure 11.2. Figure 11.2a illustrates the Log magnitude characteristics of the S_{11} of the filter, i.e. the reflection of the transmitted signal from the input of the filter, and Figure 11.2b shows the polar plot of S_{11}. The polar plot includes both the Log magnitude and the phase information of the filter.

The filters used for this study were supplied by Ferranti at Dundee in Scotland. As mentioned, the design and the construction of the filters are fully automated and in the production environment, the operator tunes the filters manually by looking at the log magnitude of S_{11}. The procedure adopted at Ferranti for the manual tuning of these filters can be summarized as follows.

(1)   All the screws are removed.

(2)   The tuning screws are inserted one at a time starting from the input to the filter. Each time a screw is inserted, it is turned clockwise to bring the resonant frequency of the corresponding cavity within the filter bandwidth.

(3)   When all the tuning screws are inserted, there must be n resonant frequencies in the passband, where n is equal to the number of cavities in the filter. Thus each tuning screw corresponds to a notch in Figure 11.2a. However, the return loss characteristic of

the filter does not always show all the resonant frequencies clearly. At this stage, the tuning screws are adjusted to minimize the return loss response of the filter as far as possible before the coupling screws are inserted.

(4)   Finally, the coupling screws are inserted. At this stage the operator needs to adjust all the screws in such a way that the S_{11} of the filter meets all the customer specifications.

This process can be divided into two main stages. In the first stage, the operator performs a rough tuning of the filter to bring the response of the filter close to the specifications. This stage can be done quickly and easily and does not require any skill. The second stage of the tuning process involves fine adjustments of the screws to meet the specification. This stage requires great amount of expertise and most of the tuning time is taken by this stage.

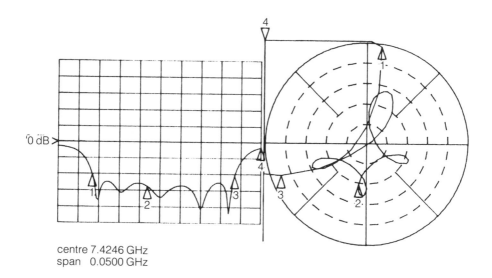

centre 7.4246 GHz
span 0.0500 GHz

Figure 11.2- S_{11} polar and log magnitude characteristics of a good filter. For the log magnitude, vertical scale is 10 dB per division and horizontal scale 5 MHz per division. Centre line corresponds to 0 dB return loss. For polar plot, return loss is displayed radically from the centre on a linear scale and phase information is measured as angular rotation from the right hand horizontal axis. Filter centre frequency = 7.4256 GHz, bandwidth = 35.0 MHz and minimum loss = -24.48dB.

3 Intelligent Filter Tuning

The adaptation of the MLS for fault diagnosis in microwave digital radio was described in the previous chapter and WGFs are chosen as another application for this system. There are two main reasons for this choice. One is the fact that these filters are very sensitive to small maladjustment of their tuning screws and there is a high level of interaction between the screws. Therefore it provides a challenging problem for the MLS. The second reason is the fact that these filters take a very long time to be tuned manually. As a typical example, a six-cavity filter would take approximately 35-45 minutes to be tuned by a skilled operator. Therefore there is a demand for a computer-based filter tuning system with the objectives of reducing the tuning time and not requiring a skilled operator to tune the filter.

The principle of the MLS, as described in Chapter 5, is based on the manipulation of some raw data to extract a set of salient features which have strong relationship to the behaviour of the filter. These features are derived visually by comparing the characteristics of a tuned filter with a faulty filter with known level of maladjustments. Therefore, the first two steps in the adaptation of the MLS to this problem, are to decide on a reference characteristic for the filter and a set of salient features.

When WGFs are tuned manually, the log magnitude of S_{11} is taken as a reference and the specifications of the filter are based on this characteristic. However the information in the log magnitude of S_{11} is not sufficient. In other words, there may be a filter whose log magnitude meets all the specifications but it has very poor group delay and phase characteristics. Thus, it has been decided to take the polar plot of S_{11} as the reference characteristic for the WGFs, since it contains both the log magnitude and the phase information (Figure 11.2).

The manual tuning of the WGFs was described in the previous sections. This procedure can be divided into two main stages. In the first stage the operator performs a rough tuning of the filter using a standard procedure while in the second stage the operator needs to finely adjust the screws so that the filter response meets all the customers specifications. The fine tuning of the filter takes most of the time due to the sensitivity of the filter and high level of interaction between the screws. Therefore it has been decided to let the operator perform the rough tuning of the filter and in next section we illustrate how the combiners of the MLS has been adapted to perform the fine tuning of the filter. It must be mentioned here that due to this sensitivity and interaction it is not possible to use a classical ES approach since the relationships between the screws and the filter response cannot be defined explicitly. For the adaptive combiners it is not necessary to define these relationships since the combiners learn them by looking at a number of feature sets and the corresponding desired values for the screws.

3.1 Use of Adaptive Combiners

It has been decided to take the polar plot of S_{11} as the reference characteristic for the filter. Now we need to decide on a set of salient features which will be used in the system. Let us now assume that the polar plot in Figure 11.3a meets all the specifications. In order to decide on a feature set, it is necessary to investigate the effects on this polar plot when the tuning screws are maladjusted from their correct positions. Figure 11.3b-d show the polar plots of S_{11} for maladjustment of selected tuning screws. The rest of the screws have very similar effects. From these polar plots we can conclude the following points,

    (1)   Figure 11.3b illustrates translation of the polar plot,
                i.e. the geometric mean of the polar plot has moved.
    (2)   Figure 11.3c illustrates deformation and compression of
                the polar plot, i.e. the circular shape of the polar
                plot has been deformed into a elliptical shape.
    (3)   Figure 11.3d illustrates the expansion and the contraction
                of the loops in the polar plot.

The salient features which are selected to describe these geometric changes are as follows,

    (1)   Position of the mean of the polar plot, two features (x and y
                coordinates).
    (2)   Position of the beginning and the end of the polar plot,
                four features (two x-coordinates and two y-coordinates).
    (3)   Centre frequency of the filter, one feature.
    (4)   Area of the loops, (n-1) features.
    (5)   Distance between the centre of the loops, (n-1) features.

Where n is the order of the filter, i.e. number of cavities. These features are calculated using the real and the imaginary parts of S_{11}. The feature extraction technique is described in detail in the following section.

3.2 Feature Extraction

Figure 11.4 illustrates how the filters have been connected to a commercial network analyser (Hewlett Packard 8510). The analyser communicates with a HP300 series computer through a HP-IB interface cable. The network analyser provides the real and imaginary parts of the polar plot, i.e. x and y coordinates, in a discrete form. These points are manipulated in order to generate the features listed in the previous section.

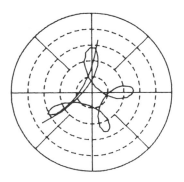

a) good filter

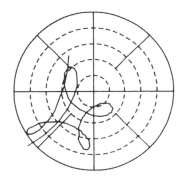

b) 1 anti-clockwise

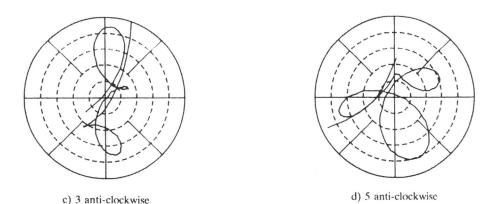

c) 3 anti-clockwise

d) 5 anti-clockwise

Figure 11.3- (a) S_{11} polar characteristics of a good filter; (b), (c) and (d) polar plots of S_{11} with selected anti-clockwise maladjustment of individual tuning screws.

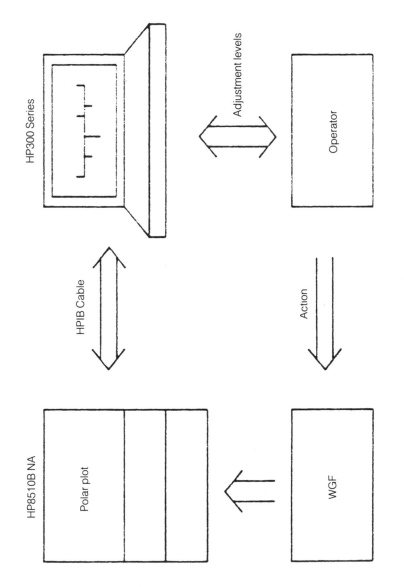

HP300 Series

HP8510B NA

Polar plot

HPIB Cable

Adjustment levels

Operator

Action

WGF

Figure 11.4 Schematic diagram of the instrumentation configuration used in the WGF tuning application.

The computer spans the pass band of the filter and collects between 60 and 101 points. The mean of the polar plot can be calculated by averaging the x-y coordinates of the polar plot. The beginning and the end of the polar plot correspond to the first and the second edge frequencies of the filter. The area of the loops are calculated by first estimating the points of intersections in the polar plot and then by performing numerical integration over the loops. A number of different techniques have been used to estimate the point of intersections in the polar plot. The Appendix describes one technique which generated the intersection points for all the different shapes of the polar plot. After obtaining the points of intersection, the centre of the loops can be found by averaging the x-y coordinates for each loop. The distance between the centres of the loops can then be found using the coordinates of the loop centres.

The data collection and feature extraction part of the MLS takes about 35 seconds to complete. The time taken by the adaptive combiners to come up with a set of adjustments is negligible compared to the above time. Thus, a new adjustment can be made by the operator in under one minute.

3.3 Learning and Use Mode

As mentioned in the previous sections, the MLS is capable of learning the relationships between the screws and the response of the filter by looking at a number of feature sets with their corresponding desired values. This is achieved by first tuning a filter to meet the required specifications. The features listed in the previous section are extracted from the polar plot of the tuned filter and presented to the combiners. The desired values for all the screws at this stage should be set equal to zero since no adjustment is required. Then each screw is maladjusted in both clockwise and anti-clockwise direction and the desired value for the maladjusted screw is set equal to -1 and +1 respectively while the desired values of the other screws are set equal to zero. This will provide 13 feature sets for the training mode. It must be mentioned here that the training of the MLS is performed in real time when the filter is connected to the network analyser and the computer. In other words, once a screw is maladjusted the MLS is presented with the feature set and the corresponding desired values for the screws and then the recursive least squares (RLS) algorithm is applied to estimate the new value of the weight matrix for the combiners (Chapter 5).

In the use mode the MLS provides the operator with a graphical display of the adjustment levels for each of the screws which gives the magnitude and the direction of the adjustments, the number of iterations, the maximum error and the screw which has generated the maximum error. At any time the operator can ask the system to provide him with the values of the centre frequency, bandwidth and the insertion loss of the filter. This enables him to stop the tuning process as soon as the specifications are met. Usually in each iteration a maximum of three screws are adjusted and as mentioned each iteration takes approximately one minute.

4 Results

In this section, we illustrate how the adaptive combiners have been used for fine tuning of a filter. we also illustrate the application of the analysis program developed in Chapter 5 for WGFs.

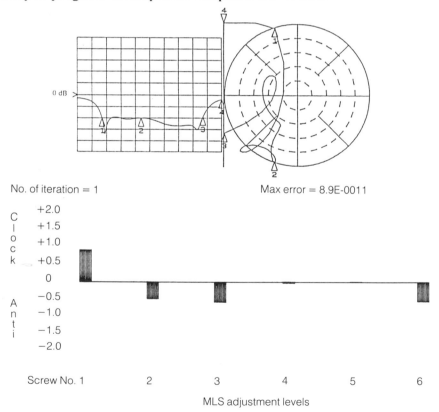

Figure 11.5- (a) The S_{11} characteristics of an untuned filter (scale as Figure 11.2): Centre frequency = 7.4253 GHz, bandwidth = 34.5 MHz and minimum loss = -19.11 dB. (b) The MLS output for filter in (a).

4.1 Filter Tuning

Figure 11.2 shows the magnitude response and the polar plot of a filter which has been taken as the reference filter in the training mode, i.e. a good filter. Figure 11.5a shows the S_{11} of an untuned filter and Figure 11.5b shows the output of the MLS for this filter state. The maximum error is due to screw number 1 and it is equal to 0.89 units. Figure 11.6a shows the output of the MLS after seven iterations and Figure 11.6b shows the filter response at this stage. It can be seen that the adjustment levels for all the screws are very close to zero and the maximum error is due to screw number 6 and is equal to 0.23. At this stage the response of the filter is within the specifications set by the reference filter.

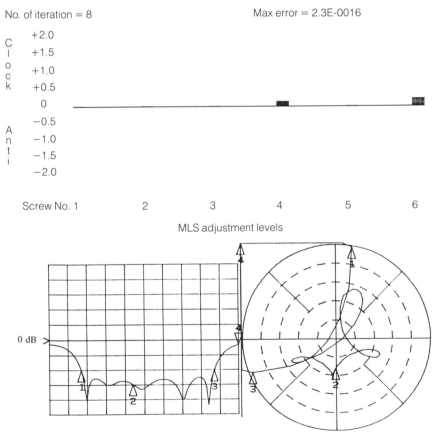

Figure 11.6- (a) The MLS output after seven adjustments. (b) The S_{11} characteristics corresponding to the tuned filter (scale as Figure 11.2): Centre frequency = 7.4256 GHz, bandwidth = 35.0 MHz and minimum loss = -25.03 dB.

4.2 Feature Analysis

Here the performance of the analysis system is checked by testing it on a set of data generated from the waveguide filter problem. First, the MLS was trained using the single fault training sequence. The analysis section has been included in the main body of the MLS and when the training mode is completed, the operator can move to the analysis section directly. Figure 11.7 illustrates the output of the expert system when the analysis of the inputs is completed.

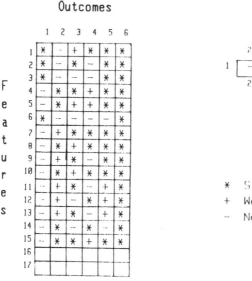

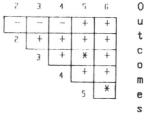

Figure 11.7- The output of the data analysis program (DAP).

The dependency table can be used to improve the chosen feature set. If there are features which are not significant for all of the outcomes, then they can be removed from the feature set. On the other hand, if all the features are strongly significant for any of the outcomes, then the outcome will be very sensitive to small changes in the values of any features. Thus, it is necessary to include some other features to reduce this sensitivity. It must be mentioned that the feature set must be kept the same for all the outcomes since otherwise the adaptive algorithm will be made more complex, i.e. R_{xx}^{-1} has to be calculated for each of the outcomes as described in Chapter 5.

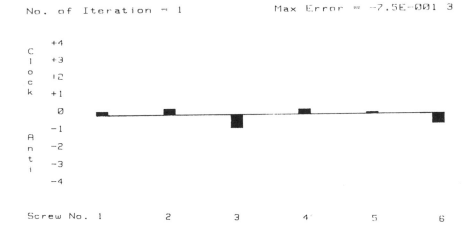

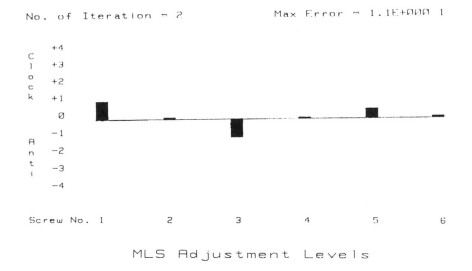

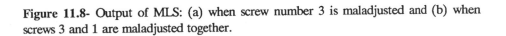

Figure 11.8- Output of MLS: (a) when screw number 3 is maladjusted and (b) when screws 3 and 1 are maladjusted together.

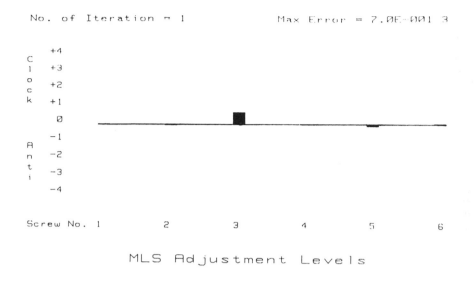

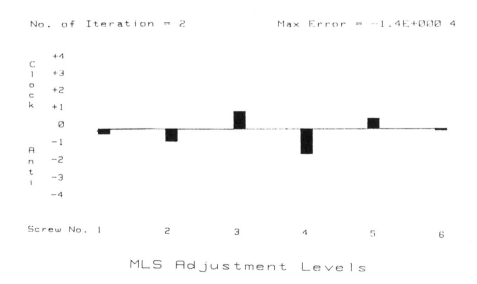

Figure 11.9- Output of MLS: (a) when screw number 3 is maladjusted and (b) when screws 3 and 5 are maladjusted together.

The interaction table is used to find out the interactions between the screws. This table may be checked by maladjusting the screws in pairs and observing the response of the MLS. From Figure 11.7, the system suggests that there are no interactions between screws (1 & 2), (1 & 3) and (1 & 4) and a high level of interaction exists between screws (3 & 5) and (5 & 6). Figure 11.8a illustrates the output of the MLS when screw number 3 was maladjusted in a clockwise direction. The system has been trained to recognize this maladjustment as seen in Figure 11.8a. Figure 11.8b illustrates the output of the MLS when both screws 3 and 1 were maladjusted. As expected from the dependency table in Figure 11.7, there is no interaction between screws 1 and 3 since the system has correctly detected both the maladjustments. On the other hand, Figure 11.9a and b show the same set of results for screws 3 and 5 which have a high level of interaction. In this case, the system has not been able to detect the maladjustments correctly. The suggestion made by the system failed in some cases and the reason for the failure is due to the limited number of training examples fed into the analysis section. The output of the expert system will be improved when a knowledge base is added to its structure (Chapter 5).

5 Conclusion

The MLS described in Chapter 5 can be thought of as an expert-system shell. The overall structure of the system is unchanged when adapting the system for a wide variety of problems. This chapter illustrated how the combiners in the MLS can be adapted to assess an unskilled operator to perform fast and accurate tuning of the WGFs. Of course the operator first requires to perform the rough tuning of the filter before using the combiners. The following limitation has been experienced when adapting the combiners for this problem.

WGFs are very complex and the level of interaction between the screws is very high. In order to model this complexity it is necessary to provide a large set of training examples. Also it is necessary to generate features when screws are maladjusted together. This is not possible due to the present structure of the filter and the sensitivity of the screws. As mentioned in Section 3, at the moment the screws are maladjusted in a clockwise and an anti-clockwise direction and the desired values are set to +1 and -1 respectively. This would give 13 feature sets for the six tuning screws on the filter. Of course these sets are only for single maladjustments. This training sequence is not sufficient to model the complexity of the filter and the interactions between the screws. This is evident by looking at the output of the MLS in Figure 11.10.

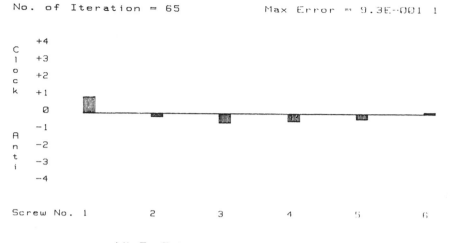

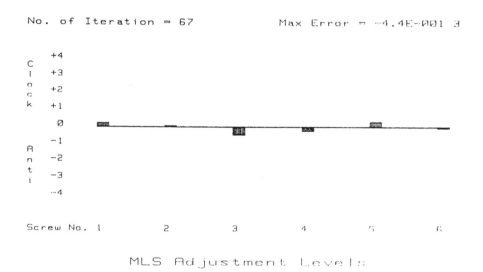

Figure 11.10- Output of MLS when screw number 1 is maladjusted to (a) the full amount and (b) half the amount as in the training mode.

Figure 11.10a illustrates the output of the MLS after training with the first screw maladjusted to the same level as in training mode. As it can be seen the MLS has been able to detect this maladjustment correctly. Figure 11.10b shows the output of the MLS when the same screw, i.e. number one, has been maladjusted by half of the amount in the training mode. This time, due to interactions between the screws, the MLS has failed to give the correct level of maladjustments for the screws.

A screwdriver has been built which gives a digital reading for the amount the filter screws are turned. This has slightly improved the training procedure but it is still very sensitive and also not very accurate since it is operated by humans. It is essential to design and construct a step motor for turning the screws on the filter. This will give full control during the training and the use mode.

The other problem with the combiners is illustrated in Figure 11.11. Figure 11.11a shows the polar plot of a filter and Figure 11.11b illustrates the output of the MLS. The polar plot in Figure 11.11c looks very similar to that of Figure 11.11a but its filter band is shifted in frequency. Figure 11.11d shows the output of the MLS for this polar plot and it can be seen that it is very similar to Figure 11.11b. The centre frequency of the filter has been used as a feature when training the combiners but it appears that the centre frequency does not have strong significance in the output of the MLS. This means that the operator needs to keep the filter response within the specific range when he is performing the rough tuning of the filter. The other alternative would be to introduce more features describing the position of the polar plot in frequency.

In conclusion, this chapter has presented an alternative approach for the tuning of WGFs. There are a number of standard procedures which can be used for rough tuning of these filters but due to the complexity of the problem the fine tuning of the filters has remained a black art. The application of the adaptive combiners illustrates that it is possible to automate the fine tuning of the filters. Since there are no defined sets of rules by which a skill operator performs the tuning of the filters a classical ES approach would be very difficult to adapt. In our approach, the combiners are presented by a set of examples which includes features and required desired response and a learning strategy is used to work out the relationships between the inputs and the outputs of the filter.

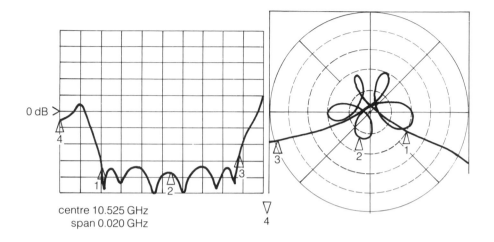

centre 10.525 GHz
span 0.020 GHz

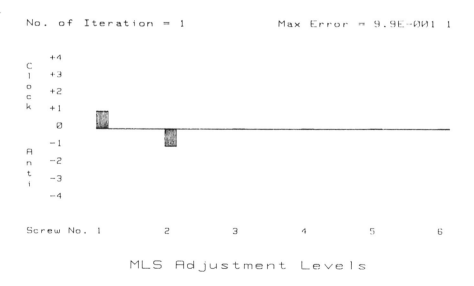

No. of Iteration = 1   Max Error = 9.9E-001 1

MLS Adjustment Levels

Figure 11.11- (a) Polar plot of the first filter and (b) its corresponding MLS output.

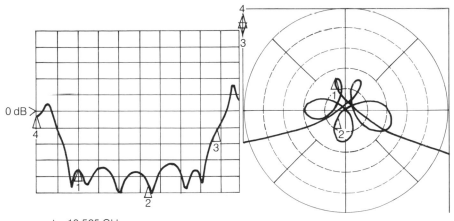

centre 10.525 GHz
span 0.020 GHz

No. of Iteration = 2   Max Error = 8.9E 001 1

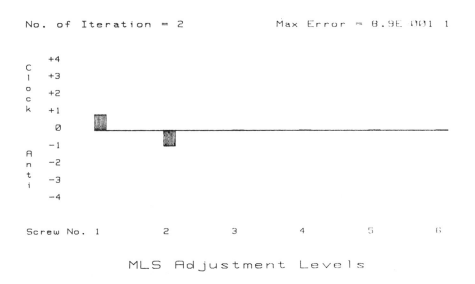

MLS Adjustment Levels

Figure 11.11- (c) Polar plot of the second filter and (d) its corresponding MLS output.

References

[1]   P M. Dishal, "Alignment and Adjustment of Synchronously Tuned Multiple Resonant Circuit Filters", *Proc. IRE.* , **Vol-39**, pp 1448-1455, Nov 1951.

[2]   A.E. Atia and A.E. Williams, "Nonminimum Phase Optimum-Amplitude Band Pass Waveguide Filters", *IEEE Trans. on MTT* , **Vol-22**, pp 425-431, April 1974.

[3]   A.E. Atia and A.E. Williams, "Measurements of Intercavity Couplings", *IEEE Trans. on MTT* , **Vol-23**, pp 519-522, June 1975.

[4]   H.L. Thal, "Computer Aided Filter Alignment and Diagnosis", *IEEE Trans. on MTT* , **Vol-26**, pp 958-963, Dec 1978.

[5]   S.B. Cohn, "Direct Coupled Resonator Filters", *Proc. IRE* , **Vol-45**, pp187-196, Feb 1957.

[6]   R.D. Wanselow, "Design Relations for Resonant Post Waveguide Filters", *J. Frankin Inst.* , pp 94-107, Feb 1961.

[7]   R. Levy, "Theory of Direct Coupled Cavity Filters", *IEEE Trans. on MTT* , **Vol-15**, pp 340, June 1967.

Appendix

In order to calculate the area of the loops and the distance between the loops it is necessary to estimate the interception points on the polar plot. The network analyser provides the real and the imaginary parts of the polar plot in a discrete form, Figure A.1a. Figure A.2b illustrates these points for one of the loops in the polar plot. It is not necessary to find the exact position of the interception point and it will be sufficient to associate the points (8,57) as the point of interception for this loop. A number of techniques were used to find these points and the following method worked for all different forms of polar plots.

One way of finding the points (8,57) would be to check which of the line segments from point 1 to 62 intercept. In other words we start from line segments (1,2) and (62,61) and check for a point of interception. For any two lines with a point of interception, Figure A.3,

we can write the following equations,

$$c = \lambda \underline{b}_1 + (1-\lambda)\underline{a}_1 \qquad \text{(A.1a)}$$

(A.1b)

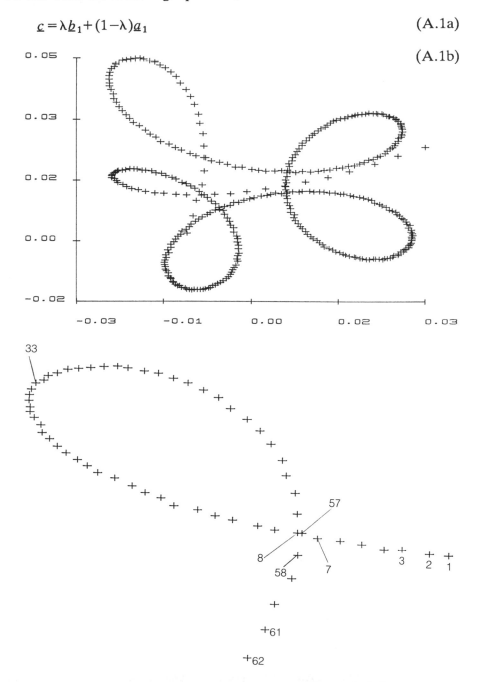

Figure A.1- (a) Polar plot in discrete form and (b) one single loop.

where $\underline{c}$ represents the coordinates of the interception point and λ and μ are scaler values. The conditions for the interception point to lie between the line segments $(\underline{a}_1\underline{b}_1)$ and $(\underline{a}_2\underline{b}_2)$ are as follows,

$$0<\lambda<1 \quad \text{and} \quad 0<\mu<1 \tag{A.2}$$

Equations (A.1a) and (A.1b) can be solved for λ and μ and these values may be checked to see if the two line segments intercept. As mentioned, this process will start from the line segments (1,2) and (62,61) and the next two lines would be (2,3) and (62,61). Before starting this process, the local maxima of the loop, i.e. point 33 in Figure A.1b, is calculated therefore when this point is reached we know that we have passed the interception points and the search is reassumed with line segments (1,2) and (61,60). This process terminates when the two line segments (7,8) and (57,58) are reached. At this stage the distance between the points (7,57), (7,58), (8,57) and (8,58) are calculated and the points which are closest to each other are chosen to represent the point of interception, i.e. 8 and 57. A 2D numerical integration technique is then used to find the size of the loop and the centre of the loop is calculated by averaging the x-y coordinates between the two points.

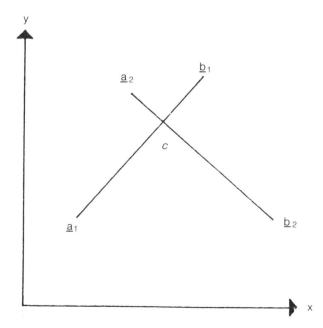

Figure A.2- Interception of two line segments.

Index